Politics as Exchange

Political institutions have been depicted by academics as a marketplace where citizens transact with each other to accomplish collective ends difficult to accomplish otherwise. This depiction supports a romantic notion of democracy in which democratic governments are accountable to their citizens and act in their best interests. In *Politics as Exchange*, Randall G. Holcombe explains why this view of democracy is too optimistic. He argues that while there is a political marketplace in which public policy is made, access to the political marketplace is limited to an elite few. A small group of well-connected individuals – legislators, lobbyists, agency heads, and others – negotiate to produce public policies with which the masses must comply. Examining the political transactions that determine policy, Holcombe discusses how political institutions, citizen mobility, and competition can limit the ability of elites to abuse their power.

Randall G. Holcombe is DeVoe Moore Professor of Economics at Florida State University. He is past President of the Public Choice Society and the Society for the Development of Austrian Economics. His previous books include *Political Capitalism: How Economic and Political Power Is Made and Maintained* (2018) and *Following Their Leaders: Political Preferences and Public Policy* (2023).

CAMBRIDGE STUDIES IN ECONOMICS, CHOICE, AND SOCIETY

Founding Editors

Timur Kuran, *Duke University*
Peter J. Boettke, *George Mason University*

This interdisciplinary series promotes original theoretical and empirical research as well as integrative syntheses involving links between individual choice, institutions, and social outcomes. Contributions are welcome from across the social sciences, particularly in the areas where economic analysis is joined with other disciplines such as comparative political economy, new institutional economics, and behavioral economics.

Books in the Series:

PAUL DRAGOS ALIGICA
Public Entrepreneurship, Citizenship, and Self-Governance

TERRY L. ANDERSON and GARY D. LIBECAP
Environmental Markets: A Property Rights Approach

ADAM CREPELLE
Becoming Nations Again: The Journey Towards Tribal Self-Determination

SHELBY GROSSMAN
The Politics of Order in Informal Markets: How the State Shapes Private Governance

MORRIS B. HOFFMAN
The Punisher's Brain: The Evolution of Judge and Jury

RANDALL G. HOLCOMBE
Political Capitalism: How Political Influence is Made and Maintained

ROGER KOPPL
Expert Failure

PETER T. LEESON:
Anarchy Unbound: Why Self- Governance Works Better Than You Think

MICHAEL C. MUNGER
Tomorrow 3.0: Transaction Costs and the Sharing Economy

JENNIFER BRICK MURTAZASHVILI AND ILIA MURTAZASHVILI
Land, the State, and War Property Institutions and Political Order in Afghanistan

ALEX NOWRASTEH AND BENJAMIN POWELL
Wretched Refuse?: The Political Economy of Immigration and Institutions

BENJAMIN POWELL
Out of Poverty: Sweatshops in the Global Economy (First Edition)

BENJAMIN POWELL
Out of Poverty: Sweatshops in the Global Economy (Second Edition)

JEAN-PHILIPPE PLATTEAU
Islam Instrumentalized: Religion and Politics in Historical Perspective

JARED RUBIN
Rulers, Religion, and Riches: Why the West Got Rich and the Middle East Did Not

VERNON L. SMITH AND BART J. WILSON
Humanomics: Moral Sentiments and the Wealth of Nations for the Twenty-First Century

CASS R. SUNSTEIN
The Ethics of Influence: Government in the Age of Behavioral Science

ANDREAS THIEL, WILLIAM A. BLOMQUIST AND DUSTIN E. GARRICK
Governing Complexity: Analyzing and Applying Polycentricity

CAROLYN M. WARNER, RAMAZAN KILINÇ, CHRISTOPHER W. HALE and ADAM B. COHEN
Generating Generosity in Catholicism and Islam: Beliefs, Institutions, and Public Goods Provision

TAIZU ZHANG
The Laws and Economics of Confucianism: Kinship and Property in Preindustrial China and England

TAISU ZHANG
The Ideological Foundations of Qing Taxation: Belief Systems, Politics, and Institutions

Politics as Exchange

An Analysis of the Political Marketplace

RANDALL G. HOLCOMBE
Florida State University

CAMBRIDGE
UNIVERSITY PRESS

CAMBRIDGE
UNIVERSITY PRESS

Shaftesbury Road, Cambridge CB2 8EA, United Kingdom

One Liberty Plaza, 20th Floor, New York, NY 10006, USA

477 Williamstown Road, Port Melbourne, VIC 3207, Australia

314–321, 3rd Floor, Plot 3, Splendor Forum, Jasola District Centre,
New Delhi – 110025, India

103 Penang Road, #05–06/07, Visioncrest Commercial, Singapore 238467

Cambridge University Press is part of Cambridge University Press & Assessment,
a department of the University of Cambridge.

We share the University's mission to contribute to society through the pursuit of
education, learning and research at the highest international levels of excellence.

www.cambridge.org
Information on this title: www.cambridge.org/9781009693974

DOI: 10.1017/9781009693967

© Randall G. Holcombe 2026

This publication is in copyright. Subject to statutory exception and to the provisions
of relevant collective licensing agreements, no reproduction of any part may take
place without the written permission of Cambridge University Press & Assessment.

When citing this work, please include a reference to the
DOI 10.1017/9781009693967

First published 2026

A catalogue record for this publication is available from the British Library

*A Cataloging-in-Publication data record for this book is available from
the Library of Congress*

ISBN 978-1-009-69393-6 Hardback
ISBN 978-1-009-69397-4 Paperback

Cambridge University Press & Assessment has no responsibility for the persistence
or accuracy of URLs for external or third-party internet websites referred to in this
publication and does not guarantee that any content on such websites is, or will
remain, accurate or appropriate.

For EU product safety concerns, contact us at Calle de José Abascal, 56, 1°, 28003
Madrid, Spain, or email eugpsr@cambridge.org

Dedicated to the memory of Jim Buchanan, Gordon Tullock, Jim Gwartney, and Bob Tollison. May their ideas and influence live on.

Contents

Preface		*page* xi
1	The Political Marketplace	1
2	Market Institutions	14
3	Transaction Costs and Institutions	33
4	The Characteristics of Authority	50
5	The Ruling Class	71
6	The Institutional Structure of the Political Marketplace	87
7	Political Transactions	105
8	Interest Groups: Elites and Masses	127
9	Welfare Maximization, Redistribution, and Governance	144
10	The Scope of Authority	164
11	Mobility and Authority	182
12	Democracy and Authority	207
13	Constraining Leviathan: Competition among Elites	230
14	Politics as Exchange	250
References		269
Index		281

Preface

In an essay written in 2003, James M. Buchanan, Nobel laureate and the father of the public choice research program, listed politics as exchange as one of the three hardcore presuppositions that supported that research program. (The other two were rational choice and methodological individualism.) Buchanan said, "A research program incorporates acceptance of a hard core of presuppositions that impose limits on the domain of scientific inquiry while, at the same time, insulating such inquiry from essentially irrelevant criticism."

Buchanan's brief statement of these presuppositions leaves much room for interpretation. Politics as exchange is often taken to suggest a political marketplace that operates much like markets for goods and services, coordinating people's political actions so that demands for collective goods and collective action are met in a manner similar to the way demands for private goods are satisfied in the marketplace. A brief summary of this volume's message is that there is a political marketplace in which well-connected individuals negotiate to design public policy, but that access to the political marketplace is limited to an elite few. This divides members of a society into two groups: the rulers and the ruled. An elite few make the rules. The masses are forced to comply with them. This volume explains why that must be the case, and explains how the political marketplace operates.

Readers in the United States, Western Europe, and other advanced democracies might view the analysis that follows with skepticism, thinking that their governments are accountable to the citizens and that democratic political institutions constrain their governments to act in the interests of their citizens. How do those constraints operate? Why are they able to be effective? Why are those Western democracies more constrained than the early twenty-first-century governments in Venezuela, Russia, and North Korea?

Members of the ruling elite are more constrained in Western democracies, to be sure, but they are not constrained by democratic institutions that convey power to the masses. Rather, those democratic institutions, to the extent that they are effective, enable a competition for power among members of the elite, which constrains their abuse of power by any one individual or group of individuals. Any notion that the elite are constrained by the power of the masses is an illusion.

The American Founders clearly understood that the biggest threat to the freedom of the masses was government. The Declaration of Independence is mostly a list of grievances against the King of England. It declared that because the King was violating their rights, they had the right to establish a government that would protect their rights. The Constitution of the United States gives the federal government limited and enumerated powers, and designs a system of checks and balances to enable some members of the political elite to constrain the abuse of power by others.

In the twenty-first century, that distrust of government power that the American Founders expressed has receded, replaced by a vision of a paternalistic state that takes care of its citizens and acts in their interests. As governments have become a larger economic influence, people look to the government for support, seeing the benefits they get from the government but overlooking the costs that are imposed on others to pay for the benefits. The programs that convey those benefits – and costs – are designed by an elite few who negotiate in the political marketplace.

There are serious political disagreements within the elite, to be sure, and those disagreements may be greater in the twenty-first century than in the twentieth century. But the disagreements are over who should hold the power of government and how that power should be used, rather than whether that power should be held by anyone.

The political freedoms enjoyed by residents of advanced democracies have only existed since the ideas of the Enlightenment took hold in the eighteenth century. Preservation of that freedom requires a recognition of the potential abuse of power by the political elite – a recognition the American Founders had – in order to maintain effective constraints against that abuse. Even then, success is not guaranteed. Adolf Hitler was democratically elected. Hugo Chavez was democratically elected. Vladimir Putin was democratically elected.

Preface

The title of this volume repeats a presupposition in the academic research program of public choice – the presupposition of politics as exchange. Public choice is a relatively new research program that uses economic methods to analyze political decision-making. James Buchanan, its most prominent founder, depicted politics as exchange, and the Public Choice Society, cofounded by Buchanan, prominently lists politics as exchange on its website as a key element in the public choice research program.

Public choice often takes the presupposition of politics as exchange too literally and depicts democratic decision-making as a collective choice process that aggregates citizen preferences to enable government to act in the interests of its citizens. There are many exceptions within the public choice literature, and this volume presents a more unified theory to connect those exceptions.

The main argument in this volume is that politics as exchange applies only to an elite few, that the masses are excluded from the political marketplace, and that democratic political institutions, unconstrained, are more likely to benefit the elite few who make public policies than the citizens who are governed by those policies. In many countries the abuse of power by elites is constrained, and later chapters in the volume discuss those constraints – constraints that are necessary to have a government that furthers the interests of the governed.

I have been fortunate, over my career as an economist, to have been able to benefit from the insights and guidance of many individuals. I dedicate this volume to four of them: Jim Buchanan, Gordon Tullock, Jim Gwartney, and Bob Tollison, all of whom have passed away. My hope is that their ideas and influence live on. Readers familiar with their work should see some of their influence in this volume.

I

The Political Marketplace

In 2005 the United States Congress passed its National Appropriations Bill, which included $398 million to fund a bridge to Alaska's Gravina Island, which was inhabited by fifty residents and serviced by a ferry. The bridge, which was intended to replace the ferry, was widely criticized as a "bridge to nowhere." Critics depicted the bridge as a pork-barrel project that was a political payoff to Alaska's Senator Ted Stevens and Congressman Don Young. Having received widespread negative publicity, funding for that project was ultimately withdrawn in 2015.

For those who follow politics, the biggest surprise in this story is that the funding for the bridge was withdrawn. The second-biggest surprise was that the story garnered such widespread publicity. Politicians regularly bargain with each other, and with lobbyists and interest groups, to pass legislation. Pork-barrel projects are often created to grease the wheels of political exchange. The bridge to nowhere was, in this regard, not that remarkable or unusual. But it received enough publicity that pork-barrel projects are sometimes referred to as "bridges to nowhere."

This political exchange among legislators, referred to as logrolling, may be as simple as trading votes. "I'll vote for your bill if you will vote for mine." It can also occur through pork-barrel spending, like the bridge to nowhere. "I'll vote for your bill if you modify it to include funding for a project in my district." More indirectly, if a legislator asks a colleague to vote in favor of some legislation and the colleague agrees, the soliciting legislator incurs a debt which must eventually be repaid. "Remember when I supported the bill you wanted passed? Now I want your support for this bridge in my district." Legislators accumulate power when they accumulate IOUs from other legislators.

Debts must be honored, or legislators will not be able to engage in future exchanges. Legislators will not take IOUs from colleagues who develop reputations for not paying their debts. These legislative exchanges are necessary for legislators who want to see their legislative proposals enacted. Passage of legislation ultimately requires support of a majority of the legislative body, so legislators must cooperate with each other to get anything done. Details about these exchanges will be analyzed later. The initial point is to acknowledge the commonly known fact that legislators bargain with each other to produce legislation. The idea of a political marketplace is not an analogy. There is an actual market, and the currency in that market is votes. This is politics as exchange.

The political marketplace is broader than just exchange among legislators. Legislators also bargain with lobbyists and interest groups that seek legislative support. Interest groups can offer campaign contributions to legislators, favorable publicity that can elicit votes from their membership, jobs for legislators' family and associates, and any number of other payoffs to gain legislative support for the issues they want to see passed.[1] Those interests that transact in the political marketplace are hoping to receive, in exchange, political support – votes – that will benefit them.

While interest groups lobby for legislation they want to see passed, they also lobby to try to prevent legislation that would have a negative impact on them. That negative impact may be an unintended consequence of legislation that has other goals, but often it is intentional. Recognizing that they can get interest groups to offer something in exchange for killing legislation that would harm the group, legislators will sometimes introduce legislation deliberately targeted to harm some interest groups, with no intention of seeing it passed. Legislation like this, referred to as a milker bills, is intended to push the targeted interest group into paying off legislators to kill it.[2] Much as the Mafia operates, legislators tell interest groups to pay up to avoid having costs imposed on them.

Legislation that would benefit an interest group typically does so by imposing costs on some other group. (Legislation that benefits some at no cost to anyone else should be an easy sell.) Thus, legislators must weigh

---

[1] Many examples appear in Peter Schweizer, *Extortion: How Politicians Extract Your Money, Buy Votes, and Line Their Own Pockets* (Boston, MA: Houghton Mifflin, 2013).

[2] Schweizer, *Extortion*, discusses this, as does Fred S. McChesney, "Rent Extraction and Rent Creation in the Economic Theory of Regulation," *Journal of Legal Studies* 16, no. 1 (January 1987), pp. 101–118, and McChesney, *Money for Nothing: Politicians, Rent Extraction, and Political Extortion* (Cambridge, MA: Harvard University Press, 1997).

the benefits they can receive from one interest against the costs they may incur by imposing costs on another.[3] Transacting with the highest bidder might be justified as promoting legislation for those who value it the most, but not all interests are well-organized. An organized interest will have an obvious bargaining advantage over an unorganized group. Setting aside details for now, there is a political marketplace in which the well-connected transact to produce public policy.

Interest group lobbying has been going on since the founding of the country,[4] but was an "open secret" that was rarely discussed until 1913, when the *New York World* ran a series of articles revealing that various interests were paying lobbyists to represent their interests to legislators.[5] In 1913, the public was outraged that this was occurring, but in the twenty-first century, people accept lobbying and interest group politics as the way the political system operates. Despite frequent criticism about the influence of powerful interests, lobbying is viewed as a legitimate way for interest groups to participate in the political process.

These transactions among legislators, lobbyists, business leaders, agency heads, and other well-connected individuals constitute the political marketplace. This is politics as exchange. It is worth emphasizing that politics as exchange is not an analogy; the political marketplace is an actual market, in which bargains are struck and favors exchanged for the benefit of those who are engaged in the transactions.

THERE IS A POLITICAL MARKETPLACE

The analysis of government decision-making often focuses on the formal processes through which those decisions are made. A bill is passed through a committee of the US House of Representatives and forwarded to the entire House for a vote. After a similar process in the Senate, any differences are reconciled by committee, and if the bill receives majority approval of both Houses, it is sent to the president for final approval.

---

[3] Gary S. Becker, "A Theory of Competition among Pressure Groups for Political Influence," *Quarterly Journal of Economics* 98, no. 3 (August 1983), pp. 371–400, considers the possibility that transactions in the political marketplace weigh the costs and benefits of legislation to arrive at an efficient outcome.

[4] Some evidence is offered by Jonathan R. T. Hughes, *The Governmental Habit: Economic Controls from Colonial Times to the Present* (New York: Basic Books, 1977).

[5] Grant McConnell, *Private Power and American Democracy* (New York: Alfred A. Knopf, 1966) describes lobbying as an open secret prior to the *New York World* articles in 1913.

Bills that are vetoed by the president can be overridden by a two-thirds vote of the legislature. This description of the formal procedure overlooks the bargaining that takes place among legislators, and between legislators and the president.

This process of political exchange determines more than just how individual legislators will vote, and whether the president will sign the bill. Political bargaining first determines what provisions the legislation to be voted on contains. Legislators may insist that to gain their support, some provisions must be added to legislation (such as projects in their districts) or that some provisions be deleted. Although the president is not formally involved in drafting legislation, legislators also bargain with the president in an attempt to avoid a presidential veto. Ultimately, legislation that is enacted is more the product of the political bargaining that takes place among legislators and other well-connected individuals than the product of a formal voting procedure. Legislative votes are mostly a formality, to approve legislation the legislators already negotiated and agreed they would support.

On the surface, voting in legislatures appears similar to voting by the general public. Votes are counted to determine whether a candidate is elected or legislation is approved. In fact, the processes are very different. Voters in general elections have no say over the choices they are offered, and they have no opportunity to negotiate with other voters to bargain for outcomes they would prefer. Meanwhile, members of a legislature can trade away votes on issues they care little about to gain the votes of their colleagues on issues they care most about – and they can bargain to determine what provisions will be in the bills that will come up for a vote. Politics as exchange describes the way legislation is created, but in general elections, the masses have no access to the political marketplace. Their only choice is to vote on the options that appear on the ballot – options that are determined by those elite few who transact in the political marketplace.

A romantic notion of democracy depicts democratic governments as accountable to their citizens and acting in the best interests of their citizens. Citizens can vote elected officials out of office if they are dissatisfied with their performance, which should provide some discipline to push elected officials to do what voters want.[6] While there is an element of

---

[6] An influential and more formal explanation of those democratic constraints on political candidates and parties is offered by Anthony Downs, *An Economic Theory of Democracy* (New York: Harper & Row, 1957).

truth in this vision of democracy, democratic institutions provide only limited constraints on the actions of those who actually make and enforce the laws. One goal of this volume is to explain why those institutional constraints are necessarily limited in their power to direct government action toward the public interest. Negotiations made in the political marketplace ultimately determine public policy.

The negotiations that occur among legislators, between legislators and lobbyists, between interest groups and government regulators, and that include government agency heads and well-connected business interests, are widely recognized. The first step in analyzing the political marketplace is to recognize that these transactions take place within an actual marketplace in which individuals bargain with each other, transacting for their mutual benefit. Politics as exchange is not an analogy. There is a real market in which real transactions take place.

MOST PEOPLE ARE EXCLUDED FROM THE POLITICAL MARKETPLACE

One characteristic of the political marketplace stands out: Most people are excluded from participating in it. When one considers the actual political exchanges that take place, among legislators, between legislators and lobbyists, with participation of agency heads, well-connected corporate executives, and the leaders of interest groups, political exchange takes place only among an elite few. Most people are unable to participate.

The average citizen has no way to participate in this process of political exchange. As individuals, they have no access to those who actually make public policy. An attempt to contact a legislator directly may result in a meeting with a legislative staffer. Legislators sometimes hold "town hall" meetings in which citizens may be granted a minute or two in front of a microphone. But such meetings have little chance of affecting public policy. Most individuals have nothing to offer in exchange, so cannot participate in the political marketplace.

Individuals can vote, and all the votes taken together will determine who holds elective office. But each individual has only one vote, and one vote will not change an election outcome. Ultimately, the actions of individual citizens will have no effect on public policy. Voters must realize this, even if they are reluctant to acknowledge it. When they cast their votes, they know that the election outcome will be the same regardless of how they vote, or even whether they vote.

The result is that voters tend to be rationally ignorant.[7] Knowing that their one vote will have no effect on an election outcome, voters have no incentive to seek out information to cast an informed ballot. Some voters will seek out information just because they are interested, in the same way that sports fans will seek out information about teams and players, but the incentive to do so is limited because outcomes, in sports and in politics, will be unaffected by the actions of individual voters and sports fans.

When an individual goes to a restaurant and chooses to order salad rather than pizza, the individual gets a salad. When that same individual decides to vote for candidate A rather than candidate B, the same candidate will be elected regardless of the individual's vote. Most individuals are unable to engage in the type of political exchange that was described in the previous section. This divides people into two groups: elites and masses. Political elites are those who are in a position to bargain to produce public policy. Most people, the masses, do not have this ability.

Well-connected lobbyists can negotiate with legislators to affect public policy, and in many cases the lobbyists will even write the legislation that later will be voted on. Most readers of this book (as well as the author) have no ability to affect public policy. Citizens can vote, they can join interest groups that do have some influence, and they can donate money and volunteer to work on political campaigns. Still, as individuals, they have no influence. A romantic notion of democracy depicts democratic governments as accountable to their citizens and acting in their interests. An analysis of the political marketplace questions the degree to which this is true.[8]

Members of the political elite are those who are able to enter the bargaining process – to engage in political exchange – to affect public policy. Different governments will have different sets of elites. An individual might be a member of the local elite in a city government, but have no influence and be excluded from the elite in the national government. Even at the local level, only a small fraction of the population is in the elite. Most people are members of the masses who are excluded from the political bargaining process that produces public policy. When analyzing politics as exchange, once we recognize that there is a political marketplace, the next thing to recognize is that only an elite few are able to participate in it.

---

[7] This term was used by Anthony Downs, *An Economic Theory of Democracy*.
[8] James M. Buchanan, "Public Choice: Politics without Romance: A Sketch of Positive Public Choice Theory and Its Normative Implications," in *The Collected Works of* James M. Buchanan, vol. 1 (1999), pp. 45–59, characterizes public choice in his title as politics without romance.

THE COASE THEOREM AND POLITICAL EXCHANGE

The Coase theorem emphasizes the role that transaction costs play in determining whether people are able to participate in mutually advantageous exchanges. One way to state the Coase theorem is: In the absence of transaction costs, resources will be allocated to their highest-valued uses. A transaction cost is anything that stands in the way of a mutually advantageous exchange. The simple logic of this statement of the Coase theorem is that if nothing stands in the way of mutually advantageous exchanges, then every mutually advantageous exchange will take place. That logic also implies that if transaction costs are too high, those transaction costs will prevent some potentially advantageous exchanges from taking place.

Consider a simple example. Someone in New York is willing to sell a used car for $10,000, and someone in Seattle is willing to pay $10,500 for that same car. There is a potential mutually advantageous exchange, but if it would cost more than $500 to ship the car from New York to Seattle, that transaction cost – the shipping cost – would prevent the exchange from being made. The Coase theorem, and more generally, transaction costs, play an important role in laying a theoretical foundation for the ideas in this volume.

The Coase theorem comes from an article published by Nobel laureate Ronald Coase in 1960, but the article itself contains no theorems.[9] The first place that Coase's idea was referred to as a theorem was in a 1966 book by Nobel laureate George Stigler.[10] As Steven Medima notes, the Coase theorem has been stated in many different ways, often contradictory, over the decades,[11] so the theorem as stated earlier is not necessarily the definitive statement of the theorem, but for present purposes, it lends a good deal of understanding to the nature of the political marketplace.

Most people are excluded from participating in the political marketplace because high transaction costs prevent their participation. The primary source of high transaction costs in politics is the large number of people who are affected by political decisions. When large numbers of people would have to be involved for an exchange to take place, bargaining among them becomes a costly undertaking, preventing people

---

[9] Ronald H. Coase, "The Problem of Social Cost," *Journal of Law & Economics* 3 (1960), pp. 1–44.
[10] George J. Stigler, *The Theory of Price*, 3rd ed. (New York: Macmillan, 1966).
[11] Steven G. Medima, "The Coase Theorem at Sixty," *Journal of Economic Literature* 53, no. 4 (December 2020), pp. 1045–1128.

from being able to negotiate with each other. A good example that illustrates the role of transaction costs in political exchange is the mandate by the US government that motor fuels contain ethanol.

Ethanol is produced mostly from corn, and lobbyists for corn farmers and processors – led by agricultural processing firm Archer Daniels Midland – lobbied Congress to mandate that motor fuels contain ethanol, a mandate that was approved in 2005. The mandate increased the demand for ethanol because without a mandate, few motor fuel consumers would choose to add ethanol to their fuel. If consumers would buy ethanol without the mandate, there would be no reason to mandate its inclusion in motor fuel. Ethanol producers received a benefit because the demand for their product increased. Purchasers of motor fuels were left to bear the cost of purchasing the ethanol they would prefer not to buy.

The example illustrates both sides of the importance of transaction costs to political exchange. Legislators and lobbyists faced low transaction costs, so they were able to negotiate an agreement beneficial to them both. Motorists faced high transaction costs because there is a large number of motorists, making it difficult for them to organize as an effective lobbying group to oppose the mandate. Low transaction costs enable political exchange. High transaction costs prevent political exchange. The most significant source of high transaction costs in political markets is large numbers of participants.[12] That is why the political elite – those who participate in the political marketplace to make public policy – will necessarily be a small subset of society, and why the masses necessarily are excluded from the political marketplace.

This idea that when large numbers of people must agree to undertake mutually advantageous activities, high transaction costs will stand in the way of their ability to do so dates back at least to David Hume. Who wrote in 1740,

Two neighbours may agree to drain a meadow, which they possess in common; because 'tis easy for them to know each other's mind; and each must perceive, that the immediate consequence of his failing in his part, is, the abandoning of the whole project. But 'tis very difficult, and indeed impossible, that a thousand

---

[12] Macur Olson, Jr., *The Logic of Collective Action* (Cambridge, MA: Harvard University Press, 1965) explains why large groups are more difficult to organize for collective action than small groups. James M. Buchanan and Gordon Tullock, *The Calculus of Consent* (Ann Arbor, MI: University of Michigan Press, 1962), ch. 6, explain that as the number of people required to agree to take collective action increases, decision-making costs increase. Those decision-making costs, in this context, are transaction costs.

persons shou'd agree to any such action; it being difficult for them to concert so complicated a design, and still more difficult for them to execute it; while each seeks a pretext to free himself of the trouble and expense, and wou'd lay the whole burden on others.[13]

When groups are small, low transaction costs enable them to negotiate to maximize the value of transactions to the members of the bargaining group. When groups are large, high transaction costs prevent negotiations from taking place.

THE TRIADIC NATURE OF THE POLITICAL MARKETPLACE

Richard Wagner has emphasized that most public policy measures benefit some by imposing costs on others. He refers to this as the triadic nature of the political marketplace.[14] Market exchanges typically involve two parties. Government transactions typically involve three. Two members of the political elite bargain with each other for their mutual benefit. The third party lies outside the political elite and bears the cost of the bargain struck by the first two. The ethanol mandate discussed in the previous section is a good example.

Legislators and lobbyists negotiate to pass the mandate. That is politics as exchange. The purchasers of motor fuels bear the cost of this bargain struck between legislators and lobbyists. Transaction costs prevent motorists from organizing and negotiating with legislators to reduce or eliminate the mandate. This is but one example of the mandates, subsidies, tax breaks, tariffs, and regulations that interest groups bargain to obtain by imposing costs on those who are excluded from the political bargaining process.

Market exchanges typically involve only two parties who voluntarily transact for their mutual benefit. In most market transactions, third parties are unaffected. In some cases, third-party effects, labeled externalities, do occur. The prototypical example is a smoke-polluting factory. A steel manufacturer negotiates with an auto manufacturer to sell steel, and in the process, smoke from the steel mill creates air pollution that imposes a cost on others not involved in the transaction between the steel mill and the auto manufacturer.

---

[13] David Hume, *A Treatise on Human Nature*, 2nd ed., Sir Lewis Amherst Selby-Bigge, and P. H. Nidditch, eds. (Oxford: Oxford University Press, 1978 [orig. 1739–40]), p. 538.
[14] Richard E. Wagner, *Politics as Peculiar Business: Insights from a Theory of Entangled Political Economy* (Cheltenham, UK: Edward Elgar, 2016).

An economic inefficiency arises because there are many individuals who are affected by the polluted air, and members of that large group find it too costly to organize to negotiate with the steel mill to reduce its emissions. High transaction costs stand in the way, so those who suffer from the pollution are left out of the bargaining process. When an externality exists, market transactions between two parties can impose a cost on a third party. Steel producers and auto manufacturers face low transaction costs, so they can bargain for their mutual benefit. Those breathing the polluted air face high transaction costs, so they are unable to bargain to reduce the air pollution.

This is what happens in most political exchanges. Lobbyists make bargains with legislators, just as steel mills make bargains with auto companies, and in each case a third party bears a cost as a result of the exchange. The big difference is that with most private exchanges, the costs and benefits are all borne by the transacting parties. When that is not the case, the legal system makes people liable for damages they inflict on others. In politics, the triadic nature of political exchange is a standard part of the process. Most political bargains entail imposing a cost on people who do not participate in the exchange. Often, in the private sector, when people's activities cause harm to others, the reason those activities are allowed to continue is that political bargains have been made to allow them to continue.

Most people are excluded from bargaining in the political marketplace. This enables those members of the political elite who bargain with each other for their mutual benefit to impose costs on third parties – the masses – who are excluded from the bargaining process. The elite do not intend to impose costs on the masses. Those costs are a by-product of their transactions, just as air pollution is an unintended by-product of steel mills.

A FEW MAKE THE RULES THAT GOVERN EVERYONE

Another difference between the political marketplace and the marketplace for goods and services is that the political marketplace produces the rules that govern everyone. When consumers make purchases in markets, the transactions only affect those who are participating in them. Even if externalities exist, the affected group remains limited. Political actors make rules that affect the masses. Most people who are affected have no say in the rules that affect them. Political elites make the rules. The masses are mandated to obey them. With market transactions, those engaged in the transactions do not have the ability to tell other people what they must do, or what they are prohibited from doing. Transactions made in the political marketplace do exactly that. Some people write the rules that others are required to obey.

Externalities resulting from market activity are unintentional by-products of productive activity. When the steel mill produces steel to sell to auto makers, the people running the steel mill do not intend to harm surrounding residents by creating air pollution. That pollution is just a by-product of the steel mill's production. In contrast, many of the costs that result from political exchange are intended to impose costs on others. The ethanol mandate, discussed earlier, has characteristics much like externalities generated by market activities. It is intended to benefit those involved in the production of ethanol, and the cost imposed on the purchasers of motor fuels is an unintended (but easily recognized) by-product. But when the political elite levy taxes, the intention is to impose a cost on the masses to finance the activities designed by the political elite.

One hopes that the net effect of both the taxes and the expenditure programs they finance will be positive, but hope is not a good foundation for analyzing human action. A more accurate picture can be drawn by looking at the incentives faced by decision-makers and the constraints they face as they act. People who transact in the political marketplace should be expected to negotiate deals that benefit those who are transacting, just as one would expect for transactions in markets for goods and services.

One can look at activities like environmental regulations and zoning laws, and again hope that, on net, they add more value than they cost. But, as is common, rules like these impose costs on some to provide benefits to others. Zoning regulations are often designed and modified to benefit narrow interests,[15] and environmental regulations are championed by environmental groups that bear none of the costs that they advocate imposing on others. Leaders of these groups are well-connected members of the political elite who are able to bargain to create policies that result in uncompensated takings.[16] The political elite make the rules. The masses are compelled to follow them.

---

[15] Richard F. Babcock, *The Zoning Game: Municipal Practices and Policies* (Madison, WI: University of Wisconsin Press, 1966).
[16] Richard A. Epstein, *Takings: Private Property and the Power of Eminent Domain* (Cambridge, MA: Harvard University Press, 1985).

POLITICAL BARGAINS ARE BACKED BY FORCE

The masses are compelled to follow the rules designed by the elite because the political elite threaten the use of force against those who do not comply. To be effective, the political elite must control institutions of coercion that have more power behind them than the power of those who are being coerced. Douglass North says, "a state is an organization with a comparative advantage in violence, extending over a geographic area whose boundaries are determined by its power to tax constituents. The essence of property rights is the right to exclude, and an organization which has a comparative advantage in violence is in the position to specify and enforce property rights."[17]

Everybody knows that government mandates are backed by the threat of force to be used against those who do not comply. Government threatens to impose costs on those who do not pay their taxes, or who do not comply with government regulations. This points toward a number of questions with regard to political institutions. Why do the masses not revolt, or at least resist the mandates of government? How do political elites gain control over institutions with a comparative advantage in violence? The political elite themselves do not enforce government mandates. They employ enforcers who have that comparative advantage in violence. Why do those who have the actual comparative advantage in violence not take over and control government? One answer is that sometimes they do. Military coups occur from time to time, but not in established democracies. How do the political elite maintain that control?

POLITICS AS EXCHANGE

This introduction to politics as exchange notes several significant features of the political marketplace. First, it emphasizes that the idea of a political marketplace is more than an analogy. There is an actual political marketplace in which members of the political elite engage in transactions with each other to create public policy. Legislators, lobbyists, agency heads, corporate leaders, and other well-connected individuals negotiate with each other, each offering something the others want, to determine the rules under which society is governed.

---

[17] Douglass C. North, *Structure and Change in Economic History* (New York: Norton, 1981), p. 21.

Second, most people are excluded from participating in the political marketplace. Transaction costs prevent them from entering the political bargaining process. They can vote. They can join interest groups that share their views. But these are expressive acts that do not give individuals any influence over political outcomes. One vote will not change the outcome of an election. One more member of an interest group will not make that group more effective. While it is true that all the votes taken together determine an election outcome, and the contributions of all the members of interest groups taken together can make a difference, one individual's participation will not have any measurable effect. Most individuals cannot negotiate with legislators, as can well-connected lobbyists, to affect public policy.

Third, political exchanges typically involve three parties, unlike market exchanges which typically involve only two. Market transactions involve two parties, exchanging for their mutual benefit. Political exchanges involve two members of the political elite exchanging for their mutual benefit and a third party that bears the cost of the agreement made by the first two.

That third feature of political exchange is the consequence of the fourth. Transactions made in the political marketplace produce the rules that govern the masses. Unlike market exchange, where the costs and benefits are concentrated on those who participate in the exchanges, political exchange involves an elite few who write the rules and regulations that govern everyone. When government is involved, an elite few impose costs on some and convey benefits to others.

A fifth characteristic of the political marketplace is that those who transact in the political marketplace have the ability to enforce compliance with their mandates. People participate in market exchanges only if they voluntarily agree to do so. The political marketplace imposes mandates on people who do not participate in the exchanges. Their edicts are backed by the threat of force against those who do not comply.

The political marketplace, as an actual marketplace in which mutually advantageous exchanges occur, is open to the same type of economic analysis as any other market.

2

Market Institutions

People who transact in the political marketplace are negotiating to trade access to the government's power to coerce. Lobbyists and interest groups negotiate with legislators to employ government's coercive power for their benefit, or sometimes to escape government's coercive power. Legislators bargain with each other to give up some power on legislation they care less about to gain power to pass legislation more important to them. In the market for automobiles, suppliers of automobiles sell automobiles to demanders of automobiles. In the market for groceries, suppliers of groceries sell groceries to demanders of groceries. In the political marketplace, legislators, regulators, and others who have access to the coercive powers of government supply that coercive power to demanders who offer payment to access it.

The triadic nature of most political exchanges means that often, legislation that is the result of bargains made by the well-connected to benefit themselves imposes costs on the masses. In markets for goods and services, the costs and benefits of exchange are mostly confined to those who participate in exchanges. People who transact in markets do so voluntarily because they benefit from the transactions. Externalities sometimes exist, which impose costs on unwilling third parties. In political markets, most exchanges produce externalities.

James Buchanan points out that under majority rule politics, majorities are able to impose their preferences on minorities.[1] This volume paints an even more pessimistic picture in which minorities are able to

---

[1] James M. Buchanan, "Politics, Policy, and the Pigouvian Margins," *Economica* n.s. 29, no. 113 (February 1962), pp. 17–28.

impose their preferences on majorities. Exchanges in the political marketplace benefit the elite few who participate in the exchanges while imposing costs on those who are excluded from the political marketplace due to high transaction costs.

The reason access to government power is sought by demanders is to coerce people to act in ways they would not choose without being coerced. Regulation either mandates that people undertake activities they otherwise would not choose to do or prohibits people from undertaking activities they otherwise would choose to do. Taxation forces people to pay for government programs. People would not have to be forced to pay their taxes or comply with regulations if they thought that doing so would benefit them. Whether people are better off, on net, from government taxes, spending, and regulation is beside the point. There is always some component of government action that is forced on people. If people would voluntarily choose to do what the government mandates, there would be no reason for the mandates.

Access to the political marketplace is access to the government's power to coerce others. Ultimately, that is all those on the government side of transactions have to sell. Legislators can trade with each other, giving up some power on one issue to gain power on another. Lobbyists and interest groups can offer benefits to legislators and other government officials in exchange for access to their coercive power. Those in government have nothing else to offer in the political marketplace.

The political marketplace gives an obvious advantage to members of the elite, who can trade for their mutual advantage, over the masses who are excluded from transacting in it. Why do the masses tolerate this? One answer is that government has a comparative advantage in the use of force. The masses have little alternative but to yield to the power of government and abide by the mandates of the elite. While there is much truth in this, the coercive power of government also provides an essential benefit to the masses. It imposes order and enables people to cooperate with each other for their mutual benefit.

The elite want an orderly and compliant citizenry because it lowers the cost of ruling and makes it easier for them to extract tribute. Indeed, disorder can lead to an overthrow of those in power. The masses want an orderly society to enable them to engage in productive interaction with each other and to be protected from harm. Thus, the masses are inclined to support their governments, which propagandize their citizens with the vision of democratic governments as being accountable to their citizens and acting in the best interests of their citizens.² The masses are exchanging protection for tribute, an exchange that improves their welfare, even if they are forced into it.³

Steven Pinker has made the case that the remarkable progress and prosperity that have occurred since the beginning of the Industrial Revolution have been the result of the rise of strong governments that have imposed order on the populations they govern.⁴ Citizens identify with their governments and patriotically support their governments, viewing the political elite as leaders they chose to follow. In part, this may be because they have no choice. The political elite will force those who do not voluntarily comply. But by imposing order, government institutions complement market institutions, enabling productive activity and mutually beneficial exchange.

Libertarian anarchists might argue that absent the state, market institutions could maintain an equally orderly society, and do a better job, without the coercion of government.⁵ Whether this is true is beside the point. The fact is that, since the Enlightenment, strong governments, typically with the support of their citizens, have imposed an order on societies that has enabled their members to interact peacefully and productively with one another. This is what actually has happened.

The orderly and productive society that effective government makes possible generates popular support for elite rule, especially when the masses believe that democratic institutions make those elites accountable to the masses. There is a close relationship between productive economic institutions and the political institutions that govern those economic institutions. The masses yield to authority because they perceive that it protects them, in addition to constraining them. The acceptance by the masses of the institutions of authority and governance run by a political elite rests on the interaction of political and economic institutions that enable people to engage peacefully and productively with each other.

---

² See Murray Edelman, *The Symbolic Uses of Politics* (Urbana: University of Illinois Press, 1964) for an insightful analysis.
³ Randall G. Holcombe, *The Economic Foundations of Government* (New York: New York University Press, 1994) says that this is the economic foundation of government.
⁴ Steven Pinker, *Enlightenment Now: The Case for Reason, Science, Humanism, and Progress* (New York: Viking, 2018).
⁵ See, for examples, Murray N. Rothbard, *For a New Liberty: A Libertarian Manifesto* (New York: Macmillan, 1973), David D. Friedman, *The Machinery of Freedom: Guide to Radical Capitalism* (Chicago, IL: Open Court Publishing Company, 1973), and Michael Huemer, *The Problem of Political Authority: An Examination of the Right to Coerce and the Duty to Obey* (New York: Palgrave Macmillan, 2013).

This chapter focuses heavily on economic institutions for two reasons. First, the political marketplace is an actual market, and the same principles that apply to markets for goods and services lend insight into the operation of political markets. Second, there is a close interaction and mutual interdependence between economic and political institutions. One of the benefits of the institutions of authority and governance – those institutions controlled by the political elite – is that they enable economic institutions to operate. Meanwhile, political markets, which produce no goods and services themselves, depend on the tribute they collect from productive economic activity for their existence.

ECONOMIC AND POLITICAL INSTITUTIONS

One of the insights Adam Smith offered in his great book, *The Wealth of Nations*, is that market economies coordinate people's activities so that individuals pursuing their own interests are led by an invisible hand to further the interests of others. Smith observes, "It is not from the benevolence of the butcher, the brewer, or the baker, that we expect our dinner, but from their regard to their own interest."[6] Exchange takes place for the mutual benefit of those involved in the exchanges. This applies to political exchange just as much as to the exchanges of goods and services, so understanding how economists have analyzed the exchange of goods and services lends insight into the nature of exchanges in the political marketplace.

People's opportunities are constrained, as everyone recognizes. Some constraints are facts of the physical world. Some constraints come from social institutions. This applies to political markets just as much as to markets for goods and services. Exchanges are structured within formal institutions which require that interactions take place in a certain way. For example, institutions are designed to prevent fraud and theft, and more generally, to protect property rights. Going back to Adam Smith's insight, markets are designed so that people further their own interests by creating value for others, in political markets just as in markets for goods and services.

Formal institutions also structure and constrain political exchange. For example, in the US Congress, legislation is approved by majority rule, so legislators who seek to pass legislation must gain the support

---

[6] Adam Smith, *The Wealth of Nations* (New York: Modern Library, 1937 [orig. 1776]), p. 14.

of a majority of their colleagues. These formal institutions affect informal institutions in the political marketplace. The logrolling and vote trading that take place are aimed at designing legislation to surpass that majoritarian bar.

In the political marketplace and in the marketplace for goods and services, people do not just hope to find others with whom they can profitably exchange. Institutions help to match up those who can profitably trade with each other. The general principles underlying market transactions apply both to markets for goods and services and to the political marketplace. The primary difference – and it is a big one! – is that the ultimate goal for those who transact in the political marketplace is to harness the coercive power of government for their benefit.

Someone who wants to acquire groceries does not just wander about hoping to find someone willing to trade them away. Grocery stores exist to make it easy for buyers and sellers to find each other. People who want to borrow money for investment do not just go from person to person seeking willing lenders. Banks and other financial institutions make it easy to match the suppliers of loanable funds with the demanders of loanable funds. Political institutions serve the same function of connecting individuals who can make mutually advantageous exchanges.

Interactions in political markets and in markets for goods and services take place within an institutional framework that structures those interactions. To see the functions of those institutions, the next section looks at the way that people would interact in a hypothetical environment in which there are no transaction costs, so people are able to complete all mutually advantageous exchanges without institutions to guide them. This framework was developed to describe the way that markets for goods and services allocate resources. This is a good starting point for analyzing political markets because it embodies the way that economists have depicted the ideal outcome of market exchange.

Understanding the way that markets in general work lays the foundation for understanding political markets. The same principles apply. This economic analysis begins in a hypothetical institution-free environment. Beginning with that foundation, the analysis can then be extended to see what institutions have developed to enable markets to allocate resources in the way the model describes. The framework that follows describes an outcome that is, in one sense, economically ideal. This provides a benchmark to evaluate what institutional arrangements would be necessary to facilitate such an outcome.

THE PROPENSITY TO TRUCK, BARTER, AND EXCHANGE: COMPETITIVE GENERAL EQUILIBRIUM AS A BENCHMARK

Adam Smith remarks on the human "propensity to truck, barter, and exchange one thing for another,"[7] and economics as a discipline has had a continuing interest in analyzing the way that individuals in market economies, pursuing their own interests, coordinate their economic activities with those of others. People specialize in narrow economic activities and exchange with others who specialize in different activities, enhancing the well-being of everyone as a result. Smith, again, says, "The greatest improvement in the productive powers of Labour, and the greater part of the skill, dexterity, and judgment with which it is any where directed, or applied, seem to have been the effects of the division of labour."[8]

One feature of a market economy is that the quantity supplied tends to equal the quantity demanded for all goods. As Smith states it, "The quantity of every commodity brought to market naturally suits itself to the effectual demand."[9] Smith discusses the operation of the forces of supply and demand, concluding, "the natural price, therefore, is, as it were, the central price, to which the prices of all commodities are continually gravitating."[10] The natural price corresponds, in modern terminology, to the equilibrium price.

One issue in early nineteenth-century economics was whether markets could equate the quantity supplied with the quantity demanded in all markets. Some economists thought so, while others predicted that increased productivity combined with low wages would produce gluts.[11] An economy would supply more goods than people could afford to buy. Continuing down this path of inquiry, Leon Walras developed a mathematical model of general equilibrium in markets, showing that there is a set of prices that can equate the quantity supplied with the quantity demanded in all markets.[12] This general equilibrium framework was further developed by John R. Hicks and Paul Samuelson.[13] Kenneth Arrow

---

[7] Smith, *The Wealth of Nations*, p. 13.
[8] Smith, *The Wealth of Nations*, p. 3.
[9] Smith, *The Wealth of Nations*, p. 57.
[10] Smith, *The Wealth of Nations*, p. 58.
[11] A well-known (at the time) defense of this idea is found in Thomas Robert Malthus, *Principles of Political Economy* (London: William Pickering, 1836).
[12] Leon Walras, *Elements of Pure Economics* (London: Routledge, 2003 [orig. 1874]).
[13] John R. Hicks, *Value and Capital* (Oxford, UK: Clarendon Press, 1939) and Paul Anthony Samuelson, *Foundations of Economic Analysis* (Cambridge, MA: Harvard University Press, 1947).

and Gerard Debreu prove that under ideal conditions there is a unique stable equilibrium vector of prices that will match up all suppliers and demanders to extract all possible gains from trade.[14]

Arrow notes, "There has long been a view that the competitive price equilibrium is efficient or optimal in some sense … it was held that a competitive equilibrium necessarily yielded a Pareto–efficient allocation of resources."[15] J. de V. Graaf and Francis Bator explain that a competitive general equilibrium maximizes welfare in the sense that in a competitive general equilibrium, nobody can be made better off without making someone else worse off.[16] The competitive general equilibrium model represents an ideal end point that will be approached when all possible opportunities for mutually advantageous exchanges implied in that propensity to truck, barter, and exchange play themselves out.

This competitive general equilibrium provides a good benchmark for analysis because it depicts an ideal state of affairs, in that all possible gains from trade have been realized. It is an idealized outcome, but one that, in theory, is the best that could be produced as the result of the real-world activity of market exchange. In a society without coercion and predation, that general equilibrium depicts an outcome that maximizes welfare.[17]

This general equilibrium model was designed to depict the market for goods and services, but these principles of market exchange apply to political markets as well. Those who have access to the political marketplace exchange with each other to maximize the value of those exchanges to those in that market. If there are no impediments to mutually advantageous exchanges – transaction costs are zero – the outcome maximizes the welfare of those in the trading group.

A significant difference is that whereas in markets for goods and services, most costs and benefits accrue to those who participate in the exchanges, political exchanges typically have large impacts on those who are excluded from the political marketplace. The competitive general equilibrium outcome maximizes welfare for those who participate in the market, but most

---

[14] Kenneth J. Arrow and Gerard Debreu, "Existence of an Equilibrium for a Competitive Economy," *Econometrica* 27, no. 3 (1954), pp. 265–290.
[15] Kenneth J. Arrow, "General Economic Equilibrium: Purpose, Analytic Techniques, Collective Choice," *American Economic Review* 64, no. 3 (June 1974), p. 255.
[16] J. de V. Graaf, *Theoretical Welfare Economics* (Cambridge: Cambridge University Press, 1957) and Francis M. Bator, "The Simple Analytics of Welfare Maximization," *American Economic Review* 47, no. 1 (March 1957), pp. 22–59.
[17] A caveat at this point is that one could conceive of a situation in which resources could be forcibly transferred from some and given to others (e.g., from rich to poor) that might be judged an improvement in welfare. This possibility is the subject of Chapter 8.

people are excluded from participating in political markets. So in political markets, the welfare of the elite, who face low transaction costs, is maximized, but this is not necessarily the case for the masses.

IMPEDIMENTS TO GENERAL EQUILIBRIUM

The model of general equilibrium contains no explicit institutions, but some institutional structure is necessary to enable people to truck, barter, and exchange with each other when transaction costs are present. In the real world, two major impediments stand in the way of realizing this ideal outcome. First, there is the challenge of matching up suppliers and demanders. How do people who want to sell goods and people who want to buy them find each other so they can engage in exchange? Institutions facilitate the linking of suppliers with demanders, and more generally, provide a structure within which people interact with each other. These are institutions of organization, which lower transaction costs. Second, the framework assumes that individuals have clear ownership rights over resources, and that ownership changes hands only through mutually advantageous exchanges. There is no predation. Institutions of authority and governance enforce those conditions.

Institutions of organization facilitate mutually advantageous exchanges. They operate through voluntary agreement. Institutions of authority and governance define and enforce people's rights. They operate through the threat of force to be used against those who do not comply.

Most institutions of organization have emerged bottom-up, developed by those who participate in exchange. Many are, as Friedrich Hayek noted, the results of human action but not of human design, although many also are consciously designed.[18] The institutions of authority and governance are designed by the political elite and enforcement is under their control. Those institutions prevent fraud and theft and establish property rights. The force of government stands behind those institutions, which are designed by the political elite in the political marketplace. People voluntarily participate in the institutions of organization because it is to their advantage to do so. People are forced to conform to the institutions of authority and governance.

The institution-free competitive general equilibrium is a good benchmark for institutional analysis for several reasons. First, it is the collective

[18] Friedrich A. Hayek, *Individualism and Economic Order* (London: Routledge and Kegan Paul, 1944).

outcome that would result from that propensity to truck, barter, and exchange, if no impediments stood in the way of mutually advantageous exchanges. Second, it depicts an efficient allocation of resources, making it a good normative benchmark. If an economy could reach that benchmark, nobody could be made better off without making someone else worse off.

Because there are impediments that prevent individuals from making all potentially advantageous exchanges, individuals have the incentive to look for arrangements that overcome those impediments to facilitate those exchanges. They will adopt those arrangements as an institutional framework that defines the way they interact. Institutions enable some types of activity and prohibit others. They address the challenge of approaching that theoretical general equilibrium by defining and enforcing property rights and contracts, and by lowering transaction costs to facilitate the matching of suppliers with demanders. By using a competitive general equilibrium as a benchmark, the analysis that follows describes the institutions necessary to facilitate the movement toward that benchmark – the outcome toward which economies naturally gravitate.

THREE ECONOMIC FUNCTIONS OF INSTITUTIONS

Institutions define the way that people within a society interact with each other. Institutions include social conventions, religious institutions, family relationships, and more. They give people expectations about the behavior of others, constrain people's actions, and enforce those institutional constraints. Institutions extend well beyond their economic functions, but institutions have three basic economic functions. First, some institutions lower transaction costs to facilitate mutually advantageous exchanges. These are institutions of organization. Second, institutions define and enforce the constraints on individual action that are required for the operation of the first category of institutions. These are institutions of authority and governance. Third, institutions redistribute from some individuals to others. Institutions of redistribution are built upon the institutions of authority and governance.

Douglass North says, "Institutions are the humanly devised constraints that structure political, economic, and social interaction."[19] Economic institutions structure the economic interactions that occur in an economy. Institutions of organization, like grocery stores and banks, lower

---

[19] Douglass C. North, "Institutions," *Journal of Economic Perspectives* 5, no. 1 (Winter 1991), p. 97.

the transaction costs of matching up suppliers with demanders. Rules can also serve as institutions of organization. An example is the set of rules that define what constitutes a contract. Money is an institution that facilitates trade when people do not have a mutual coincidence of wants. These institutions of organization are free of coercion because people can choose not to participate in them, and when they do participate, they do so because they believe that it improves their welfare. Institutions of authority and governance are imposed on people by force, even if those people benefit from them. Institutions that define property rights and that prohibit fraud and theft have the threat of force standing behind them.

Institutions of authority and governance do more than this. They prohibit certain types of interactions and require that other types of interactions occur in a certain way. A minimum wage law, for example, prohibits people from working for less than the specified minimum. Consumer protection laws may prevent certain products from being sold and specify required or prohibited characteristics of some goods and services, even if people might prefer the prohibited goods or services. Collective bargaining laws may require that employers and employees determine employment terms through collective bargaining, even if the result is that some employers and some employees may prefer other terms.

While institutions of authority and governance often stand in the way of transactions that might be beneficial, laws against physical assault, against theft, and against fraud enable people to deal with each other through voluntary agreement. They are necessary prerequisites for a market economy.

The general equilibrium framework that provides the foundation for this analysis assumes that individuals engage with others only when they voluntarily choose to do so. But the general equilibrium model that depicts the result of voluntary exchange does not specify any institutions that enable suppliers and demanders to locate each other, or that prevent coercion. Those are the institutions of organization, and the institutions of authority and governance. The masses voluntarily participate in institutions of organization for their own benefit and accept the constraints that come with the institutions of authority and governance because they are necessary for the operation of the institutions of organization.

ACHIEVING GENERAL EQUILIBRIUM

The competitive general equilibrium framework shows the outcome that would result if all mutually beneficial exchanges were to take place, but while that framework depicts the outcome, it does not describe a process that would enable that outcome to occur. Walras resorted to an imaginary and unrealistic auctioneer who would call out prices. Twentieth-century writers did not even go that far, depicting the general equilibrium outcome without describing a process that would produce it. As Samuelson says, "This in brief is the method of *comparative statics*, meaning by this the investigation of changes in a system from one position of equilibrium to another without regard to the transitional process involved in the adjustment."[20]

Walras imagined a process whereby an auctioneer would call out prices for all goods, and suppliers would declare how much they would be willing to supply at those prices while demanders would announce how much they would be willing to demand at those prices. If the quantity supplied exceeded the quantity demanded for a good, that was an indication that the announced price was too high, and if the quantity demanded exceeded the quantity supplied, that was an indication that the price was too low. So, the auctioneer would lower the prices that were too high and raise the prices that were too low, and call out another set of prices which would be closer to the general equilibrium set of prices. The process would continue until it arrived at that set of prices at which the quantity supplied would equal the quantity demanded for all goods.

Walras knew he was not describing the actual process by which markets adjusted. The purpose of his general equilibrium model was to demonstrate that there was a set of prices that would equate the quantity supplied to the quantity demanded for all goods. In the twentieth century, however, advocates of central economic planning argued that economic planners could act just like the auctioneer described by Walras and engineer a centrally planned economy to mimic a market economy.[21]

This line of reasoning, attempting to adapt Walras's auctioneer to become a central planner, began a lively debate about the viability of central economic planning, with some pressing the argument that it was superior to the market mechanism[22] and others arguing that it was

---

[20] Paul Anthony Samuelson, *Foundations of Economic Analysis* (Cambridge, MA: Harvard University Press, 1947), p. 8.

[21] See, for example, Oskar Lange and Fred M. Taylor, *On the Economic Theory of Socialism* (Minneapolis, MN: University of Minnesota Press, 1938).

[22] See Abba P. Lerner, *The Economics of Control: Principles of Welfare Economics* (New York: Macmillan, 1944).

doomed to failure.[23] The debate continued until the collapse of the Berlin Wall in 1989, followed by the break-up of the Soviet Union in 1991, which tilted the advantage toward those who argued against the effectiveness of central economic planning.

Setting the main issue of that debate aside, it does point out something about the market mechanism's tendency toward a general equilibrium, which is that it is not centrally planned by an auctioneer or anyone else. Everyone makes their own plans and, guided by market institutions, is led to that aggregate outcome in which the quantity supplied equals the quantity demanded in all markets. That outcome is generated through the autonomous behavior of all the individuals who determine their own actions and make their own choices, interacting within a market. People have an incentive to seek out mutually beneficial interactions with others. And they have an incentive to design institutions that make it easier to find others with whom they can exchange.

GENERAL EQUILIBRIUM AND THE REAL-WORLD MARKET ECONOMY

This general equilibrium outcome, in which the quantity supplied equals the quantity demanded for all goods, is descriptive of real-world market economies. The quantity supplied does come very close to equaling the quantity demanded for all goods, as long as prices are free to adjust. General equilibrium models are descriptive of the outcome one actually sees in market economies, even if the models do not depict the processes that lead to that outcome.

Explicit recognition of this link between general equilibrium models and the real-world market economy is worthwhile because people are so accustomed to it that they take it for granted. A supermarket stocks tens of thousands of items, and there is always just about the right amount of all of them in the store: a remarkable feat that shoppers have come to expect. If they want milk, or bananas, they just go to the store to get them. Similarly, drivers can run their cars until their gas tanks are nearly empty, confident that when they want gas, they can just drive up to a gas station and get it.

---

[23] For examples, Ludwig von Mises, *Socialism: An Economic and Sociological Analysis* (New Haven, CT: Yale University Press, 1951) and Friedrich A. Hayek, "The Use of Knowledge in Society," *American Economic Review* 35 (1945), pp. 519–530.

The remarkable ability of market institutions to coordinate the plans of everyone in an economy so that everyone gets as much as they want of all goods, as long as they are willing to pay the market price, is not explained by the general equilibrium framework. It describes the outcome without explaining the process that produces that outcome. The value of the general equilibrium model is that it demonstrates the possibility that the quantity supplied will equal the quantity demanded in all markets at a point in time. The demonstration that this outcome is possible and that, if it is realized, is desirable, makes it a good benchmark for understanding what is necessary for it to be realized.

Another way to look at the general equilibrium outcome depicted in economic models is through the lens of the Coase theorem, described in Chapter 1. The Coase theorem says that if no transaction costs stand in the way of mutually beneficial exchanges, all potential mutually beneficial exchanges will be made. The result would be the outcome described by the competitive general equilibrium model. The Coase theorem says that in the absence of transaction costs, suppliers and demanders will find each other and all those exchanges will be made, resulting in a general equilibrium. This is the ultimate end point of Adam Smith's observation about the propensity to truck, barter, and exchange. If there is nothing preventing mutually advantageous exchanges from being made, that propensity will propel them to be made. The result is an optimal allocation of resources, in the sense that at the general equilibrium, nobody could be made better off without making someone else worse off.

In the real world, there are impediments that stand in the way of mutually advantageous exchanges, which is why institutions of organization have evolved to overcome them. Some of those institutions have been purposefully designed, while others have emerged as a by-product of people's pursuit of mutually beneficial interactions.

TWO SHORTCOMINGS OF THE GENERAL EQUILIBRIUM MODEL

The general equilibrium model that has served as a framework for this chapter's discussion falls short of describing the way that markets work in (at least) two important ways. First, as already noted, it depicts an outcome without describing a process that can produce that outcome. That process is driven by the human propensity to truck, barter, and exchange that Adam Smith mentioned, which pushes people to look for ways to transact with others for their mutual benefit. The market matches up suppliers and demanders because they are looking for each other. There is an institutional framework that aids the pairing of suppliers with demands, which the general equilibrium model assumes without explicitly recognizing the institutions that facilitate the connecting of suppliers with demanders.

A second way that the general equilibrium model falls short of describing the market process is that it leaves no room for innovation and progress. The competitive general equilibrium model describes a static equilibrium outcome that, once reached, is the best the economy can do. In an economy that has been characterized by continuing economic progress since the beginning of the Industrial Revolution, a model of static equilibrium omits an explanation of economic progress – the most important economic phenomenon in human history.

As Joseph Schumpeter observed, "The essential point to grasp is that in dealing with capitalism, we are dealing with an evolutionary process. It may seem strange that anyone can fail to see so obvious a fact.... Capitalism, then, is by nature a form or method of economic change and not only never is but never can be stationary."[24] The model of competitive general equilibrium depicts a stationary economy, not one characterized by continual economic progress.

This is the primary reason why attempts to extend Walras's auctioneer to undertake the job of central economic planning fall short. That mechanism might apply to an economy in which underlying economic conditions never change, but things are always changing in a market economy. That propensity to truck, barter, and exchange does more than just equate the quantity supplied with the quantity demanded. It produces economic progress.

PROGRESS AND PROSPERITY

General equilibrium models describe an equilibrium outcome, but with reference to the real-world economy, that outcome is better characterized as market-clearing than as equilibrium. Markets clear in the sense that the quantity supplied equals the quantity demanded in all markets. Equilibrium refers to a situation that, if disturbed, tends to return back to its predisturbed condition. Markets are not like that. Many factors that disturb markets initiate permanent changes, so the market never returns back to its former state. When automobiles replaced horse-drawn

[24] Schumpeter, *Capitalism, Socialism and Democracy*, p. 82.

transportation, stables permanently closed, while gas stations multiplied. Market economies are characterized by continual progress – continual evolution – not equilibrium.

The market process that leads markets to clear is the same process that generates economic progress. Individuals in a market economy do well for themselves when they find ways to create value for others. As Israel Kirzner has explained, individuals prosper by discovering unexploited profit opportunities in an economy, and their entrepreneurial actions move an economy toward that outcome described by the general equilibrium model.[25] That same search for profit opportunities generates economic progress as individuals introduce new and improved goods and more efficient production processes into the economy.[26]

That propensity to truck, barter, and exchange both serves to clear all markets, so that the quantity supplied equals the quantity demanded, and to introduce the innovations into the economy that lead to economic progress. Joseph Schumpeter described a market economy as characterized by creative destruction.[27] New and improved products and more efficient production methods displace the old. Automobiles replace horse-drawn transportation. Flat-screen televisions replaced tube televisions, which replaced some of the functions of radios. Smart phones replace landlines. Even in something as mundane as food, one can see the evolution of restaurants and of items available at grocery stores. The new displaces the old.

This is relevant to the political marketplace because institutions of authority and governance created in the political marketplace enforce those institutions of organization that enable the market process to operate. The masses tolerate, and even appreciate, the protection those institutions of authority provide them, because it allows them to truck, barter, and exchange to generate economic progress. Should institutions of authority stand in the way of progress, the masses may decide to knock them down, much as they did with the Berlin Wall in 1989. The ruling class must be aware of the impact their authority has on the masses, lest they lose that authority.

Meanwhile, economic progress can undermine existing political arrangements and open the opportunity for new ones. Governments

---

[25] Israeil Kirzner, *Competition and Entrepreneurship* (Chicago, IL: University of Chicago Press, 1973).
[26] This idea is discussed in detail in Randall G. Holcombe, *Entrepreneurship and Economic Progress* (London: Routledge, 2007).
[27] Schumpeter, *Capitalism, Socialism, and Democracy*.

have a history of regulating taxi cabs, for example, to create barriers to entry for the benefit of incumbent taxi operations. The development of ride-sharing companies like Uber and Lyft has undermined those old bargains and opened the opportunity for new political transactions. The production of electricity from solar and wind sources opens a potential opportunity for new producers to compete with existing electric utilities, pushing those utilities to enter the political marketplace to try to keep those new technologies off the grid. Economic progress means that there are always new profit opportunities for the well-connected in the political marketplace.

INSTITUTIONS TO SUPPORT GENERAL EQUILIBRIUM

Markets are ubiquitous. Even when governments try to suppress them, underground markets emerge to enable suppliers and demanders to exchange for their mutual benefit. Markets require clearly defined and enforced property rights to function. Buyers must recognize that sellers have the right to sell what they are offering, and those property rights must be enforced to prevent fraud and theft.

This is true even in underground markets. People will buy goods they acknowledge as stolen only if they have some assurance that the original owner will not be able to reclaim the goods. People will buy illegal drugs only if they recognize that the seller has the ability to transfer ownership. For rights to be effective, people must be able to claim and enforce them.[28]

When government does not protect people's property, as is the case with illegal drug dealers, for example, those who have such property develop institutions to protect them.[29] The violence that tends to be associated with these underground markets shows, first, the role that the threat of violence plays in enforcing property rights, and second, the actual violence that occurs when those who threaten to use it cannot display an overwhelming advantage. One might be able to get away with robbing a drug dealer, despite the fact that the dealer is armed, but is less likely to get away with robbing a jewelry store, which has government police and courts protecting it.

---

[28] This idea is more fully developed in Randall G. Holcombe, "The Economic Theory of Rights," *Journal of Institutional Economics* 10, no. 3 (September 2014), pp. 471–491.
[29] See David Skarbek, *The Social Order of the Underworld: How Prison Gangs Govern the American Penal System* (Oxford, UK: Oxford University Press, 2014) for an insightful analysis.

An orderly society requires institutions that define and protect rights. This is true of the market economy depicted in the general equilibrium model, but is equally true of centrally planned economies and any other type of economic organization. And those institutions that define and protect rights also exist in political markets, as Chapter 6 discusses in more detail. Market orders are more self-organizing than planned orders because everyone interacts voluntarily for their mutual benefit. But even when institutions of organization facilitate mutually advantageous exchanges, supporting institutions are required to prevent opportunistic individuals from using force against others.

THE ROLE OF POLITICAL MARKETS

All that government does rests on its comparative advantage in the use of force. Institutions of authority and governance are necessary for the operation of economic institutions, so the masses depend on them, even as they are designed and controlled by a ruling elite, and despite the advantages they give the elite over the masses. Those same institutions of authority and governance that define and protect people's rights can also be used to provide targeted benefits to those who are able to transact in the political marketplace. The only thing those on the government side of those transactions have to offer is access to government's power to coerce.

Despite theories of natural rights, the rights people actually are able to exercise are determined by the political elite, as a result of negotiations in the political marketplace. Public choice theories of rent-seeking[30] and regulatory capture[31] depict individuals and firms negotiating for privileges that transfer resources from others to those interests. Those interests enter the political marketplace to negotiate for access to government power that can be used for their benefit. As with markets for goods and services, prices are determined through negotiation. Those who make the rules weigh the benefits they can get from rent-seeking interests against the costs they impose on others to produce those benefits.[32]

---

[30] These theories were developed by Gordon Tullock, "The Welfare Cost of Tariffs, Monopolies, and Theft," *Western Economic Journal* 5, no. 3 (June 1967), pp. 224–232 and Anne O. Krueger, "The Political Economy of the Rent-Seeking Society," *American Economic Review* 64 (1974), pp. 291–303.

[31] This idea is explained by George J. Stigler, "The Theory of Economic Regulation," *Bell Journal of Economics and Management Science* 2, no. 1 (1971), pp. 3–21.

[32] A model of the political marketplace along these lines is developed by Gary S. Becker, "A Theory of Competition Among Pressure Groups for Political Influence," *Quarterly Journal of Economics* 98, no. 3 (August 1983), pp. 371–400.

Political markets – those that trade in access to government power – are necessary to define and enforce rights, which enables an orderly and productive society. Those same institutions of authority and governance that define and enforce rights open the door to transactions among the well-connected elite for their benefit. Ideally, the elite would use their power to further everyone's common interests, and would be constrained from using it to provide targeted benefits for the well-connected elite. One challenge is that the elite themselves design and enforce the rules, and it is likely that the rules will be designed to benefit their designers. Possible constraints on the abuse of power by the elites who exercise it are considered later in the volume.

CONCLUSION

Economic theory has developed a formidable theoretical framework to describe the outcome that results when individuals engage in that propensity to truck, barter, and exchange, if no transaction costs stand in the way of mutually beneficial exchange. The real-world economy is sure to fall short of this state of affairs because transaction costs that the model assumes away exist in the real world. But, that propensity to truck, barter, and exchange that was observed by Adam Smith pushes people to develop institutions that organize the interactions of individuals to facilitate exchange and move toward that efficient allocation of resources – the competitive general equilibrium that this chapter has used as a benchmark.

This chapter has emphasized two different types of institutions that are required to approach this result. Institutions of organization lower transaction costs to facilitate mutually advantageous interactions among people. People choose to cooperate within these institutions – they do not have to be forced – because doing so works to the advantage of everyone. For these institutions to operate, property rights need to be defined and enforced, and people must be prevented from coercing others. Institutions of authority and governance fulfill this role. Those institutions, designed by the political elite in the political marketplace, are based on the threat of force to be used against those who do not comply.

Political markets operate under the same principles as markets for goods and services. Two big differences, however, are that most people are excluded from participating in the political marketplace, and that most transactions within the political marketplace have large effects on those who are excluded from participating in it. Access to government power is the good that is bought and sold in the political marketplace. This naturally gives an advantage to the elite few who are able to transact to gain access to that power. Much as with externalities in markets for goods, those who are able to transact in the political marketplace often agree to transactions that impose costs on those who are excluded from transacting.

3

Transaction Costs and Institutions

Chapter 2 noted three economic functions of institutions. Some institutions are designed to lower transaction costs. Some institutions are designed to enforce institutional constraints. Some institutions are designed to redistribute income. This chapter builds on the previous one to consider those first two economic functions of institutions. Institutions that redistribute income are analyzed in Chapter 9. Institutions facilitate the exchange of goods and services and, in similar ways, facilitate political exchange, so it makes sense to look at the way institutions, generally, facilitate exchange as a way of understanding the institutions that structure the political marketplace.

Institutions can also inhibit exchange, to be sure. A minimum wage law prohibits employers from hiring employees at a wage lower than the legal minimum, for example. In other cases, there are outright bans on the exchange of some goods. Tariffs are often implemented specifically to discourage the importation of goods, and transaction-based taxes such as sales taxes or value-added taxes impose transaction costs and discourage exchanges that would be mutually beneficial absent the tax cost. Despite some institutional barriers to exchange, by far the most important function of institutions is to facilitate mutually beneficial interactions among individuals.

Transaction costs play a large role in this analysis of political markets and political institutions. This chapter describes the role of institutions, both in markets for goods and services and in political markets. While transaction costs play similar roles in both types of markets, the characteristics of the political marketplace make transaction costs a greater barrier to exchange than is the case in markets for goods and services.

The first step is to see how institutions in markets for goods and services lower transaction costs to promote mutually advantageous exchange and move toward that optimal allocation of resources described in Chapter 2.

INSTITUTIONS THAT LOWER TRANSACTION COSTS

In the general economic equilibrium framework described in Chapter 2, suppliers and demanders somehow find each other so that all mutually advantageous exchanges take place, and the economy allocates resources efficiently, in the sense that nobody can be made better off without making someone else worse off. For this outcome to be approached, suppliers and demanders must have some way to discover potential opportunities for exchange. This is the role of institutions of organization.

In the real-world economy, someone who wants to buy a gallon of milk does not just wander off into "the economy," hoping to run into someone who wants to sell a gallon of milk. Grocery stores are institutions that facilitate the matching of suppliers of milk with demanders of milk. The real-world market is more complicated than this simple example lets on. Wholesale and retail markets that have developed for milk, along with markets to transport milk from dairy farms to final consumers. Futures markets for milk allow people to lock in prices and quantities for future delivery. The actual market economy comes very close to facilitating all the mutually advantageous exchanges for that commodity. Everyone who wants to sell milk finds it easy to do so. Everyone who wants to buy milk finds it easy to do so. Similar observations could be made about all markets. Institutions arise to enable suppliers and demanders to find each other.

Because institutions develop to facilitate the matching of suppliers with demanders, the general equilibrium model is a fairly realistic representation of the outcome produced by a market economy, even though it does not describe the process that leads to that outcome. That process takes place within the framework provided by market institutions, which facilitate the matching of suppliers with demanders in all markets. These are institutions of organization.

The institutions of organization serve the function of lowering transaction costs so that suppliers and demanders can more easily locate each other and engage in exchange. They provide information to suppliers and demanders, and they also provide structure to their interactions. Institutions of organization provide people with an expectation of how others will interact with them. This is true in the political marketplace just as it is in the market for goods and services. As Chapter 2 emphasized, people voluntarily engage within these institutions of organization because doing so is beneficial for everyone. And, people continually look out for institutional innovations that can lower transaction costs, because doing so creates a profit opportunity.[1]

INSTITUTIONS OF ORGANIZATION

Douglass North says transaction costs are "the costs of measuring and enforcing agreements."[2] Accepting North's description, measurement costs and enforcement costs differ from each other in an important way. Measurement is important because people must have a good idea of what is agreed upon in an exchange. This is straightforward in simple exchanges. When A exchanges an apple for an orange with B, both parties can see what is being exchanged, so measurement is not an issue. When A agrees to build a house for B in exchange for a sum of money to be paid at some time in the future as the house is completed, the measurement issue arises in many dimensions, including the physical characteristics of the house, the time when the house will be completed, and what benchmarks must be met for payment to take place. Both parties will want a clear understanding of what they are giving up and what they are getting in return before they agree to an exchange.

Contracts serve to specify the terms of an exchange. Contracts address the measurement issue. They are institutions of organization, and both parties to an exchange want the terms to be clearly specified. There is always some incompleteness and ambiguity in a contract, and when parties disagree about what they agreed to, institutions of enforcement come into play. Enforcement arises as an issue when one party believes the other is not living up to the terms of the agreement. Institutions of measurement are the product of agreement between transacting parties. Institutions of enforcement typically involve a third party that sorts out any disputes. Enforcement is undertaken by institutions of authority and governance.

Measurement costs involve identifying mutually advantageous transactions. Enforcement costs involve ensuring that both parties to a transaction live up to their contractual obligations. The transaction will not

---

[1] Israel Kirzner, *Competition and Entrepreneurship* (Chicago, IL: University of Chicago Press, 1973) depicts entrepreneurship as the noticing of previously unnoticed profit opportunities.
[2] Douglass C. North, "A Transaction Cost Theory of Politics," *Journal of Theoretical Politics* 2, no. 4 (1990), p. 362.

occur if it costs more to provide this assurance than the gains from trade that would result from the transaction.

Both measurement and enforcement are more concretely defined in markets for goods and services than they are in the political marketplace. When legislators promise lobbyists they will introduce and promote legislation the lobbyist desires, legislators get payment up front, but because ultimately any legislation requires majority approval, a legislator can always say, "I tried, but the support just wasn't there." Lobbyists will not get refunds if they do not get what they anticipated, although lobbyists may be reluctant to deal with that legislator in the future.[3] Similarly, when legislators accumulate IOUs by asking fellow legislators to support some legislation, there is some ambiguity in what constitutes repayment. And if a legislator reneges on repaying a debt, there are no formal sanctions for what amounts to breach of contract.

The public choice literature on rent-seeking embodies this ambiguity. Rent-seeking is depicted as a contest in which the rent-seekers pay up-front with the hope of "winning" a rent. Many contestants pay the rent-seeking costs but come up empty-handed.[4] In markets for goods and services, measurement issues are resolved so that people get what they pay for.

The new institutional economics, as described by Oliver Williamson, focuses primarily on the institutions of organization – institutions that lower transaction costs.[5] Institutions as varied as firms,[6] retail stores, money, banks, contracts,[7] and advertising lower transaction costs to help suppliers and demanders in markets to locate and trade with each other.

---

[3] Political transactions are in this sense similar to those in the market for health care. When one purchases an automobile, it comes with a warranty, and should defects later become apparent, automobiles are often subject to recalls to fix the defects at the seller's expense. Health care transactions typically come with no warranties. Health care providers get paid up front and health care professionals get paid the same amount regardless of whether their treatments make their patients better.

[4] See Roger D. Congleton and Arye L. Hillman, eds., *Companion to the Political Economy of Rent-Seeking* (Cheltenham, UK: Edward Elgar, 2015), who include eight chapters from different authors on rent-seeking theory, all of which characterize rent-seeking as a contest.

[5] Oliver E. Williamson, "A Comparison of Alternative Approaches to Economic Methodology," *Journal of Institutional and Theoretical Economics* 146, no. 1 (1990), pp. 595–613.

[6] Ronald H. Coase, "The Nature of the Firm," *Economica* n.s. 4, no. 16 (November 1937), pp. 386–405.

[7] Michael C. Jensen and William H. Meckling, "Theory of the Firm: Managerial Behavior, Agency Costs, and Ownership Structure," *Journal of Financial Economics* 3, no. 4 (October 1976), pp. 305–360.

Because these institutions facilitate mutually advantageous exchange, people do not have to be forced to participate in them. They want to, for their own benefit. And, people have an incentive to look for ways to improve existing institutions of organization and to discover new institutions of organization. This is as true in the political marketplace as it is in markets for goods and services. Legislators, lobbyists, and other well-connected interests look for ways to negotiate with others for their mutual advantage.

BILATERAL EXCHANGE AND TRANSACTION COSTS

By far the most important mechanism for lowering transaction costs is the development of institutions that reduce transactions to bilateral exchanges. When large numbers of people must be involved for a mutually advantageous exchange, there is a good chance that the exchange will not occur because transaction costs are too high. This was the major point that Ronald Coase was making in his famous paper on externalities.[8] If one person imposes a cost on another, the two can bargain to reach an efficient allocation of resources. When large numbers of people must be involved – for example, thousands of people breathing polluted air from nearby industries – transaction costs will likely be too high for them to be able to negotiate to reach an agreement to limit the pollution.

Consider, in the framework of the general equilibrium model, the production of Toyota automobiles for American consumers. Thousands of Japanese autoworkers must organize to produce automobiles for thousands of American consumers who are thousands of miles away. Mutually advantageous exchanges can be made if institutions can be designed to facilitate them – to coordinate the activities of all these thousands of people. Readers already know how markets solve this problem, but explicitly stating it shows the challenge. How do thousands of Japanese autoworkers find a way to organize their labor to produce cars and get them to American consumers who are willing to buy them? How do thousands of potential American car buyers organize to strike a deal with those autoworkers to build cars for them? The short answer is that institutions arise to transform that organizational problem into a large number of bilateral exchanges.

---

[8] Ronald H. Coase, "The Problem of Social Cost," *Journal of Law & Economics* 3 (1960), pp. 1–44.

Those thousands of workers who cooperate to produce automobiles do not negotiate collectively with each other, but rather engage in bilateral agreements with the Toyota motor company regarding their individual employment. One employee negotiates with one employer. Similarly, Toyota does not bargain collectively with a large number of buyers, or even directly with consumers at all, but bilaterally with American auto dealers who buy the cars from Toyota. Those dealers then deal bilaterally with each individual auto buyer. One auto dealer negotiates with one auto purchaser. This undertaking, which matches up thousands of suppliers of labor and owners of capital with thousands of demanders of automobiles, occurs because institutions have been developed to break down that large undertaking into a large number of bilateral exchanges.

Michael Jensen and William Meckling have characterized firms as a nexus of contracts, and one function of those contracts is to distill the cooperative efforts of, in many cases, thousands of workers into a set of bilateral exchanges, lowering transaction costs.[9] With one buyer and one seller in each transaction, transaction costs can be kept low. One individual autoworker deals with one individual employer, and one individual auto buyer deals with one individual dealer.

The primary way that institutions of organization lower transaction costs is by decentralizing transactions to minimize the number of transacting parties, ideally to two. Banks match up a large number of borrowers with a large number of lenders, but acting as a financial intermediary reduces that matching to bilateral transactions. Each borrower transacts individually with the bank, and each lender transacts individually with the bank. Institutions can be more complex to provide greater gains from trade – fractional reserve banking is an example – but the most significant way that institutions lower transaction costs to facilitate mutually advantageous exchange is by reducing more complex transactions into bilateral exchanges.

These institutions of organization arise from the bottom up, as entrepreneurs find ways to contract with buyers and sellers for their mutual advantage. All parties want to enter into the transactions because they benefit. The autoworkers at Toyota take those jobs because they believe they are better off doing so, and the buyers of autos at the other end choose to buy the autos because they believe they are better off as a result. Some of those gains from trade go to the owners and managers

---

[9] Michael C. Jensen and William H. Meckling, "Theory of the Firm: Managerial Behavior."

of the firms that facilitate those mutually beneficial exchanges. The end result occurs because the activities of many autoworkers producing automobiles for many consumers can be divided into a large number of bilateral exchanges, each with low transaction costs.

CONTRACTS

To clarify the distinction between institutions of organization – those that lower transaction costs – and institutions of governance – those that enforce institutional constraints – consider a contract as a straightforward example. A person contracts with a carpenter to build a table, for example, but the project will take time. The carpenter wants to make sure to get the money in exchange for building and delivering the table, and the person buying the table wants to make sure to get the table in exchange for the money. One can see the potential for a breach of contract. If the buyer pays the money in advance, the buyer risks not getting the table, and if the buyer agrees to pay once the table is delivered, the carpenter risks not receiving the money after having built the table.

Contracts in general, including this one, are institutions of organization designed to lower transaction costs by specifying the terms of a mutually beneficial exchange. Both the buyer and the seller view it as in their interest to agree to the contract. The carpenter anticipates being better off with the money in exchange for making the table, and the buyer anticipates being better off having the table in exchange for the money. Nobody has to force these individuals to contract. They voluntarily agree to the contract because both believe they will be better off.

Should one side breach the contract, institutions of governance are then called upon to resolve the issue. Because there is a disagreement (at least) one of the parties will not be satisfied with the resolution, requiring some threat of force should one party not want to resolve the dispute as those with authority have decreed. Two different types of institutions are at work here. Institutions of organization bring together the buyer and the seller, but if there is a breach or disagreement between them, institutions of governance enforce the constraints that come with institutions of organization. Characterizing institutions this way is especially helpful in clarifying what constitutes institutions of governance – those institutions that are designed in the political marketplace.

Envisioning a firm as a nexus of contracts, contracts are mutually agreed to for the benefit of all parties. Nobody is forced to enter those contractual arrangements. They are designed to lower transaction costs for the mutual benefit of the contracting parties. Firms are institutions of organization, formed through contractual arrangements. Firms are not institutions of governance.

However, the nexus of contracts has institutions of governance standing behind it in case one party breaches the terms of the contract, or if there are disagreements about the obligations that the contracting parties have to each other. In case of breach or disagreement, parties can go to court to resolve the issue. What if the employer does not pay the employee? Institutions of governance stand behind the institutions of organization to enforce the institutional constraints.

In the political marketplace, many agreements are informally made and do not have clear terms. If one legislator agrees to a colleague's request to support some legislation, what does that colleague owe to the legislator who agreed? The answer is often deliberately not stated. If a lobbyist provides a benefit to a legislator in exchange for supporting some legislation, what does the legislator owe the lobbyist? Just introducing a bill in a committee? Negotiating for support to pass the legislation? Actually getting the legislation passed? Clearly, one legislator cannot pass legislation alone, and the legislator might be reluctant to accumulate IOUs to further the lobbyist's cause.

The competitive markets in a general equilibrium model characterize participants as price takers. Participants consider the terms of exchange as given, determined by market forces. In the political marketplace, where the parameters of exchanges are not so clearly defined, those who have accumulated more political power can use it to capture more of the gains from trade for themselves. Political markets are less "competitive" than competitive markets for goods and services, in the sense that the political marketplace does not typically determine how the gains from trade are divided. That is determined by the individuals who engage in exchanges.

Even when legal contracts are formally written, there can be ambiguities that result in disagreements and lawsuits. Agreements in the political marketplace typically have more ambiguities and no method of third-party enforcement. Once a legislator cashes that campaign contribution check, the only thing that pushes the legislator to fulfill the agreed-upon bargain is the legislator's reputation. That is one reason why the political elite must remain a small subset of the total population. Participants must know each other well enough to rely on those reputations.

RULES AND ORGANIZATIONS

Institutions consist of rules that structure interactions and organizations that define and enforce those rules. Some rules allow people to engage in certain actions. Other rules require people to do things they might otherwise choose not to do, while still others prohibit people from doing things they might otherwise choose to do. Because rules are constraints on people's behavior, they can only act as constraints if they are enforced. Organizations define and enforce the rules.

Consider a retail store as an organization that structures a set of processes – rules – that facilitate transactions they make with their customers. Retailers may specify that customers go to cashiers who total the purchases and make the exchange of money for goods. If many buyers converge at the same time, retailers will have procedures for customers to queue up to make their purchases. Stores, as organizations, enforce the rules by employing security guards and requiring that customers leave the stores only at certain points where they can be monitored. Retailers are organizations that design rules to structure the interactions between their customers and themselves. This example illustrates that institutions are a combination of rules for social interaction and organizations that both facilitate that interaction and enforce the rules.

Organizations typically embody both institutions of organization that facilitate mutually advantageous activities and institutions of governance that enforce those mutually advantageous activities. Retail stores provide an organizational mechanism to bring together suppliers and demanders, and also governance mechanisms to prevent fraud and theft.

In addition to the store's own enforcement mechanisms, it also relies on government enforcement mechanisms such as police and courts, operating within a legal structure – a set of rules – that constrains the actions of those who transact in the market. The organization that makes the rules might also enforce them, but often, third-party enforcement stands behind the rules, and often, that third party is the government.

Similarly, banks are organizations that define procedures – rules – that enable transactions between suppliers and demanders of loanable funds. In the absence of institutions, it would be difficult for borrowers and lenders to find each other. Banks lower transaction costs to facilitate making those exchanges. Legal institutions are the same in this regard. They are a set of rules enforced by organizations – courts, and if required, police.

Organizations establish rules to structure how individuals interact with them. Similarly, the creation of rules requires organizations to enforce them. Banks establish procedures to interact with their customers, but the government also creates rules that structure those transactions, enforced by the Federal Reserve, the Federal Deposit Insurance Corporation, and other organizations. Legislators create minimum wage laws, and those rules require organizations (such as the Department of Labor) to enforce them.

Institutions have the same general functions in the political marketplace. Rules structure organizations such as Congress and regulatory agencies, which are organizations that enforce, and often design, the rules. Within that structure, those who face low transaction costs can negotiate with each other to their mutual advantage.

TRANSACTION COSTS AND GOVERNANCE

The primary way institutions lower transaction costs is by reducing complex transactions down to a series of bilateral exchanges. That presents an insurmountable challenge when designing the institutions of governance, because those institutions are designed to enforce constraints on a large number of people. To illuminate the problem, consider the nature of externalities in markets for goods. In markets for goods and services, the costs and benefits of transactions mostly are confined to those who are engaged in the transactions. When externalities are present – smoke-polluting factories provide the classic example – transactions affect people who are not engaged in them. When the auto manufacturer agrees to buy steel from the steel mill, the air pollution from the steel mill creates an external cost imposed on those who have to breathe the polluted air. The problem is that with large numbers of people bearing those external costs, transaction costs are high, so they cannot negotiate to mitigate the externality.

In political transactions, almost all of them affect large numbers of people who are not party to the transactions. An elite few make and enforce the rules. The masses are subject to those rules. An elite few decide how much in taxes people are obligated to pay. The masses pay those taxes. Members of the political elite are like the auto manufacturer and the steel mill in the previous example. They face low transaction costs and bargain to maximize the value of their exchanges to those who participate in the political marketplace. The masses are like those who breathe the polluted air. High transaction costs prevent them from negotiating to mitigate any costs imposed on them by the elite.

Individuals who contemplate engaging in market transactions for goods and services can decide not to undertake the transaction if the terms appear unfavorable. But most of those who are affected by political exchanges are third parties who have no ability to exempt themselves from the transactions made by others in the political marketplace. The masses cannot opt out of the institutions designed by the elite. Individuals buy their own automobiles, and one person's purchase of an automobile does not determine what automobiles (if any) other people will buy. Individuals can have their own individual automobiles, but not their own individual laws. Laws that apply to one person apply to (almost) everyone.

Many people have observed that an elite few make and enforce the rules that most people are forced to follow. An understanding of the role of transaction costs in the design of institutions of governance and authority explains why this must be the case. Despite populist visions of democratic government that is under the control of the masses, this cannot happen because transaction costs prevent it.

INFORMAL GOVERNANCE

Formal enforcement of institutional constraints is undertaken by third parties who have the power and authority to impose costs on those who violate the rules. If someone violates the rules by assaulting another person, police, courts, and prisons are formal institutions designed to impose costs on the assailant. Ideally, the display of potential force by the authorities will be sufficient to deter people from violating the rules. With a sufficient display of the potential to use force, the need to use actual force should be rare.

Informal governance relies on the members of the group who are subject to the group's rules to enforce them through social sanctions. People who violate social norms can be subject to disapproval by others, shunning, or ostracism. Even in high-value market transactions, if there is a small group of traders who know each other and trust each other based on their reputations, those people have an incentive to abide by the norms of the group so they can remain a part of it. Robert Axelrod makes a case that an environment in which people acquire reputations with others they interact with is sufficient to overcome opportunistic behavior.[10] People risk losing their good reputations and being excluded from future exchanges if they act underhandedly. This works for some types of transactions, but not for others.

---

[10] Robert Axelrod, *The Evolution of Cooperation* (New York: Basic Books, 1984).

A small group of diamond traders in New York relies on the doctrine of continuous dealings because they all know each other and are included in the group based on their reputations.[11] They have an incentive to be fair and honest with each other to avoid being expelled from the group. They can rely on informal enforcement of their rules because everyone in the group is aware of the reputations of everyone else. Retail stores that have many customers who are personally unknown to the retailers must rely on intentionally designed formal enforcement mechanisms to prevent fraud and theft. They do not know the reputations of all the customers with whom they deal. The mechanisms they use to enforce institutional constraints may rely partly on their own actions, such as locking up valuable merchandise, but also rely on third-party enforcement from police and courts.

Oliver Williamson uses Adam Smith's invisible hand, leading people who are pursuing their own interests to act in the interests of everyone, as an example of spontaneous governance.[12] This is an example of spontaneous order, but not an example of spontaneous governance. The invisible hand falls under the heading of organization, not governance. People voluntarily engage in exchange because they benefit from doing so. Governance enforces the agreements people voluntarily make, to prevent fraud or theft.

The invisible hand does not prevent opportunistic individuals from engaging in fraud and theft when opportunities present themselves. Market exchange among individuals who do not know each other well enough to have the trust exhibited by New York diamond traders is supported by governance institutions – police and courts – in addition to the efforts of the traders themselves. Retailers lock up valuable goods and employ security guards to try to limit such opportunistic behavior.

Spontaneous institutions of governance can emerge without anyone planning them out, but Adam Smith's invisible hand mechanism is not, on its own, such an institution. People voluntarily agree to engage in exchange for their mutual benefit, and nobody needs to force them to do so. These market institutions emerge spontaneously, without anybody planning them out. Companion institutions to enforce property rights and mitigate breach of contract may also emerge spontaneously, as the

---

[11] See Barak D. Richman, *Stateless Commerce: The Diamond Network and the Persistence of Relational Exchange* (Cambridge, MA: Harvard University Press, 2017).

[12] Oliver E. Williamson, *The Mechanisms of Governance* (New York: Oxford University Press, 1996), ch. 6.

diamond trader example shows, but often, third-party enforcement is necessary to prevent opportunistic behavior.

The political marketplace is a combination of formal and informal institutions. Formal rules structure government, specifying different branches of government, how they are organized, and how they operate. For example, Congress passes legislation by majority vote of both houses, which then requires the president's approval. If the president vetoes the legislation, the veto can be overridden by a two-thirds vote of both houses. Within the institutional framework of those formal procedures is the political marketplace in which legislators negotiate with each other, with lobbyists, and with other interests to produce a legislative outcome. Logrolling and vote trading are well-established but informal institutions.

Much political exchange is enforced informally. When a legislator asks a colleague to support some legislation, if the colleague agrees, the legislator incurs a debt that must be repaid. The legislator trusts the colleague to vote as promised, and in exchange, the colleague can come back to say, "Remember when I supported your bill? Now I'd like your vote on mine." Legislators who do not repay those debts develop reputations that keep them from engaging in future political exchanges, but there is no formal sanction or penalty that is levied on legislators who do not pay their debts.

The rule that legislation requires majority approval from Congress is formally enforced, but political exchanges made among legislators are not. If a legislator decides not to follow through on a bargain – say, voting against a bill the legislator promised to support – the group may express disapproval, and members might decide not to participate in exchanges with that legislator in the future. Sanctions come only from the legislator's loss of reputation, which is why the group participating in politics as exchange must always remain small. Those engaged in political exchange do so based on their reputations, and large groups, in which members cannot know the reputations of all of those with whom they are transacting, have no way to verify that those they bargain with will actually follow through.

THE OMNISCIENT BENEVOLENT DICTATOR

The general equilibrium models developed in the mid twentieth century derived with mathematical precision the conditions under which a competitive general equilibrium will exist. This led to an analysis of situations in which those conditions would not be met, which economists then defined as market failures. According to the economist's definition, a market failure exists whenever an economy does not reach a welfare-maximizing competitive general equilibrium. Common examples of market failures are externalities, public goods, and monopolies.[13] The term is not descriptive because it labels outcomes as failures when there may not be any possible outcome that would be better. In theory, the optimal welfare-maximizing general equilibrium outcome would be ideal. In practice, there may be no way for a real-world economy to achieve that theoretical ideal.

A common approach economists take to addressing market failure is to derive conditions for the optimal allocation of resources and then assume that government will design policies that satisfy those conditions. Government, in this approach, acts as an omniscient benevolent dictator. But, government is not omniscient, it is not benevolent, and it is not a dictator.

Often, the conditions for the optimal allocation of resources would require policymakers to use information that is not available to anyone. To optimally correct for an externality requires knowing the external cost, but that information is not observable, so it is not available to policymakers. Efficient provision of a public good by government would require knowing the optimal quantity of the public good, which would require knowing how much value individuals place on it. That information is not available to anyone. Government cannot implement optimal corrections for market failure because the information it would require is unavailable. Government is not omniscient.

Government also is not benevolent. Most members of the general public are well aware that politicians will support policies to gain political support, even if those policies are inefficient. Their motivation is to win elections, which sometimes leads them away from efficient policies. Meanwhile, government bureaucrats seek job security, higher pay, and budget increases for their agencies, again leading to inefficiencies.[14] People in the public sector are looking out for their own interests, just as are people in the private sector. Those in government may try to further the

---

[13] See Francis M. Bator, "The Anatomy of Market Failure," *Quarterly Journal of Economics* 72, no. 3 (August 1958), pp. 351–379 for a taxonomy built on the general equilibrium framework.

[14] On this matter, see William A. Niskanen, *Bureaucracy and Representative Government* (Chicago, IL: Aldine-Atherton, 1971).

public interest as they see it, as long as it does not impose too much cost on themselves, but government is not benevolent.

And, government is not a dictator. No one individual in government has the power to dictate government policy. In democracies, political outcomes are the product of a political marketplace in which individuals negotiate to produce public policies. To understand political outcomes, one must understand the political marketplace that produces them. Even in dictatorships, the dictator must remain aware of potential challengers and must maintain a group of loyal supporters to remain in power. The purpose of analyzing the political marketplace is to understand the process by which individuals interact to produce public policy.[15]

One problem with this approach to public policy – deriving optimality conditions and then hoping government will implement them – is that it offers the false hope that with good leadership, it would be possible to do this. Academic economists promote the idea and politicians campaign on it. Politicians essentially say that what is needed for better government is an omniscient, benevolent dictator, and if they are elected, they will fill that role. Of course, they cannot use those exact words, or citizens would see that their message amounts to wishful thinking. But political campaigns often are built on that type of wishful thinking.

There is a parallel between the theory of market failure and the real-world political demands of the masses. When people perceive social or economic problems, they are quick to demand that those in authority do something to address them. If the political elite do not try, that opens the door to challengers who claim that if elected, they would address those problems. How could they do this? The general equilibrium framework offers a mathematically precise model of optimality – a model the political elite would be able to implement, if they were omniscient benevolent dictators. This approach to public policy – political promises to address perceived real-world problems – finds academic support in economic models of market failure.

There is a bias in the selection of expert policy advisors for this reason. Politicians promise to solve problems. If one potential policy advisor says it would not be possible to design institutions to address those problems because the information needed to reach an optimal solution would not be possible to acquire, while another claims to know what to do to solve

---

[15] See Richard E. Wagner, *Fiscal Sociology and the Theory of Public Finance* (Cheltenham, UK: Edward Elgar, 2007), who makes the case that interactions within the political marketplace are more complex than at first they appear.

the problem, the second policy advisor will get the job, even if the first policy advisor is correct. Then, if the problem remains unsolved, the government will throw more money at it, more regulations, and hire more personnel. In markets, when firms fail to meet their goals, they go out of business. In government, when agencies fail to meet their goals, they get budget increases so they can hire more bureaucrats and increase their scope of authority.

THE PROBLEM OF LARGE NUMBERS

In markets for goods and services, institutions that lower transaction costs decentralize economic interactions, often reducing them to bilateral transactions. This allows individuals who participate in exchanges to agree on their terms. If satisfactory terms cannot be agreed upon, the transaction will not take place. Institutions that enforce institutional constraints cannot be decentralized. One set of rules applies to (almost) everybody. Because the same rules necessarily apply to a large number of people, the large numbers involved preclude bargaining among those who are covered by the rules.

If an individual interested in buying a good finds the terms a seller offers to be unacceptable, the buyer can opt out and not complete the transaction. Institutions that lower transaction costs simply make transactions feasible, but do not require that people complete them. However, people cannot opt out of rules that enforce institutional constraints. Rules against fraud and theft and rules that prohibit people from assaulting or killing other people apply to the masses. Individuals cannot negotiate their own terms for those rules, because large numbers of people are governed by those rules, and transaction costs prevent those who are covered by the rules from negotiating over their content.

Some institutions stand in the way of mutually advantageous exchanges. Institutions that specify employment conditions, such as minimum wage laws, that require that products have certain characteristics or are prohibited from having other characteristics, such as requiring ethanol in motor fuels, impose costs on some for the benefit of others. The rules apply generally, and high transaction costs mean that those who are governed by them have no say in their design.

An elite few are in the low transaction cost group that can negotiate to design the rules, and those elite few are in a position to design exceptions to the rules for themselves. Most people are not in this position. The problem of large numbers goes in two directions. It prevents the masses from having a meaningful say in the rules under which they are governed, and it allows the elite to design rules such that they are not constrained by the rules that apply to the masses.

CONCLUSION

Institutions of organization are designed to lower transaction costs. Transaction costs tend to be prohibitively high when large numbers of people would be required to engage in a transaction, so because of transaction costs, those transactions will not occur. Classic cases of externalities, such as when large numbers of people in an area suffer the externality of air pollution from nearby industries, are good examples. Large numbers prevent those suffering from pollution from negotiating with those who are causing it.

One way that market institutions deal with the problem of large numbers is to reduce those large number cases down to a set of bilateral exchanges. With two parties engaged in transactions, transaction costs are lower and that facilitates mutually advantageous exchange. That works well for institutions of organization, but is difficult to apply to institutions of governance because one set of rules applies to the entire population. Transaction costs are necessarily high, which means that only an elite few will be able to negotiate in the design of those institutions of authority and governance.

Many people have observed that government is run by an elite few, sometimes following that observation with ideas on how to shift control of government to those who are governed. Looking at the effect of transaction costs reveals that not only is it the case that an elite few control government, it must be the case. High transaction costs prevent the masses from negotiating the design of institutions of authority and governance.

4

The Characteristics of Authority

The primary benefit institutions bring to a society is that they lower transaction costs, to enable people to interact with each other productively for their mutual advantage. People voluntarily interact within these institutions because they gain by doing so. These institutions that lower transaction costs depend upon institutions of authority – institutions of governance – in two ways, both of which are based on the threat of force. First, before people can interact productively with each other, their rights and obligations toward each other must be defined. Second, those rights and obligations, along with any agreements people have made with each other, must be enforced.

Economic exchange requires that property rights be defined so that people know what they have a right to exchange, and that those who offer to trade with them have the right to sell what they are offering. Governments establish land titles, for example, to specify who owns specific pieces of land. Even with title established, there may be restrictions on how owners can use their land.[1] Patent and copyright laws establish rights to intellectual property.[2] Labor laws establish restrictions on the ability of people to buy or sell labor services. Beyond economic activities, people have other obligations, such as prohibitions against assaulting one another and restrictions on activities that are allowed in public places.

---

[1] Hernando de Soto, *The Other Path: The Invisible Revolution in the Third World* (New York: Harper & Row, 1989), discusses problems that arise without clearly defined and government-enforced land titles.

[2] See N. Stephan Kinsella, *Against Intellectual Property* (Auburn, AL: Ludwig von Mises Institute, 2008) for a thought-provoking discussion of intellectual property rights.

4 The Characteristics of Authority

Those institutions are imposed on people regardless of whether they agree. Going back to Douglass North's definition of institutions as constraints that structure people's interactions with each other, a constraint implies that there is a limit placed on people's behavior. Some people may feel they should have the right to play music at a loud volume in their own homes, while others feel they should have the right to a quiet environment free from the sound of their neighbors' music. Some people may feel that businesses should have the right to sell their inventory at whatever prices the market will bear, whereas others believe that they should not be allowed to raise their prices during emergencies, such as those caused by hurricanes or earthquakes. Institutions of authority and governance determine what rights people actually are able to exercise.

An orderly society requires that prior to people interacting with each other, a set of rights, including property rights, must be established specifying allowable interactions.[3] A buyer in a market must be assured that the seller actually has the right to sell what is being offered. People must have an assurance that they will not be assaulted by others to prevent interpersonal interactions from devolving into a war of all against all, as Thomas Hobbes described anarchy. Because some people might disregard those institutional constraints that are imposed on everyone, the threat of force must stand behind them.

Even when people have agreed to transactions, a method of ensuring that all parties live up to their agreements must be in place. Even with simple transactions – two people agree to exchange an apple for an orange – there must be a mechanism to prevent theft. For more complex transactions – labor contracts or construction contracts – there may be misunderstandings in addition to the possibility that one of the parties decides not to fulfill their part of the bargain. A complex economy requires sophisticated enforcement mechanisms.

Institutions that lower transaction costs do not require force, because all parties agree to transactions that make them better off, and because nobody is required to transact with others. Before those mutually agreeable transactions occur, institutions that assign rights require the threat of force against those who would violate the rights people are given by the institutions of authority and governance. During and after those transactions occur, the threat of force may be required to compel people to follow through on what they have agreed to deliver to others. The

---

[3] Murray N. Rothbard, *The Ethics of Liberty* (Atlantic Highlands, NJ: Humanities Press, 1982), explains that all rights are property rights.

institutions of authority and governance rest on their ability to coerce. Those institutions are designed through negotiations that take place in the political marketplace and controlled by the political elite.

INSTITUTIONS OF GOVERNANCE

If institutions are humanly devised constraints, as Douglass North stated, they must be enforced to be constraining, which is the role of institutions of authority and governance. To be effective, those who administer the institutions of authority must have enough power to overpower those who are governed by them. Those who control them must have the obvious capability to marshal sufficient force that those who are subject to institutional constraints believe that resistance would be more costly than compliance. That way, actual force rarely has to be used.

Actual use of force is costly to those who use it, so those who administer the institutions of governance always want to display sufficient power to make resistance appear futile. Then, as Douglass North says, "The costs to the individual of opposing the coercive forces of the state have traditionally resulted in apathy and acceptance of the state's rules, no matter how oppressive."[4] The apathy that North refers to was called rational ignorance by Anthony Downs.[5] If citizens have little choice but to comply with government mandates, they have little incentive to analyze or question them. Those mandates become part of the environment within which they act.

North says, "A state is an organization with a comparative advantage in violence, extending over a geographic area whose boundaries are determined by its power to tax constituents. The essence of property rights is the right to exclude, and an organization which has a comparative advantage in violence is in the position to specify and enforce property rights."[6] This passage illustrates the relationship between institutions that lower transaction costs and institutions of governance. The latter are the enforcement mechanisms for the former.

That benchmark social goal of competitive general equilibrium rests on the unstated assumptions that institutions that eliminate transaction costs are in place so that suppliers and demanders can costlessly find each

---

[4] Douglass North, *Structure and Change in Economic History* (New York: Norton, 1981), p. 31.
[5] Anthony Downs, *An Economic Theory of Democracy* (New York: Harper & Row, 1957).
[6] Douglass C. North, *Structure and Change in Economic History*, p. 21.

other and that institutions of authority and governance are in place to constrain all individuals to act only within market institutions. The element of force begins with the definition of property rights. Whereas the general equilibrium model assumes that property rights are well-defined, that often is not the case. One role of institutions of governance is to define and enforce property rights.

Jon Pierre and Guy Peters say, "The best way to understand governance is as a process of steering and control."[7] The language they use makes governance sound benign, but steering means telling people what to do, and control means enforcing their mandates so that people have little choice. Those who steer and control make the rules. Those who are subject to the rules are forced to obey. Those who steer and control are the political elite, who design public policies in the political marketplace.

Erik Furubotn and Rudolph Richter observe that "the decisive difference between economic and political competition is that economic competition is the struggle for economic advantages through economic exchange. It occurs on the basis of secure property rights. Political competition, on the other hand, is the struggle for authority, that is, the power to change exactly these property rights – unilaterally, without any economic quid pro quo."[8] Rights, including property rights, are not in any sense given, despite any arguments people make about what rights people should have. Rights are assigned by those who control the institutions of authority, and citizens must comply with their mandates regardless of whether they agree.

RIGHTS EXIST ONLY TO THE EXTENT THAT THEY ARE CLAIMED AND ENFORCED

Any discussion of rights has normative issues lurking in the background. People talk about the rights they and others should have, and often speak about rights they have but are unable to enforce. In a purely positive sense, people only have the rights they are able to claim and enforce. People might claim, for example, that they have the right to walk down a public street without being assaulted, but in some cities at some times of day, walking down a particular street is likely to result in the walker

---

[7] Jon Pierre and B. Guy Peters, *Advanced Introduction to Governance* (Cheltenham, UK: Edward Elgar, 2021), p. 2.
[8] Erik G. Furubotn and Rudolph Richter, *Institutions and Economic Theory: The Contributions of the New Institutional Economics* (Ann Arbor, MI: University of Michigan Press, 2000), pp. 420–421.

being assaulted. People often know this, to the extent that they will avoid walking in those places where they are likely to be assaulted. Perhaps people should have the right to walk down a street without being assaulted, but if they are aware that they cannot claim and enforce that right, they do not actually have the right, even if they should. People do not actually have rights they are unable to exercise, even if people widely agree that they should have those rights.

Institutions of governance define and enforce rights. The analysis in this volume is strictly positive and does not consider what rights people should have; only the rights they actually do have. If you own a bicycle and know that if you leave it in a particular location, it is very likely to be stolen, you do not have the right to leave it in that location. Perhaps you should, but if you leave it there, someone else will take it and you will have lost the right to ride that bicycle. Regardless of any claim you make, you will no longer be able to use the bicycle that once was in your possession. You only have a right if you can claim and enforce it.[9]

A particularly harsh example can drive this point home. During World War II, the Japanese army forced Korean women into sexual slavery. Did members of the Japanese military have the right to use these women, referred to as "comfort women," in that way? If people have rights to what they can claim and enforce, then the Japanese military personnel did have that right. They could claim and enforce their right to those women. Most people would believe they should not have that right, but they were able to claim and exercise it. They did have the right, even if many would argue they should not have it.

How did Japanese soldiers gain the right to these comfort women? The Japanese government gave the soldiers the right. At the same time, they deprived those Korean women of rights most people would argue they should have had. One role of government is to assign and enforce property rights. Similarly, in the pre-Civil War United States, some people had the right to own others as slaves. The right to own slaves was given and enforced by government.

As a more straightforward example, do women have the right to vote? In most places in the nineteenth century, the answer would have been no. In the United States, women were guaranteed the right to vote in 1920, with the passage of the Nineteenth Amendment to the Constitution. This example illustrates the government's power to determine the rights people

---

[9] This idea is elaborated in Randall G. Holcombe, "The Economic Theory of Rights," *Journal of Institutional Economics* 10, no. 3 (September 2014), pp. 471–491.

actually have. That right was negotiated in the political marketplace, as a result of agreement by two-thirds of both the House and Senate and three-quarters of the state legislatures.

This positive theory of rights defines those rights people actually can exercise, as opposed to a normative theory that considers what rights people should have. A purely positive theory of rights is appropriate to the present study because the political elite define and enforce rights. The rights people actually can exercise are negotiated in the political marketplace. Those rights that actually exist are not necessarily the rights everyone thinks should exist. The rights people can actually exercise are not the same as those that, by some normative standard, they should have. Ultimately, institutions of authority and governance determine what rights people actually have – what rights they actually are able to exercise.

THE ASSIGNMENT OF RIGHTS

There are potential ambiguities in defining property rights over physical assets, which are settled by those who control the institutions of governance. Zoning laws, building codes, and environmental regulations determine the rights of those who own real estate; agricultural regulations limit the ownership rights over livestock and regulate the planting and harvesting of crops. Owners of businesses are constrained by workplace regulations and regulations on the characteristics of products they produce. The general equilibrium model assumes that suppliers have clearly defined rights to sell the goods that they are supplying, and that demanders have the clear right to buy what suppliers are offering. Those ownership rights that are assumed in the general equilibrium model are, in the real world, determined by the institutions of authority and governance that fall under the control of the political elite.

Many governments have implemented "land reform," in which the ownership rights to land were forcibly transferred, typically from large landholders to agricultural workers who worked on the land. This occurred in Bolivia in 1952, Chile from 1964 to 1973, Cuba in 1959, Guatemala from 1944 to 1954, Zimbabwe in 2000, and in many other nations. Land reform provides a clear illustration that the rights people actually do have are not necessarily the rights they should have. If the assignment of property rights was just after the land reform, it was therefore unjust before, and if it was just before, it was therefore unjust afterward. Setting aside what rights people should have, land reform offers a clear example in which those who control the institutions of authority and governance determine the rights that people actually do have.

Enforcement often requires a third party, which is accomplished through the institutions of governance. Consider, for example, the right to intellectual property. That right is defined and enforced by governments. In the United States, patent and copyright law gives the creators of (some) intellectual property ownership rights over the use of their ideas. Institutions of governance enforce those rights. Owners of intellectual property can take those who make unauthorized use of their ideas to court and receive compensation for rights violations. Still, piracy is common, so those rights are only partially protected. Much like the stolen bicycle, copyright holders can claim that pirates are violating their rights, but they only have those rights to the extent that they can be claimed and enforced.

The ownership of intangible property is even more heavily influenced by the rules drawn up by those who control the institutions of governance. Patents and copyrights give rights to intellectual property that would be very difficult to claim and defend without government enforcement. Rights to financial assets are also heavily influenced by legislatively designed institutions. As intellectual property and financial assets become an increasingly larger share of total wealth, the way that rules are drawn up for patents, copyrights, bankruptcy, shareholder rights, financial institutions, and so forth has a major influence on what someone can own and what the owner can do with that property. Rights, in general, are determined through negotiations in the political marketplace.

GOVERNMENTS ARE NOT AGENTS OF THEIR CITIZENS

The relationship between citizens and their governments is sometimes depicted as a principal–agent relationship, but this is misleading. As typically understood, principals hire their agents and a potential problem is that the incentives of agents can conflict with the best interests of the principals. This gives both principals and potential agents the incentive to look for ways to minimize those incompatible incentives. But institutions of governance are forced on their citizens. Citizens do not choose governments to be their agents, and citizens have little alternative but to take the terms their governments offer them.

Governments are not agents who act on behalf of their citizens. Those who exercise the power of government impose the rules on their citizens, and citizens are not given the choice of whether to comply. Citizens are not hiring an agent who can be terminated if the terms of their interactions are unfavorable. Governance institutions must work this way. They must offer the credible threat to force compliance in cases where individuals resist complying.

Democratic elections offer citizens the opportunity to replace those who exercise the power of governance, but even when this happens, the replacements have the same authority over their citizens as did those they replaced. One group of elites is replaced by another. The institutions of governance remain largely the same, regardless of which individuals have control of them. While competition among elites can constrain the exercise of power by those who have it, electoral competition leaves the institutions of governance unchanged, and only changes who oversees those institutions.

From the standpoint of the masses, the challenge is to create institutions of governance that protect them and result in an orderly society, but that constrain those who govern from abusing their power to the detriment of the citizens. To understand the possibilities, one must first understand how institutions of governance operate, to avoid wishful thinking and consider only realistic possibilities. Institutions of authority are not designed by the masses.

From the standpoint of the ruling elite, they want to use the power they have to protect their own interests. Realistically, any analysis of potential effective constraints on the abuse of government power must be analyzed from the standpoint of the ruling elite, not from the standpoint of the interests of the ruled, because the rulers are the ones who have the power, and they are the ones who make the rules. The ruling elite are not agents of the citizens over whom they rule.

TRANSACTION COSTS LIMIT THE SIZE OF THE RULING ELITE

The Coase theorem, which illustrates the way in which market institutions lower transaction costs, says that in the absence of transaction costs, resources are allocated to their highest valued uses. Transaction costs are anything that stands in the way of mutually advantageous exchange. The simple logic of the Coase theorem is that if nothing stands in the way of a mutually advantageous exchange, whoever places the highest value on a resource will negotiate to obtain it. In the absence of transaction costs, transactions continue to be made until resources end up in their highest valued uses.

Transaction costs are higher when large numbers of people must be involved in an exchange, as Chapter 3 noted. One of the ways that market institutions lower transaction costs is to design institutions so that one buyer interacts with one seller. Small numbers lower transaction costs. When large numbers of people must be involved in an exchange, transaction costs tend to be too high, so the exchange does not take place.

Coase's article on the subject deals directly with this issue of small versus large numbers of people as he analyzes the economic literature on externalities.[10] Recall the example from Chapter 3, in which residents who suffer air pollution from factories near them are unable to organize to bargain for a reduction in pollution because large numbers made organizing to try to bargain too costly. Recall that the same framework was applied to actions by government. Legislators and lobbyists face low transaction costs, so they bargain with each other to create legislation that maximizes the benefits to those in the low-transaction group. The masses often bear the costs of these bargains because large numbers prevent them from organizing to have their interests represented in the political marketplace. In the political marketplace, the masses are analogous to those individuals who suffer pollution as a by-product of market exchange.

Those who transact in the political marketplace do not intend to harm the masses, just as those who transact in markets for goods do not intend to impose external costs such as pollution on others. Rather, those who face low transaction costs engage in exchange for their mutual benefit, which can impose costs on third parties who face high transaction costs and cannot negotiate to mitigate the costs those who face low transaction costs impose on them. As Mancur Olson explained, small groups have an advantage over large groups in organizing to further their interests.[11]

Some people face low transaction costs and are able to participate in the political marketplace. They are the political elite. Most people face high transaction costs and are prevented from entering the political marketplace. They are the masses.

The masses recognize their inability to influence public policy, which is why they tend to be rationally ignorant about public policy matters,[12]

---

[10] Ronald H. Coase, "The Problem of Social Cost," *Journal of Law & Economics* 3 (1960), pp. 1–44.

[11] Mancur Olson, Jr., *The Logic of Collective Action* (Cambridge, MA: Harvard University Press, 1965).

[12] The concept of rational ignorance was explained by Anthony Downs, *An Economic Theory of Democracy* (New York: Harper & Row, 1957).

and even rationally irrational.[13] The masses are not excluded from the political marketplace by institutional constraints, but by high transaction costs. This is an important observation. If institutions were designed to exclude the masses from participating in the political marketplace, that would offer the possibility that institutions could be redesigned to allow them to participate. The masses are prevented from participating in the political marketplace by high transaction costs, and lowering those transaction costs is problematic because those high transaction costs result from the large number of people who are subject to the institutions of authority.

James Buchanan and Gordon Tullock reach a similar conclusion in the context of voting rules.[14] They note that when the number of persons who have to agree to take collective action increases, that results in an increase in decision-making costs. Those decision-making costs are an example of transaction costs, and their framework shows why, as groups get larger, they move away from decision-making by consensus. The decision-making costs in large groups are too high to allow everyone to negotiate a collective outcome.

People sometimes suggest that governance could be improved if citizens would become more informed about the issues and be more politically involved. But millions, or even thousands, of people cannot enter the political marketplace within which public policy is designed. People recognize this, which is why they tend to be rationally ignorant about politics and appear apathetic. For many, it is not that they do not care; it is that they recognize that there is nothing they, as individuals, can do to affect public policy.

GOVERNMENT INSTITUTIONS THAT LOWER TRANSACTION COSTS

In their study of governance, Jon Pierre and B. Guy Peters observe that "several theoretical and methodological issues persist [that] plague the study of governance and prevent it from reaching its full potential."[15] One of the biggest issues is that often, no clear distinction is made

---

[13] For an elaboration, see Bryan Caplan, *The Myth of the Rational Voter: Why Democracies Choose Bad Policies* (Princeton, NJ: Princeton University Press, 2007).

[14] James M. Buchanan and Gordon Tullock, *The Calculus of Consent* (Ann Arbor, MI: University of Michigan Press, 1962), ch. 6.

[15] Jon Pierre and B. Guy Peters, *Advanced Introduction to Governance* (Cheltenham, UK: Edward Elgar, 2021), p. 116.

between governance and government. For example, David Osborne and Ted Gaebler say, "Governance is the process by which we collectively solve our problems and meet our society's needs. Government is the instrument we use."[16] Government and governance are not the same. Government does things other than governance, including finding ways to lower transaction costs to facilitate mutually advantageous exchange.

Avinash Dixit defines governance institutions broadly, saying the three functions of governance institutions are (1) securing property rights, (2) enforcement of contracts, and (3) collective action.[17] Much like Osborne and Gaebler, Dixit's definition muddies the distinction between government and governance. Institutions that facilitate collective action are not governance institutions. People voluntarily agree to act collectively. Governance institutions may be required to enforce collective agreements, but then, governance institutions may also be required to enforce private contracts. Markets, which facilitate mutually advantageous exchanges among individuals, are not institutions of governance. Governments also facilitate mutually advantageous exchanges when they facilitate collective action.

Sometimes, people organize to take collective action to achieve their goals, by forming clubs,[18] joining fraternal organizations, joining churches, and through other collective organizations, including government.[19] The same distinction between institutions that lower transaction costs and institutions of governance applies to governmentally provided goods. The provision of parks, roads, and other collective goods lowers transaction costs to facilitate collective action. They are institutions of organization. The concept behind them is that it is difficult for large numbers of people to act collectively to produce roads, parks, and other goods that are consumed by many individuals, so government can organize that production to avoid the transaction costs that come with large numbers.[20]

---

[16] David Osborne and Ted Gaebler, *Reinventing Government: How the Entrepreneurial Spirit is Transforming the Public Sector* (Reading, MA: Addison-Wesley, 1992), p. 24.

[17] Avinash Dixit, "Governance Institutions and Economic Activity," *American Economic Review* 99, no. 1 (March 2009), p. 5.

[18] See James M. Buchanan, "An Economic Theory of Clubs," *Economica* n.s. 32, no. 126 (February 1965), pp. 1–14.

[19] This is the subject of Elinor Ostrom, *Governing the Commons: The Evolution of Institutions for Collective Action* (Cambridge: Cambridge University Press, 1990).

[20] One might note the possibility of privately owned toll roads, or private parks such as those owned by the Disney company. Those roads and parks operate by disaggregating the collective demand for their use into bilateral transactions, as Chapter 3 noted.

4 The Characteristics of Authority

These government institutions of organization – the parks, the roads, the schools, and the libraries – almost always rely on institutions of governance for their existence, so government's institutions of organization and institutions of governance are not unrelated. Governments may use eminent domain to secure land for parks and roads, and typically rely on taxation to finance those institutions. Indeed, the argument for government to provide those "public goods" typically is that the private sector will not provide them because of some type of market failure.[21]

Consider government-provided entertainment, such as art museums, symphony orchestras, and professional sports stadiums. One might argue that the private sector would underprovide them, and casual observation suggests that the art museums and symphony orchestras subsidized by governments would exist, at best, at a smaller scale were it not for government finance. The evidence is less clear on pro sports stadiums because professional sports franchises appear very profitable on their own. What all these institutions have in common is that consumers of their services have been able to organize to enter the political marketplace to force others to pay for the entertainment venues they prefer. This observation is not intended to pass judgment on the merits of these activities, but merely to point out the relationship between government-provided goods and services that fall under the organizational heading of lowering transaction costs and the institutions of governance that force some to underwrite the interests of others.

Government institutions play an organizational role, not a governance role, when mutually advantageous activities would require collective action. As James Buchanan and Gordon Tullock explain it, "Collective action is viewed as the action of individuals when they choose to accomplish purposes collectively rather than individually, and the government is seen as nothing more than the set of processes, the machine, which allows such collective action to take place."[22] Buchanan and Tullock underemphasize that those who initiate collective action are members of the political elite who do so within the political marketplace.

Government production bypasses the challenge of designing those institutions, substituting a different type of organization to lower transaction costs and facilitate the production of those goods.

[21] "Public goods" has been placed within quotation marks because most of those goods produced by government's institutions of organization do not fit the economist's standard definition of joint consumption or nonexcludable goods.

[22] James M. Buchanan and Gordon Tullock, *The Calculus of Consent* (Ann Arbor, MI: University of Michigan Press, 1962), p. 13.

While symphonies, art museums, and sports stadiums seem like products aimed at interest groups, government institutions of organization produce much that benefits the masses. Beyond food, clothing, and shelter, people want roads, wastewater treatment facilities, and fire departments that typically are provided through government institutions. Some governmental institutions facilitate mutually advantageous exchanges by organizing and producing goods collectively. When collective action is required to produce goods that benefit the group, transaction costs can prevent large groups of people from bargaining among themselves to do so. Government is providing the organizational function of lowering transaction costs to enable mutually advantageous exchange to provide collective goods.

Government can undertake this organizational function of providing collective goods because it has the power to do so embodied in its institutions of authority and governance. Without its ability to force people to comply with its mandates, these institutions of organization that depend on taxation and regulatory authority would not exist. Government institutions that lower transaction costs are built on government institutions of authority and governance.

GOVERNMENT-PROVIDED GOODS AND GOVERNANCE

The goods government provides are not necessarily public goods in the way Paul Samuelson defines them, as joint consumption goods.[23] Goods like education are primarily private goods by Samuelson's definition, but often are produced collectively. When government creates institutions that facilitate collective action, these are institutions of organization, not institutions of governance.

Pierre and Peters say, "Governance is essential for the success of any society. There must be some means of setting collective goals, and of finding ways of reaching those goals."[24] This view of governance confounds government and governance. Moving toward collective goals falls under the category of reducing transaction costs, as Buchanan and Tullock describe collective action. Meanwhile, referring back to the benchmark of general equilibrium, decentralized action and exchange

---

[23] Paul A. Samuelson, "The Pure Theory of Public Expenditure," *Review of Economics and Statistics* 36 (November 1954), pp. 387–389, and "A Diagrammatic Exposition of a Theory of Public Expenditure," *Review of Economics and Statistics* 37 (November 1955), pp. 350–356.

[24] Pierre and Peters, *Advanced Introduction to Governance*, p. 17.

can enable individuals to realize their own goals and allocate resources optimally without there being any collective goals. Groups do not have goals. Individuals do. Individuals who have goals in common can join together to try to accomplish them, but those goals remain the goals of the individuals in the group.

This points toward another quibble with the previous quotation. The goals that will be pursued through the institutions of governance are those of the people who have the power to govern: the political elite. If governance is the process of steering and control, as Pierre and Peters say elsewhere, the goals that institutions of governance will further are the goals of those who hold the steering wheel and are in control.

Osborne and Gaebler say, "Governance is the process by which we collectively solve our problems and meet our society's needs."[25] This precisely misstates the governance functions of government. Collective action to further the interests of members of society is action that lowers transaction costs to enable mutually beneficial collective action. Government action that furthers collective action typically needs enforcement mechanisms standing behind it, and those mechanisms are institutions of governance.

THE OLD AND NEW INSTITUTIONALISTS

The new institutional economics, as described by Oliver Williamson, focuses heavily on institutions that lower transaction costs and facilitate mutually advantageous exchange.[26] This focus contrasts with that of the old institutionalists, and John R. Commons in particular, who focused on legal institutions as institutions of authority that affect the distribution of income.[27] The legal system specifies the rules of the game, and how they are specified can shift advantages from some people to others.

Labor law provides a good example. By enabling collective bargaining, workers have an advantage in negotiating their terms of employment, including their wages, when compared to a legal system that does not require collective bargaining, or even one that might prohibit it. In the

---

[25] Osborne and Gaebler, *Reinventing Government*, p. 24.
[26] Oliver E. Williamson, "A Comparison of Alternative Approaches to Economic Methodology," *Journal of Institutional and Theoretical Economics* 146, no. 1 (1990), pp. 595–613.
[27] John R. Commons, *The Legal Foundations of Capitalism* (Madison, WI: University of Wisconsin Press, 1924), and Commons, *Institutional Economics: Its Place in Political Economy* (New York: Macmillan, 1934).

United States, workers can join unions of employees across firms for collective bargaining, but firms are not allowed to collectively organize to bargain. The United Auto Workers (UAW) union represents workers across many automobile manufacturers, but the manufacturers themselves are not allowed to organize together to bargain with the UAW. This gives the union more bargaining power than if the workers at each auto manufacturer had to form their own unions, or if the auto firms were allowed to collectively bargain with the UAW.

Minimum wage laws and workplace requirements set by the Occupational Safety and Health Administration (OSHA) are additional examples of laws that can alter bargaining between workers and their employers and, in so doing, affect the distribution of income between workers and the owners of the firms that employ them. Labor laws provide a clear example, but the legal structure more generally has a substantial impact on economic organization and economic outcomes.

A significant example is the creation of the limited liability corporation.[28] In most cases, laws of legal liability make people liable for harm they create to others and for debts they incur. If a firm causes harm to someone, or incurs a debt to someone, the owners of the firm are liable. This is the law for partnerships, and for individuals more generally. But the creation of the limited liability corporation, as the name suggests, limits the liability placed on the corporation's owners. By forming a limited liability corporation, the owners of corporations – the stockholders – are liable for the corporation's debts only up to the amount they have invested. If a corporation goes bankrupt, the value of its stock can fall to zero, and stockholders can lose all they have invested, but not more. This stands in contrast with liability law in general, which holds people liable for their debts. If a partnership goes bankrupt, all of the partners are personally liable for the debts of the partnership.

One justification sometimes given for this limited liability is that shareholders own the corporation but do not control it. Accepting this, if control is associated with management rather than the shareholders, why are managers not liable for a limited liability corporation's debts? If a partnership or sole proprietorship goes bankrupt, the owners are liable for the firm's debts. With a limited liability corporation, nobody is liable.

---

[28] Some background on the impact of the limited liability corporation is found in Walter A. Friedman, *American Business History: A Very Short Introduction* (Oxford: Oxford University Press, 2020).

Prior to the mid 1800s, limited liability corporations were rare and received corporate charters by specific acts of state legislatures. In the mid 1800s, states began adopting incorporation laws that allowed anyone to apply for a corporate charter and operate as a limited liability corporation, without a special act of the legislature. This meant that it was easy to form a business in which the owners were liable for the corporation's debts only up to the amount they had invested.

One effect has been the separation of ownership from control in corporate organization.[29] Another effect has been the facilitating of the financing of corporations because investors, as owners of the firm, have only limited liability. This lowers the risk to investors, which facilitates the raising of equity funds by the firm's management. Modern corporations would not have the ability to grow so large so rapidly were it not for the role of limited liability that enables them to gain more investors.

One can debate whether the owners of corporations should be able to escape liability for the debts of the corporations they own. All of the corporation's profits accrue to the stockholders, but in the event that the business fails, stockholders do not bear all of the corporation's losses. The point is not to argue that limited liability corporations are good or bad, but rather that the laws enabling them have had substantial effects on the economy and on the distribution of income within the economy. The existence of limited liability corporations has altered the structure of the economy, and in the process made corporate insiders more wealthy than they would have been absent this institution.

Another example is the protection of intellectual property. One important difference between intellectual property and physical property is that, once created, intellectual property is not scarce. If person A uses an idea created by person B, that does not deprive person B of the opportunity to continue using the idea. If person A takes person B's guitar, person B can no longer use the guitar. But if person A sings a song that was written by person B, this does not deprive person B of the opportunity to sing that song. When A uses B's idea, A is taking nothing from B.[30]

It is true that if A is allowed to sing B's song in a commercial venue without compensating B, B will have a lower income, but property rights give people the right to own and use property, not a right to its value.

---

[29] This separation of ownership from control is the subject of Adolf A. Bearle and Gardner C. Means, *The Modern Corporation and Private Property* (New York: Harcourt, Brace, and World, 1934).

[30] This topic is insightfully discussed by N. Stephan Kinsella, *Against Intellectual Property* (Auburn, AL: Ludwig von Mises Institute, 2008).

If someone buys a house that subsequently declines in value, the homeowner continues to have the right to use the house, even though the house is worth less. If A can sing B's song without compensating B, that may lower the monetary value of the song to B, but it does not deprive B of the right to use the song.

The point is not to argue that the patent and copyright laws that convey intellectual property rights are desirable or undesirable, but rather to illustrate that the degree to which they are granted affects economic organization and affects the relative well-being of those in a society. Bill Gates became the richest person in the world in the 1990s because of his ownership interest in Microsoft. Microsoft, in turn, made its income by selling computer programs that were protected by patent and copyright laws. If the legal system did not grant people intellectual property rights over the computer code they created, Microsoft's programs could have been freely copied, and Bill Gates's economic fortunes would not have been as bright. This is a dramatic example of the distributional impact of laws that protect intellectual property.

In the United States, patent and copyright laws give ownership rights to people who compose songs, who write computer programs, and who develop pharmaceutical drugs. Fashion designers who create and design clothing, or those who develop new culinary recipes, cannot patent or copyright their creations. Why should computer programs and drugs be protected intellectual property when fashion designs and culinary recipes are not? Normally, economists argue that monopolies have undesirable economic effects, yet patents and copyrights convey monopoly rights to certain types of intellectual property (but not others). Again, the point is not to argue that intellectual property should or should not be protected, but to point out the distributional effects.

Institutions of governance define and enforce those property rights, and once created, markets develop in which people buy and sell intellectual property in the same way that they buy and sell physical property. In the case of intellectual property rights, it is especially clear that they can be effective only if institutions of governance stand behind them to enforce those rights. People have some ability to protect their rights to their guitars by keeping them in a safe place, and perhaps fighting off those who might try to steal them. But once people have heard someone's song, it would be very difficult for a composer to collect compensation when others sing or record their songs without government enforcement of copyright laws. Institutions of governance define and enforce rights, and market institutions evolve to facilitate their mutually advantageous exchange.

The general equilibrium model that has been used as a benchmark just assumes people have ownership rights over goods and services, but what people can own and buy and sell is determined by and enforced by institutions of governance. Those institutions have distributive effects and efficiency effects, and are under the control of the political elite. The rights people have and can exercise are determined in the political marketplace. Those rights specify a status quo from which trade can begin, and that beginning point determines what outcomes are feasible. A different distribution of rights will result in a different distribution of income.

The new institutional economics[31] focuses heavily on institutions of organization – those that lower transaction costs – whereas the old institutionalists focused more on the institutions of authority and governance. Both are necessary for a society to approach that benchmark of competitive general equilibrium.

SOCIAL BENEFITS OF AUTHORITY

The fact that institutions of governance are based on force does not imply that those who are governed are worse off because of it. Thomas Hobbes, in 1651, argued that without a government that enforced rules of social cooperation, life would be solitary, poor, nasty, brutish, and short, and a war of all against all.[32] The general equilibrium model that has been used as a benchmark for analysis depends on institutions that define property rights and that prevent fraud and theft. In that model, people interact with each other only through mutually advantageous exchange.

Surely, members of a society are better off because their government enforces rules against murder, robbery, and assault. We could imagine, as Hobbes does, that everyone is better off agreeing to a social contract in which they abide by the mandates of a government that enforces those rules. People submit to authority partly because they are forced to, but also partly because they perceive that they benefit from the mandates imposed on others.

Steven Pinker attributes the economic and social progress that has come since the Enlightenment era to strong governments that protect

---

[31] As explained by Williamson, "A Comparison of Alternative Approaches to Economic Methodology."
[32] Thomas Hobbes, *Leviathan* (New York: E. P. Dutton, 1950 [orig. 1651]).

citizens from predation from their fellow citizens and from outsiders.[33] Jared Diamond draws a similar conclusion, noting that strong government enables people to peacefully coexist among those they do not know personally.[34] Daron Acemoglu and James Robinson also attribute progress and prosperity to strong governments, noting that progress and prosperity require that government power must be constrained by a strong civil society.[35]

The challenge, from the standpoint of civil society, is to design institutions of governance so that they have sufficient power to protect the rights of the governed, but are constrained from using that power to violate the rights of the governed. This challenge is described well by the title of James Buchanan's book, *The Limits of Liberty: Between Anarchy and Leviathan*.[36] Too weak a government leads to anarchy, where, as Hobbes said, life is a war of all against all. But without constraints on its use of power, government becomes an oppressive Leviathan that uses its power for the benefit of the rulers, to the detriment of the ruled.

There is a tendency to envision ways that citizens can design their governments to act in their interest. However, citizens do not design their governments. Government institutions are imposed on them by force. One might imagine what institutions citizens would agree to if their agreement was required to implement rules of social interaction, but that is not how those institutions are created. The ruling class makes the rules. Those who are ruled must follow them. In some nations, the ruling class is more constrained in their exercise of authority than in others. The analysis that follows explores why.

Douglass North observes the "persistent tension between the ownership structure which maximized the rents to the ruler (and his group) and an efficient system that reduced transaction costs and encouraged economic growth."[37] That tension is the tension between institutions that lower transaction costs and institutions of governance. The tension exists because institutions that reduce transaction costs (and lay

---

[33] Steven Pinker, *Enlightenment Now: The Case for Reason, Science, Humanism, and Progress* (New York: Viking, 2018).
[34] Jared Diamond, *The World Until Yesterday: What Can We Learn from Traditional Societies?* (New York: Viking, 2012).
[35] Daron Acemoglu and James Robinson, *The Narrow Corridor: States, Societies, and the Fate of Liberty* (New York: Penguin, 2019).
[36] James M. Buchanan, *The Limits of Liberty: Between Anarchy and Leviathan* (Chicago, IL: University of Chicago Press, 1975).
[37] Douglass C. North, *Structure and Change in Economic History* (New York: Norton, 1981), p. 25.

a foundation for economic prosperity) facilitate voluntary agreement, whereas the institutions that enforce property rights and contracts have the threat of force standing behind them. Those who exercise government power have their own incentives to use that power for their advantage, which is not necessarily to the advantage of the masses.

A DIGRESSION ON CORPORATE GOVERNANCE

The primary interest of this volume is the governance institutions enforced by governments, focusing on the political elite, Clubs, firms, and all types of organizations also have governance institutions, and there is a substantial literature on corporate governance. However, much of the institutional structure of corporations (and other organizations) falls into the category of reducing transaction costs rather than governance. Following Ronald Coase, corporations create contractual arrangements to reduce transaction costs,[38] and Michael Jensen and William Meckling depict a firm as a nexus of contracts.[39] Those contracts define institutions that are designed to reduce transaction costs to facilitate mutually advantageous exchanges. They are not governance institutions. Standing behind them are the institutions of governance that enforce the contracts. Governance institutions stand ready to use coercion to enforce institutional constraints, including institutional constraints that lower transaction costs. Much of the corporate institutional structure (and social institutional structure more generally) is organizational and facilitates voluntary participation in mutually advantageous activity.

Agreements entered into voluntarily are not governance. The nexus of contracts that constitutes a firm is a nexus of voluntary agreements, not governance, although institutions of governance stand ready to enforce contracts in the event that people do not fulfill the contractual obligations they agreed to, or if there is a dispute about the nature of those obligations. Contracts are constraints, voluntarily agreed to, and are designed to lower transaction costs and enable mutually advantageous exchange. Constraints must be enforced. Contracts are not institutions of governance, but the enforcement mechanisms standing behind them are.

---

[38] Ronald H. Coase, "The Nature of the Firm," *Economica* n.s. 4, no. 16 (November 1937), pp. 386–405.
[39] Michael C. Jensen and William H. Meckling. "Theory of the Firm: Managerial Behavior, Agency Costs, and Ownership Structure," *Journal of Financial Economics* 3, no. 4 (October 1976), pp. 305–360.

CONCLUSION

Institutions of authority and governance are essential to the operation of an orderly society. Institutions, following North, are constraints that structure interactions among individuals, and to be effective, constraints must be enforced. Institutions of governance supply the enforcement mechanisms. Effective governance requires institutions that project sufficient threat of force that individuals will believe that noncompliance is futile. The threat of force needs to be sufficient to deter almost all violations so that actual force rarely has to be used.

The authority that the political elite has enables them to expand their reach beyond defining and enforcing rights, to produce goods for collective consumption. Some of these goods, like wastewater treatment and roads, have benefits that extend largely to the masses. Others, like symphony orchestras, are narrowly targeted to specific interest groups. What they have in common is that their production appeals to a constituency that has access to the political marketplace, so the authority of governance institutions can lay a foundation for collectively demanded goods. The production of those goods is not determined by the breadth of membership in the collectivity, but by their ability to access the political marketplace.

To create an orderly society, the rules must apply to (almost) everybody. As Chapter 5 discusses, the ruling class often designs rules that exempt themselves. Because they cover (almost) everyone, transaction costs prevent most people from being able to negotiate to determine the rules. Thomas Hobbes recognized this issue and resolved it by saying that a social contract obligates everyone to obey the government's rules; that is, the rules created by the political elite.

Many observers have noted that societies are ruled by an elite few. This chapter explains why that is necessarily so. The size of the group that makes the rules is necessarily limited by high transaction costs. Even if the elite wanted everyone to have a say – and they do not – it would not be possible for individual members of the masses to have meaningful participation. The high transaction costs that come with large numbers prevent it.

5

The Ruling Class

A distinction is sometimes made between democratic governments and authoritarian governments. That distinction is false. All governments are authoritarian. Some are more constrained than others in their exercise of authority, but regardless of the form of government, the ruling class makes the rules and requires the masses to abide by them. The political elite threaten the use of force against those who do not comply. Rule by authority is a characteristic of all governments – including those that are the most democratic. While different forms of government have different institutions that determine who controls the institutions of governance, that does not change the fact that the political elite in governments of all types claim the authority to make and enforce the rules.

The Cold War ideology that pitted capitalist democracies against socialist dictatorships painted governance institutions as ranging from "free" democratic societies, in which governments were accountable to their citizens, to "oppressive" authoritarian dictatorships in which the dictators made the rules. This distinction between democracies and dictatorships contains an element of truth, in that democratic governments tend to allow citizens more autonomy – more freedom – than dictatorships. This does not counteract the fact that regardless of the form of government, the elite claim the authority to make and enforce the rules, and the masses are required to follow them. A more accurate distinction would refer to democratic versus autocratic governments. Even the most democratic government is still authoritarian.

The elite are able to impose their rules on the masses because they control the institutions of governance – institutions that are based on coercion, not agreement. The political elite, above all, are motivated to maintain their elite status that gives them the power to force the masses to conform to their mandates. Ultimately, they do that by force. If their authority is challenged, they will use the police power of the state to put down any challenges. This is true regardless of whether the ruling class is elected. People elected to positions of power may appear to have even more legitimacy in their use of power against those who challenge it. Their authority comes from their elected positions – president, senator, member of parliament – rather than being attached to the individual. Institutions of governance protect the authority of the position rather than the authority of the individual holding the position.

The institutionalization of political power creates a perception of legitimacy in the exercise of power, but can serve as a check on its abuse, an idea considered later in this chapter. The key point is that all forms of government are authoritarian, and the ruling class maintains its power by force.

THERE IS NO SOCIAL CONTRACT

While institutions of governance are backed by force, one line of thinking in political philosophy is that people consent to the coercive power of government because they benefit from having an orderly and productive society. Government, thinking along these lines, is the product of a social contract in which everyone agrees to be bound by the government's rules as long as those same rules apply to everyone else. The social contract offers a way out of a prisoners' dilemma situation in which individuals who do what is best for themselves make the group worse off. One issue with this line of reasoning is: everyone did not agree, even if under some hypothetical circumstances they might have. Governments are not the product of agreement. They are the products of force.[1]

The social contract theory of the state has a certain plausibility to it, in that people could imagine that they would agree to form a government that would enforce rules and create an orderly society. When asked, most people would agree that they should not assault or kill each

---

[1] This argument against the social contract theory is forcefully made by Leland B. Yeager, "Rights, Contract, and Utility in Policy Espousal," *Cato Journal* 5, no. 1 (1985), pp. 259–294, and Yeager, *Ethics as a Social Science: The Moral Philosophy of Social Cooperation* (Cheltenham, UK: Edward Elgar, 2001). See also Michael Huemer, *The Problem of Political Authority: An Examination of the Right to Coerce and the Duty to Obey* (New York: Palgrave Macmillan, 2013) for a good critique of social contract theory.

other, or steal each other's property (although they may not agree on what constitutes the legitimate ownership of property). Thus, one might conclude that there is a general agreement among people that they would consent to have a government that would enforce those rules. This was the reasoning Thomas Hobbes employed, centuries ago in 1651, to argue that citizens are bound by a social contract to abide by the government's rules.[2] Otherwise, Hobbes conjectured, society would devolve into anarchy, where life would be a war of all against all.

While it is plausible that people might agree to be constrained by the coercive nature of governance institutions, in fact people did not agree, and the social contract theory makes government appear to be the product of agreement when it is actually the product of coercion. The masses will find it difficult to object to the coercive acts of government if they believe that, somehow, they have agreed to give government that power. In this way, the social contract theory offers legitimacy to elite rule.[3]

In some cases it is obvious that the ruling class established their status by force. When revolutions establish new governments, it is clear that rulers like Lenin in 1917 Russia, and Castro in 1959 Cuba took control by force. What about Lenin's successor Stalin, or Kim Jong-un of North Korea, both of whom came to power within the framework of established political institutions? Few would doubt that both ruled by force. But the same is true of elected officials in more democratic societies. American presidents, for example, are elected by a vote of the nation's citizens, but once chosen, they control the institutions of governance in a manner similar to those who seized their political power through revolution. While they share their power with other elected officials in the legislature, and appointed officials in the judiciary, the political elite as a group have just as firm control over the institutions of governance in democracies as do the political elite in dictatorships.

Nobody in the political elite is completely unconstrained in their use of power. A clear example that illustrates that is the demise of Muammar Gaddafi, Libya's dictator from 1969 to 2011. Gaddafi took power by overthrowing the Libyan monarchy and ruled with a seeming iron fist, until an uprising in 2011 displaced him and ultimately led to his

---

[2] Thomas Hobbes, *Leviathan* (New York: E. P. Dutton, 1950 [orig. 1651]).
[3] See Randall G. Holcombe, "Contractarian Ideology and the Legitimacy of Government," *Journal of Institutional Economics* 17, no. 3 (June 2021), pp. 379–391, for an elaboration of this point.

assassination while he was hiding in a drainage pipe to try to escape. Those who hold political power require the cooperation and support of others to maintain it. That is just as true of dictators as it is of elected leaders. If members of the ruling elite lose the support of those under them who enforce the rules, they will lose their power.

Again, considering the president of the United States as an example, the president is also Commander in Chief of the military, has a substantial security detail for physical protection, and – most significantly for the present line of reasoning – is recognized as the legitimate holder of that power by other members of the political elite. Regardless of how members of the political elite come to power, through democratic elections, armed revolutions, or some other means, their power comes through the ability to credibly threaten to use force against those who do not comply with their mandates.

There is no social contract, and the masses did not agree to give power to those who have it. Their power comes from the threat of force that stands behind it.

GOVERNMENT IS THE PRODUCT OF FORCE

All governments were established through force. Some people had the power to conquer and rule over others, establishing themselves as the ruling class. This is evident in the history of Europe, where Greek city-states fought each other to maintain their sovereignty. The Roman Empire controlled their substantial territory through their military superiority, and after its collapse, feudal lords maintained armies to preserve, and perhaps enlarge, their territories. The United States, often cited as an example of a nation created to preserve the liberty of its citizens, was established by winning a war – one which not all citizens favored fighting. But prior to that Revolutionary War, the colonies that united to form the United States were established by forcefully displacing the native population. The actual history of state formation shows that they were established by force, not through any agreement among their citizens.

Once established, governments claim the authority to employ force to maintain their rule. They command people to engage in certain acts, prohibit them from engaging in others, and threaten the use of force against those who violate their rules. No matter how much people like their governments, and support them, governments are the product of coercion, not agreement.

THE QUEST FOR POWER

The primary advantage that is conveyed by membership in the ruling class is the ability to exercise power over others. As C. Wright Mills observed,

> The powers of ordinary men are circumscribed by the everyday world in which they live.... But not all men are in this sense ordinary. As the means of information and power are centralized, some men come to occupy positions in American society from which they can look down upon, so to speak, and by their decisions mightily affect, the everyday worlds of ordinary men and women.[4]

Mills called those people the power elite. They write the rules, they issue commands to the masses, but often are exempt from having to follow those rules themselves. This is a benefit of power. But while power has instrumental value – it can help people accomplish other goals – people also desire power for its own sake.

John Kenneth Galbraith says, "In all societies, from the most primitive to the ostensibly most civilized, the exercise of power is profoundly enjoyed.... Power is pursued not only for the service it renders to personal interests, values, or social perceptions, but also for its own sake, for the emotional and material rewards inherent in its possession and exercise."[5] More than two centuries earlier, Adam Smith observed, "The pride of man makes him love to domineer, and nothing mortifies him so much as to be obliged to condescend to persuade his inferiors."[6] In his Nobel lecture, "What Desires are Politically Important?", Bertrand Russell notes,

> Power, like vanity, is insatiable. Nothing short of omnipotence could satisfy it completely. And it is especially the vice of energetic men, the causal efficacy of love of power is out of all proportion to its frequency. It is, indeed, by far the strongest motive in the lives of important men.... Love of power is greatly increased by the experience of power, and this applies to petty power as well as to that of potentates.[7]

Max Weber observes that "the career of politics grants a feeling of power. The knowledge of influencing men, of participating in power over them, and above all, the feeling of holding in one's hands a nerve fiber of

---

[4] C. Wright Mills, *The Power Elite* (New York: Oxford University Press, 1956), p. 3.
[5] John Kenneth Galbraith, *The Anatomy of Power* (Boston, MA: Houghton Mifflin Company, 1983), p. 10.
[6] Adam Smith, *The Wealth of Nations* (New York: Modern Library, 1937 [orig. 1776]), p. 365.
[7] Quotation found at www.nobelprize.org/prizes/literature/1950/russell/lecture.

historically important events can elevate the professional politician above everyday routine even when he is placed in formally modest positions."[8] Bertrand de Jouvenel remarks that that "Power ... can only maintain the ascendancy necessary to it by the intense and brutal love which the rulers have for their authority."[9]

Robert Michels says,

> The consciousness of power always produces vanity, an undue belief in personal greatness. The desire to dominate for good or evil is universal. These are elementary psychological facts.... He who has acquired power will almost always endeavor to consolidate it and to extend it, to multiply the ramparts which define his position, and to withdraw himself from the control of the masses.... The possession of power transformed into a tyrant even the most devoted friend of liberty.[10]

Many scholars have observed that people seek power for its own sake because they desire to exercise authority over others, that the quest for power is insatiable, that the exercise of power makes those who hold it desire it even more, and that control over the institutions of governance is the most direct way that people can acquire and exercise power. Indeed, power is the engine that drives the institutions of governance.[11]

Members of the ruling class have many goals, like everyone else, but the quest for power stands above their other goals, partly because it facilitates their achieving those other goals. Power brings with it the ability to accumulate wealth, gain respect, demand that others follow orders, and brings with it a degree of satisfaction and self-esteem. But, as Bertrand Russell noted, the quest for power is insatiable, so those who have it always want more. One would not go far wrong to characterize members of the ruling class as power maximizers, in the same way that economists often characterize individuals as maximizing income and wealth, and firms as maximizing profits.

People seek power for its own sake, but it also helps them achieve other ends. If they gain more power, new opportunities open up for them. If

---

[8] Max Weber, "Politics as a Vocation," In H. H. Gerth and C. Wright Mills, eds., *From Max Weber: Essays in Sociology* (New York: Oxford University Press), p. 115.

[9] Bertrand de Jouvenel, *On Power: Its Nature, and the History of Its Growth* (New York: The Viking Press, 1949), p. 115.

[10] Robert Michels, *Political Parties: A Sociological Study of the Oligarchical Tendencies of Modern Democracy* (Glencoe, IL: Free Press, 1915), p. 128.

[11] The concept of power is analyzed in more detail in Randall G. Holcombe, *Coordination, Cooperation, and Control: The Evolution of Economic and Political Power* (Cham, Switzerland: Palgrave Macmillan, 2020), ch. 1.

they lose power, they lose the ability to accomplish what they could have before. Power comes in many forms, and political power can be particularly intoxicating. Thinking back to Adam Smith's observation, people with economic power have to persuade others to cooperate with them. This gives an advantage to the wealthy, who have more resources to offer others to persuade them to cooperate with them, but the use of economic power still requires others to see that it is in their interest to cooperate. Political power gives its holders the ability to command that others follow their mandates, regardless of whether they agree.

The primary goal of the ruling elite is to maintain, and if they can, increase their power. That power is a means to an end, but also is an end in itself.[12]

TWO SOURCES OF POLITICAL POWER

When members of the political elite seek power, there are two ways they can obtain it. First, they could gain positions of power, through elections, through appointment to power positions, or through conquest – acquiring power that once was controlled by others. They acquire power by acquiring positions of power. Second, they could increase the amount of power associated with positions of power they already hold. Institutions of authority and governance are the sources of political power. This second route to power is to convey more power to those who already have positions of power. Higher taxes, increased regulation, and stricter enforcement can add to the power for those who already hold it. Conversely, tax cuts, deregulation, and more lenient enforcement can reduce the power of the powerful. Through these mechanisms, the total amount of political power conveyed by the institutions of authority and governance can rise or fall.

An increase in the scope of political power gives the political elite more authority over the masses and results in less autonomy for the masses. This contrasts with economic power, because people interact with those who have economic power only if they choose to. If Elon Musk gains more economic power through his sale of electric automobiles, that does not restrict the opportunities for the masses, but increases them. They can choose to buy one of his cars, or not. An increase in the scope of political power increases the authority of the political elite, and restricts the autonomy of the masses.

---

[12] Margaret Levi, *Of Rule and Revenue* (Berkeley, CA: University of California Press, 1988) depicts governments as revenue maximizers.

Absent changes in these institutions of authority and governance, the quest for power is a zero-sum game. More power for some means less power for others. Given the institutions of authority that convey certain powers to presidents, prime ministers, or legislators, if one person gains a position of authority, that excludes another person from holding that position and exercising that power. In the competition for positions of authority, if one person wins, another loses. The result is that political competition often can be vicious.

The transaction cost approach to understanding the political marketplace explains why political power is held by an elite few, and is not accessible to the masses. At the same time, those who transact within the political marketplace compete with each other for positions of power.

THE EXERCISE OF POWER

The quest for power has implications for the legal institutions that will be produced in the political marketplace. One consequence of strong government is that it produces an orderly society. It dictates the rules and enforces them by its credible threat to impose costs on violators sufficient to make compliance appear to be the best option for them. An orderly society is produced when governance institutions define clear rights for individuals and effectively protect those rights.

As noted earlier, this idea is not new. In 1651, Thomas Hobbes argued that without a government to enforce rules that protect each other from aggression from their fellow citizens, life would be a war of all against all. Life would be, among other things, poor without the authority of government, because the incentive to be productive would be absent without secure property rights to what people produce. When everyone abides by the rules of their governments, their societies will be more orderly and more productive. Steven Pinker documents the substantial decrease in human violence since the establishment of strong governments during the Enlightenment era. Murders, assaults, deaths in wars, and indeed interpersonal violence in general have steadily fallen over long periods of time because strong governments enforce rules against it, and protect their citizens from violence by other governments.[13]

An orderly society creates the potential for a more prosperous society. When people have the security to be able to interact with others they do

---

[13] Steven Pinker, *The Better Angels of Our Nature: Why Violence Has Declined* (New York: Viking, 2011).

not know personally, they are more able to engage in that propensity to truck, barter, and exchange that Adam Smith described. The result is a more productive society, which results from a greater division of labor. One caveat – how productive a society is depends on the degree to which institutions of governance allow individuals to reap the rewards from their own productivity.

The central economic planning in many nations over the twentieth century shows that productivity is hampered when those with power use it to direct people's economic activities, rather than allowing them to make their own choices, and when it prevents them from profiting from their productivity. Power that generates order aids productivity. Power that reduces people's ability to act autonomously hinders productivity.

Despite the greater productivity of market economies when compared with centrally planned economies, centrally planned economies are still more productive than a society would be in that hypothetical state of Hobbesian anarchy. People still cooperate and take advantage of the division of labor in centrally planned economies, despite their top-down economic organization that hampers the ability of individuals to be entrepreneurial.

One might view the creation of centrally planned economies, despite their demonstrated lower productivity, as a result of a "fatal conceit" on the part of their political leaders – thinking that a top-down economic organization run by those leaders will be more efficient than a reliance on the uncertainties of the market.[14] Many prominent academic economists thought so.[15] However, another reason why the political elite may favor centrally planned economies is that it gives them more power over others. This is consistent with the hypothesis that the political elite can be characterized as power maximizers. Even if society as a whole is poorer, central economic planning concentrates more power in the hands of the elite.

If decentralized market economies tend to be more productive than centrally planned economies, one advantage they bring to the

---

[14] Friedrich A. Hayek, *The Fatal Conceit: The Errors of Socialism* (Chicago, IL: University of Chicago Press, 1988).

[15] A prominent example is Nobel laureate Paul A. Samuelson, *Economics*, 9th ed. (New York: McGraw Hill, 1973), p. 883, who projects that the Soviet Union will overtake the US economy in per capita GDP perhaps as soon as 1990, and almost surely by 2010. The socialist calculation debate, discussed earlier, offers other examples such as Abba P. Lerner, *The Economics of Control: Principles of Welfare Economics* (New York: Macmillan, 1944) and Oskar Lange and Fred M. Taylor, *On the Economic Theory of Socialism* (Minneapolis, MN: University of Minnesota Press, 1938).

power-maximizing political elite is that they can use their powers of taxation and regulation to take more for themselves – to have control over more resources. A wealthier society produces more that can be taxed away by the political elite. They may (and often do) appropriate some resources for themselves. More resources flowing toward the ruling class enables them to use those resources to acquire more power. But the power they seek tends to be power over people, which indirectly gives them power over resources, rather than the direct control over resources.

The United States, sometimes referred to as the world's policeman, offers a good example of the way that prosperity can produce power for the political elite. Not content to exert power only over its own citizens, the political elite in the United States has projected its power all over the globe in a way that the political elite in most nations would be unable to duplicate. Even so, the United States is not alone. Russia, with its invasion of Georgia in 2008, and its invasion of Ukraine in 2022, is a twenty-first century example. History is filled with examples of the political elite in one nation attempting to extend its power beyond its borders. More prosperous economies generate more resources that can increase the chances of success.[16]

Prosperity can afford the ruling class the advantage of buying support for its continued rule. People are inclined to evaluate the ruling elite based on how their own situations have changed relative to the recent past. If their situation is improving, they will tend to be happier with the ruling elite. If things are getting worse, they will be more likely to be dissatisfied with the ruling class. There is good evidence that this is the case in democratic societies. Voters are more likely to support incumbents when conditions are improving and more likely to vote against incumbents when conditions are deteriorating.[17]

The concept applies to governments in general, not just to democratic governments. Chinese citizens are less likely to actively oppose China's authoritarian government in the twenty-first century because the economic progress of the Chinese economy has lessened discontent in that dimension. In the twentieth century, the Berlin Wall fell because those in Eastern Bloc countries were dissatisfied with the economic stagnation

---

[16] See Christopher J. Coyne and Abigail R. Hall, *How to Run Wars: A Confidential Playbook for the National Security Elite* (Oakland, CA: Independent Institute, 2024) for a discussion of this point.

[17] Political scientists call this retrospective voting. See Christopher H. Achen and Larry M. Bartels, *Democracy for Realists: Why Elections Do Not Produce Responsive Government* (Princeton, NJ: Princeton University Press, 2016).

under the direction of their authoritarian governments. The goal of the ruling class is to maintain and increase its power, and it does so by creating an orderly and productive society.

ORDER VERSUS JUSTICE

In protecting the rights of its citizens, the ruling class strives to create order, not justice. A legal system that promoted justice would focus on providing restitution to victims whose rights were violated by others, paid for by those who violated others' rights.[18] Government legal systems, in contrast, are oriented toward punishing those who violate the rules, not providing restitution to those whose rights are violated. If someone is found guilty of assault, that person will be put in prison, but that provides no benefit to the assault victim. Someone guilty of murder will be imprisoned, but this provides no benefit to family members who may have been dependent on the victim. A carjacker may be put in prison, but if the carjacker wrecked the car that was stolen, it will be up to the owner (or the owner's insurance company) to address the damage.

Government legal systems place heavy emphasis on punishing those who violate the government's rules rather than providing restitution to those who are harmed by rule violators. Those who are harmed can try to file civil suits to recover damages, but it is up to the harmed individual to take action. From the standpoint of the ruling class, the purpose of institutions of governance is to produce an orderly and productive society in which people obey the mandates of the political elite. This benefits the masses because it enables them to interact peacefully and productively with each other. But the masses do not make the rules. The rulers do. The goals of the rulers are order and compliance. The ruling class uses its power to create order, not justice.

RULES: DESIGNED BY ELITES; ENFORCED ON THE MASSES

The laws that govern social interaction are designed by the elite in the political marketplace and applied to the masses. Those who write the rules often are not bound by them. Noting that the rules are rigged to favor the elite, Nobel laureate Joseph Stiglitz observed, "It's one thing to win a 'fair'

---

[18] This idea is discussed by Bruce L. Benson, *The Enterprise of Law: Justice without the State* (Oakland, CA: Pacific Research Institute for Public Policy, 1990).

game. It's quite another to be able to write the rules of the game – and to write them in ways that enhance one's chance of winning. And it's even worse if you can choose your own referees."[19] Transaction costs prevent most people from negotiating when the rules are being written, but they are subject to those rules. Members of the political elite, who face low transaction costs in the political marketplace, are in a position to negotiate for favorable treatment. The idea that the rules apply equally to everyone is not quite true. They apply to most people. That is why they create an orderly society. But the rules often exempt those who write them.

Rule of law means that there is an objective set of rules that are impartially enforced, minimizing discretion on the part of the enforcers. While in some ideal sense one might hope that the same set of rules applies to everyone, that is never the case. The elite always operate under a different set of rules from the masses because they write the rules. Stiglitz goes on to say, "It doesn't have to be this way, but powerful interests ensure that it is."[20] One of the lessons of this transaction cost approach to understanding the political marketplace is that, contrary to Stiglitz's claim, it does have to be this way. The situation Stiglitz describes is the inevitable result of the necessary division between elites and masses – inevitable because of transaction costs facing the masses. One might wish that this was not the case, but institutions cannot be reformed through wishful thinking.

GOVERNANCE IS BASED ON AUTHORITY

The political elite have the threat of force standing behind their actions, but that threat of force benefits the masses as well as the elite. Consider again that general equilibrium framework that has been used to explain the role of institutions. Some institutions are designed to lower transaction costs and operate based on the voluntary actions of those involved in mutually advantageous exchange. Those institutions that lower transaction costs act as constraints that require an enforcement mechanism standing behind them. That enforcement mechanism is the institutions of governance that are controlled by the political elite.

The chapter began by observing that all governments are authoritarian. Those authoritarian institutions are a necessary foundation

---

[19] Joseph E. Stiglitz, *The Price of Inequality: How Today's Divided Society Endangers the Future* (New York: W. W. Norton, 2012), p. 59.
[20] Stiglitz, *The Price of Inequality*, p. 62.

underlying the orderly, institution-free general equilibrium model that provides a benchmark for welfare maximization. Institutions that lower transaction costs are necessary to match suppliers with demanders, and institutions of governance are necessary to define property rights and to prevent fraud and theft that would undermine those property rights. That propensity to truck, barter, and exchange can only be realized when the institutions of authority prevent people from opportunistically violating institutional constraints.

The necessity of institutions of governance to protect people's rights and enable production and exchange brings with it the necessity that those institutions fall under the control of a subset of the population – the ruling elite. Their elite status is a direct result of the fact that they control the institutions of governance, and their number is necessarily limited by transaction costs. The implied institutions of governance within the general equilibrium model define property rights, so people have a clear right to what they own and what they may sell to others, and to ensure that resources are transferred among individuals only through voluntary exchange – preventing fraud and theft. That is the ideal world of general equilibrium.

Potential conflict arises because those who control the institutions of governance can design the rules to benefit themselves at the expense of the masses. Social scientists often speculate on institutions that would maximize social welfare – institutions that would be implemented as if they were designed by an omniscient benevolent dictator. Such speculation departs from social science to engage in wishful thinking. The political elite design the institutions of governance, so an analysis of the institutions of governance requires an understanding of the motives of the ruling class, the degree to which they are able to design institutions, and the constraints on the actions of the ruling class.

CREATIVE DESTRUCTION: STABILITY VERSUS PROGRESS

Progress can solidify elite rule because the masses will be more content as they see material improvement in their lives, but progress also represents a threat to the elite. Joseph Schumpeter described capitalism as a process of creative destruction.[21] Entrepreneurs in competitive markets continually introduce new and improved products and develop more efficient production

---

[21] Joseph A. Schumpeter, *Capitalism, Socialism, and Democracy*, 2nd ed. (London: George Allen & Unwin, 1947).

methods. Those new products and production methods displace the old. That process of creative destruction benefits creative and ambitious people who have good ideas. It gives them the opportunity to get ahead, and in the process, displace those who have gotten ahead in the past.

That process of creative destruction that benefits those who want to get ahead threatens the destruction of those who are already ahead. The past beneficiaries of that process of creative destruction, who want to maintain their positions in the hierarchy, have an incentive to undermine the system that gave them their past successes. This has implications for both the marketplace for goods and services and for the political marketplace. Both the political and economic elite want to maintain their elite status, and one way to do so is to create barriers to entry for potential competitors.

The economic elite enter the political marketplace to bargain for benefits targeted to themselves – tax breaks, subsidies, tariffs on foreign competitors, and regulatory barriers to entry. While creative destruction produces the economic progress that has characterized market economies since the beginning of the Industrial Revolution, for those who have risen to the top, further progress threatens their elite status. Having risen to the top, they want to replace progress with stability, and would like nothing more than to remain in that situation described by general equilibrium, year after year, in which the same goods and services continue to be exchanged at the same prices.[22] The economic elite want to preserve the status quo. They prefer stability to progress.

The political elite likewise seek stability. They want to retain their positions of power. Elected officials want to be reelected, while challengers campaign to displace them. Agency heads and other appointed officials want to retain their positions. The political and economic elite are both threatened by the forces of creative destruction, and they are in a position to cooperate with each other to retain their elite status. The political elite can provide the economic elite with targeted benefits and regulatory protections, and in exchange the economic elite can provide the political elite with campaign contributions, political support, and even personal benefits. The elite want order and stability. Progress threatens their elite status.

Both the political and the economic elite strive to create barriers to entry to create stability and prevent the creative destruction that threatens to displace them. The political elite cooperate with the economic

---

[22] Clayton Christensen, *The Innovator's Dilemma: When New Technologies Cause Great Firms to Fail* (Cambridge, MA: Harvard Business Review Press, 1997) discusses the challenges leading firms face due to the creative destruction of capitalism.

elite, who support political incumbents in exchange for barriers to entry in the form of regulations, tax breaks, subsidies, and other impediments to innovative challengers. To the degree that they are successful, progress will erode into stagnation.[23]

POLITICAL COMPETITION

Political competition occurs across many dimensions. The most significant dimension of political competition is the competition between elites and masses – the competition between those who have power and those who want to get power. Consider an election for a seat in the U.S. House of Representatives. The obvious dimension of competition is that a Republican is running against a Democrat. Less obvious is that in most cases, an incumbent is running against a challenger. Incumbents from different political parties have more in common with each other than they have with challengers from their own parties. Incumbents work together to maintain their hold on power. Incumbents exchange with each other in the political marketplace for their mutual benefit and conspire to design barriers to entry to solidify their positions of power.

As a parallel example, businesses often set up competitions among their sales staff. The top sellers can win prizes, sometimes with substantial value. This makes it appear that the salespeople are in competition with each other, and in one sense they are. But stepping back, all those salespeople are on the same side, as their employer competes with other businesses in the marketplace. Those salespeople are working together, and their individual successes benefit the whole business. The larger dimension of competition is the competition among different businesses for a piece of the total market, not among salespeople who work for the same business.

Similarly, in the U.S. Congress, Democrats compete with Republicans, and while that competition is real, the more significant dimension of competition is between incumbents of both parties against challengers of either party. The political elite work together to maintain their elite status. Some evidence of their success is the substantial advantage that incumbents have over challengers in democratic elections. Chapter 6 discusses specific institutions that benefit incumbent power holders over challengers in more detail.

---

[23] On this theme, see Mancur Olson, Jr., *The Rise and Decline of Nations* (New Haven, CT: Yale University Press, 1982), and Randall G. Holcombe, *Political Capitalism: How Economic and Political Power Is Made and Maintained* (Cambridge: Cambridge University Press, 2018).

In this competition between the power elite and their challengers, should a challenger displace a member of the elite, that challenger then becomes a member of the elite. While challengers seek to upset the status quo, once becoming a member of the political elite, they seek to preserve the status quo. Challengers who campaign on the virtues of term limits for elected officials, for example, often change their views on term limits once elected.

Despite their differences on many issues, members of the ruling class are united in their quest to maintain and increase their hold on power.

CONCLUSION

The interests of the ruling class are often different from those of the masses. The ruling class, necessarily limited in size because of transaction costs, controls the power of government, they write the rules, and they enforce them. As Joseph Stiglitz notes, they choose their own referees, so they operate under different rules from the masses. While they rule by force, they often do not have to force themselves upon the masses. Propaganda and patriotism can lead the masses to support their rulers, but there are more instrumental reasons that the masses accept their rulers. First, the institutions of governance and authority enable them to live in an orderly and productive society. Second, they have little alternative but to comply with the mandates of their rulers, so they might as well accept that rather than resist.

The benchmark of competitive general equilibrium, the ultimate end-state of the propensity of people to truck, barter, and exchange, can only be approached if there are institutions that lower transaction costs to enable demanders and sellers to locate and trade with each other. Those institutions that lower transaction costs are in turn enforced by the institutions of authority and governance administered by the ruling class.

Just as there are institutions in markets for goods and services that lower transaction costs and facilitate exchange, there are institutions that structure the political marketplace in which the elite transact with each other. Those transactions occur for the benefit of those who are transacting and often result in providing advantages to themselves at the expense of those who are excluded from the political marketplace. Those institutions are the subject of Chapter 6.

6

The Institutional Structure of the Political Marketplace

Political markets face the same challenges to their smooth operation as markets for goods and services. Just as with markets for goods and services, institutions have developed to facilitate political exchange. The political marketplace has institutions designed to lower transaction costs and facilitate mutually advantageous exchanges. And the political marketplace has institutions of enforcement and governance that constrain those who transact in it. The biggest difference is that while markets for goods and services rely heavily on third-party enforcement, institutional constraints in the political marketplace are enforced by the same political elite who transact there.

Chapters 2 and 3, which introduced the model of competitive general equilibrium as a benchmark, noted that the way a market economy works cannot be understood simply by understanding that model. The model shows the results of mutually advantageous exchanges but does not explain the process that produces those results. Those exchanges are structured by institutions that lower transaction costs to facilitate exchange. Similarly, the political marketplace cannot be understood simply by pointing out that the political and economic elite engage in mutually beneficial exchange. They undertake those exchanges within an institutional framework that both facilitates their exchanges and constrains the exchanges they are able to make.

FORMAL AND INFORMAL CONSTRAINTS

As with institutions more generally, some institutions in the political marketplace have formal third-party enforcement mechanisms, while others are informally enforced by those engaged in the transactions. Informal enforcement takes place when those who act within institutional constraints are also the ones who enforce those constraints. Violators may be sanctioned by social disapproval, by shunning, or by ostracism. If, for example, a legislator gains a reputation for not following through on bargains made with other legislators, that legislator will be excluded from future bargaining because legislators will refuse to enter into agreements with those who fail to keep their end of a bargain. There is no formal sanction; no penalty is levied on the legislator who reneges on promises, outside of being excluded from future exchanges because other legislators will refuse to deal with that legislator.

This is one aspect of the political marketplace that necessarily limits the size of the group that can participate. People who participate in politics as exchange bargain based on their reputations for following through on what they promised, and for this to work, people in the group must be able to ascertain the reputations of those with whom they deal. Anthropologist Robin Dunbar has studied clan-based societies and concluded that individuals are capable of personally knowing about 150 other individuals.[1] That number, 150, has subsequently been referred to as Dunbar's number. When groups become larger than Dunbar's number, members lose the ability to know everyone in the group, so enforcement based on people's reputations becomes problematic. In larger groups, disreputable individuals can find people to negotiate with who are unaware of the disreputable individual's reputation.

Larger societies require other mechanisms to enforce transactions. For example, a retail store will not know or be able to trust all of its customers, but it will accept payment for goods by customers who use credit cards like Visa or Mastercard. The store has no reason to trust the individual customer, but does trust Visa to make good on the payment. Credit cards provide an institutional mechanism to facilitate transactions between parties who do not know each other personally. An individual can show up at a hotel far from where that individual lives, knowing nobody at the hotel, yet the hotel trusts that the individual will make good on the hotel bill because Visa guarantees it.

The number of participants in the political marketplace is small enough that those who transact with each other are able to trade based on their personal reputations, without any third-party assurances. Even if

---

[1] Robin L. M. Dunbar, "Neocortex Size as a Constraint on Group Size in Primates," *Journal of Human Evolution* 22, no. 6 (1992), pp. 469–493.

everyone does not know everyone else, everyone knows those with whom they transact. This requirement necessarily limits the size of the political elite. This chapter discusses institutions that facilitate those informally enforced transactions.

Formal constraints on the political elite are problematic in that the political elite themselves control the institutions of authority and governance. There is no higher authority. Political elites have designed the formal constraints that bind them. This is an issue that political philosophers have grappled with for centuries. How can the actions of the political elite be constrained so that they do not abuse the power that comes with their positions? Many of those formal constraints were designed by the predecessors of the current elite, so current elites face constraints designed well in the past. But, institutional constraints can be changed, rapidly by an explicit redesign, or slowly through evolutionary changes.

To give one clear example, the Constitution of the United States gives the federal government limited and enumerated powers. One would be hard-pressed to find any place in the Constitution that gives the federal government the power to create a compulsory retirement system. Yet, the Supreme Court ruled in 1937 that the Social Security program was constitutional. In contrast, the Court declared federal income taxation unconstitutional in 1895, leading to the passage of the Sixteenth Amendment to the Constitution to enable income taxation. If the Court, in 1937, was reading the Constitution as literally as it was in 1895, a constitutional amendment would have been required to create the Social Security program.

The United States has, for centuries, abided by the procedural constraints in its Constitution. Legislation must be approved by a majority in both the House and Senate. The president can veto legislation, but a presidential veto can be overridden by a two-thirds majority of the legislature. This is worth a remark because those procedures are enforced by those who are engaged in them. In other nations, presidents have dismissed legislatures that have opposed them, shut down courts, and established military rule. A breakdown in enforcement can occur when those who are subject to the rules also enforce them.

FORMAL CONSTRAINTS ON THE ELITE

While the previous paragraph said there is no higher authority, one option would be to create one. In medieval Europe, the higher authority was God. The masses were told that the ruling class obtained their authority from God, and the ruling class ruled with the support of the Church. If rulers lost the support of the clergy, they ran the risk that the ruled might no longer recognize the authority of their rulers, threatening their positions. Setting aside any speculation about God's views, the Church provided a check on the power of the ruling class.

Constraints on the power of political elites might come from democratic oversight and constitutional limits on the powers of government. Chapter 12 considers those possibilities in more detail. One can see, however, that constitutional rules will offer few constraints on the elite if they are not enforced, so they need to work in conjunction with some enforcement mechanism. Similarly, democratic oversight is problematic, partly because individual citizens have no power and little incentive to be informed about political matters. While it is true that in democracies, all the votes taken together determine who will be able to exercise political power, those elections do not limit the scope of power. They just allow for the possibility that the existing set of elites will be replaced by another set who exercise the same powers.

The formal constraints on the exercise of power by the political elite are enforced by the elite themselves, which requires a set of institutions within which some members of the elite have the power to prevent others from overstepping their bounds. This requires a separation of powers among the members of the elite and the ability of some members of the elite to limit the exercise of power by others. The checks and balances within the Constitution of the United States provide an example. In theory, the powers of three branches of government – legislative, executive, and judicial – check and balance the abuse of power by each other.

Centuries of experience in Western Europe and the United States suggest that an institutional structure of checks and balances can be a stable long-run method of constraining the powers of the elite. Twenty-first century examples of Putin's Russia, Maduro's Venezuela, and the Kim dynasty in North Korea indicate what can happen when there are no effective competing elites within the institutions of authority and governance.

As an example, consider the 2020 presidential election in the United States. Donald Trump, the sitting president, declared that he was the legitimate winner of the election and should remain in power. Other members of the elite disagreed, and he was replaced as president by Joe Biden. Meanwhile, in Russia, President Vladimir Putin was facing term limits that would prevent him from remaining in office, and he had the Russian constitution changed, enabling him to retain his presidency indefinitely. What made the difference between these two cases? In the

United States, there was a division of power, and the formal election rules were enforced by other members of the elite, not the sitting president. In Russia, there were no effective competing elites who were able to counteract Putin's power and enforce the constitutional term limits.

When formal constraints are placed on elites, the only mechanism to enforce them is a division of power among elites, so some elites can check and balance the power of others. Democratic elections are desirable, as are constitutional constraints on the exercise of government power, but neither are effective absent an enforcement mechanism, which must come from a division of authority. Chapter 13 discusses this in more detail.

REVOLUTION AS A CONSTRAINT

Another constraint on the power of the elite is the possibility of revolution. Citizens have the power, because of their sheer numbers, to revolt and replace their governments. But this is a rare occurrence. As Gordon Tullock notes, most instances in which governments are overthrown occur as the result of coups in which insiders within the existing government displace the old leaders.[2] Some members of the elite are displaced by other members of the existing elite. Competition among elites for power can be vicious, sometimes extending to violence. Popular uprising to gain political power through revolution is difficult and rare because even if most citizens would favor the revolutionaries over the incumbent government, they have little incentive to show their support.

The existing ruling class, with a comparative advantage in the use of violence, sees it as their first priority to use their comparative advantage to maintain their power. Demonstrations against an incumbent government are often met with the show of overwhelming force to discourage further uprisings. While all individuals collectively may have sufficient power to overthrow the government, each individual could have only an imperceptible influence in such an uprising, so individuals, even if they favor the revolutionaries, have an incentive to free ride and hope that others take the risk of opposing the government.[3] As a result, the status quo remains even if most people would be in favor of replacing it.

---

[2] Gordon Tullock, *The Social Dilemma* (Indianapolis, IN: Liberty Fund, 2005).
[3] For further discussion along these lines, see Gordon Tullock, *The Social Dilemma* (Indianapolis, IN: Liberty Fund, 2005), Peter Kurrild-Klitgaard, *Rational Choice, Collective Action, and the Paradox of Rebellion* (Copenhagen: University of Copenhagen Institute of Political Science, 1997), and Mark Irving Lichbach, *The Rebel's Dilemma* (Ann Arbor, MI: University of Michigan Press, 1995).

Everyone has this same incentive, so the likelihood of a successful revolution is small even when most people would favor it. But revolutions are also unpredictable. Should people begin to perceive that the revolution has a chance of succeeding, they will be more inclined to join, and the more people who join, the stronger the chance of success, which encourages even more people to join. Getting to that critical mass where enough people show their support is a challenge to revolutionary leaders, making it difficult to predict if or when a revolution will occur. For example, even a year or two prior to the event, few people foresaw the collapse of the Berlin Wall in 1989. People are reluctant to show their support until the success of the revolution looks likely. Then the balance of power can rapidly shift.

FORMAL INSTITUTIONS OF GOVERNANCE

James Buchanan makes the observation that economic analysis typically focuses on choices people make subject to constraints. He then refers to constitutional decision-making as choosing those constraints.[4] Some constraints on people's actions are given by the laws of nature, but many are the result of institutions. Drawing a sports analogy, Buchanan has described constitutional decisions as deciding the rules of the game, in contrast to postconstitutional decisions that are made subject to those rules.

To be effective, the rules have to be established and enforced, and in one way the sports analogy works better as a description of the political marketplace than the market for goods and services. Rules against assault and theft are imposed and enforced from the outside, by the government. But the rules of the political marketplace are imposed and enforced by those who trade in the political marketplace, much as the teams that compete against each other in sports events work together to establish and enforce the rules of the game. In many cases, contestants decide the rules under which they will compete – NBA teams collectively determine the rules of basketball under which they play, for example – but even then, they employ referees to interpret and enforce the rules. In the political marketplace, the political elite both design and enforce the rules.

Potential problems arise because contestants have an incentive to favor rules that would benefit themselves. Consider the creation of the three-point line in basketball. Basketball fans will know that prior to

---

[4] James M. Buchanan, "The Domain of Constitutional Economics," *Constitutional Political Economy* 1, no. 1 (December 1990), pp. 1–18.

1979, shots made anywhere on the court scored two points. In 1979 the NBA added a three-point line. Shots from behind that line would score three points. Clearly, this rule change favored teams that had better long shooters. The rule would seem to favor some teams over others. However, basketball rosters change and a team without good long shooters could acquire them relatively rapidly. This being the case, teams would be likely to take the long view and decide whether to favor the addition of the three-point line based on whether they thought it would be good for the game. Five years down the road, every team would have a different mix of players.

One can think of political institutions the same way. If the rules are relatively durable, individuals may have little idea about what positions they might hold in the future, so they will favor rules that will be socially beneficial rather than looking toward their own interests.[5] The Constitution of the United States has been viewed this way. Its authors designed the structure of government without knowing what positions they might take in it, or even if they would hold government positions.

If rules are general, so they apply to everyone, and if they are durable, so that people do not have a good idea of their future situations with regard to the rules, people have an incentive to create and agree on rules that are best for everyone. People will favor rules against assault to protect themselves against potential assailants, but they will also want rules of due process to convict assailants to protect themselves against being falsely accused.

Rules about government structure and decision-making processes may fall into this category. Even among the political elite, when nobody can be assured of being a dictator, they will want to agree on rules that prevent the political process from being taken over by some faction. Decision-makers find themselves behind a veil of ignorance, in that they do not know what their positions will be after the rules are imposed, so want rules that will treat them fairly regardless of their future status.[6] This appears to be descriptive of the constitutional framework in the United States and Western Europe. In contrast, when those who write the rules know they will be at the top of the political hierarchy, the result is the political structure of Castro's Cuba or Kim's North Korea.

---

[5] This idea is developed by James M. Buchanan and Roger D. Congleton, *Politics by Principle, Not Interest* (Cambridge: Cambridge University Press, 1998).

[6] This veil of ignorance framework lays the foundation for just rules, according to John Rawls, *A Theory of Justice* (Cambridge, MA: Belknap, 1971).

The sports analogy breaks down in one important way. When sports leagues write their rules, those rules apply only to the members of the leagues. When the political elite write the rules, the rules apply, perhaps to everyone, but certainly to the masses – and often exempt the elite. The externality example applies here. Those who transact in the political marketplace design rules for their mutual benefit, to maximize the value of those rules to themselves. Those who face high transaction costs are excluded from the bargaining process, and often bear the costs of the bargains made by the political elite.

The elite can write the rules to benefit themselves in two major ways. First, they can design rules that transfer income from the masses to themselves. Second, they can design rules that create barriers to entry into the political elite, solidifying their power and making it difficult for challengers to displace them. The remainder of the chapter considers rules produced by the elite that apply to the elite.

SINGLE-MEMBER DISTRICTS

Members of the United States House of Representatives are elected from single-member districts, but there is no constitutional requirement that they be elected this way. Early in the nation's history, many states elected their Representatives through general ticket elections, in which all Representatives ran statewide and all voters voted for all of the seats to be filled. General ticket elections were common until 1846, when they were discouraged by federal law, but continued to be used in some states. North Dakota used general ticket elections until 1962, and Hawaii, in 1968, was the last state to use general ticket elections for Representatives.[7]

Some states also used at-large elections to elect some of their Representatives. If a state gained Representatives as a result of population gain, they would sometimes retain their old districts and elect additional Representatives statewide. Twelve states elected at-large Representatives in 1912, and in 1964, the last time any Representatives were elected at-large, three states used the practice. Up until 1840, some states used plural districts, in which more than one Representative was elected from a district. This might make sense today in densely populated areas. Five members of Congress represent New York City, for

---

[7] Detailed information on representation can be found in Kenneth C. Martis, *The Historical Atlas of United States Congressional Districts: 1789–1983* (New York: Free Press, 1982).

example. Rather than five small districts, an alternative would be to elect five Representatives citywide.

While the Constitution does not specify single-member districts for House elections, Congress has passed legislation encouraging it going back to 1842 and continuing through 1967.[8] This system of electing Representatives is the product of legislation passed by the Representatives themselves. Single-member districts serve the function of making Representatives monopolists in their own districts. Constituents have a single Representative who represents them, and more advantageous for Representatives, it creates a system in which incumbent Representatives do not compete with each other for reelection. A rare exception may occur every ten years when congressional districts are redrawn following a census. But single-member districts are designed to minimize, if not eliminate, competition among incumbents for political office.

Single-member districts create a cartel arrangement among Representatives.[9] Rather than compete with each other for office, incumbents run against nonincumbent challengers. The political elite compete against those who want to join the political elite. This offers an interesting example of the way that the political elite design political institutions for their own benefit. A similar situation exists in the United States Senate. Although each state is represented by two Senators elected statewide, their terms are staggered so that incumbents from a state do not run for reelection in the same year.

THE COMMITTEE SYSTEM

Legislation considered by the United States Congress is initiated in congressional committees. There is no provision made for congressional committees in the Constitution, and in the 1800s much legislation was introduced before the entire House or Senate and discussed by the group. The committee system, which emerged around the turn of the twentieth century, has often been seen as a response to the increased amount of legislation dealt with by Congress, and it is the case that the committee system enables Congress to pass more legislation.

---

[8] See Randall G. Holcombe, *Liberty in Peril: Democracy and Power in American History* (Oakland, CA: Independent Institute, 2019), pp. 71–73 for a discussion.

[9] This aspect of single-member districts is analyzed by W. Mark Crain, "On the Structure and Stability of Political Markets," *Journal of Political Economy* 85, no. 4 (August 1977), pp. 829–842.

Another issue is that the legislative agenda is a common pool resource for members of Congress. There is little cost to them accessing the legislative agenda, even to propose legislation that has little chance of passage. If there were no restrictions on proposed legislation, one can envision legislators proposing legislation in response to requests from constituents and lobbyists, knowing that the legislation would not pass. The legislator, doing a favor for the lobbyist, would introduce legislation with the expectation of a payment in return. All legislators facing the same incentives, the legislative agenda would become clogged with legislation that could not win majority approval.[10] Legislation proposed by one representative would impose an external cost on the others, interfering with the ability to pass legislation.

The situation is similar to the common grazing grounds that once existed in Britain, which led to overgrazing.[11] Farmers who would bring their herds to the common grazing grounds had no incentive to conserve the grass, leading to an overgrazing so that little grass was available to anyone. The enclosure movement in the eighteenth and nineteenth centuries divided up the common grazing grounds and granted private property rights to individual herders, who then had an incentive to efficiently manage their land and preserve the grass for their herds. While some people question the facts surrounding the enclosure movement, the theory is clear. People have an incentive to overuse resources that are used in common.

The creation of congressional committees served the same purpose as the enclosure movement – privatizing the common pool of the legislative agenda. Legislators, facing low transaction costs, had the incentive to create institutions to allow them to use the legislative agenda more efficiently, for the benefit of all members. The common agenda was divided up and property rights over sections of the legislative agenda were assigned to committees. Committee members then had an incentive to manage legislation coming out of their committees to maximize its value. The institutional structure was reformed to lower transaction costs and to facilitate the ability of the legislature to maximize the value of legislative output to its members.

---

[10] This idea is discussed in Randall G. Holcombe and Glenn R. Parker, "Committees in Legislatures: A Property Rights Perspective," *Public Choice* 70, no. 1 (April 1991), pp. 11–20.

[11] The classic article on this subject is Garrett Hardin, "The Tragedy of the Commons," *Science* 162, no. 3859 (December 13, 1968), pp. 1243–1248.

The committee system is an institutional arrangement that assigns property rights to what would otherwise be a common pool resource – the legislative agenda. This gives committee members an incentive to maximize the value of the committee's sphere of authority, rather than overusing access to an agenda that otherwise would be open to all members.

The committee system also has the advantage of enabling legislators to have better knowledge of the other representatives with whom they deal. Recalling Dunbar's number, and the idea that people can only have personal knowledge about a limited number of others, committee members will know each other in that small group well, and have little reason to know the reputations of members of other committees with whom they will have limited dealings. Committee chairs deal with legislative leaders. By breaking up a larger legislature into smaller groups, transaction costs are lowered, facilitating political exchange.

SENIORITY

Committee assignments, chairmanships, and other leadership positions in Congress tend to be assigned based on member seniority, and once assigned, those positions tend to remain with the members who have the assignments. The seniority system serves much the same purpose as the committee system. It assigns property rights to the current holder of a position. If a legislator has a committee assignment, or chairs a committee, the seniority system gives the holder of that position a right to keep it.

Again drawing a parallel to the enclosure movement, if ranchers who have their herds on their private grazing land have to sit on the fence with a rifle to protect the ownership of their animals from rustlers, the time they spend guarding their property takes away from time they could use productively for other purposes. Similarly, if legislators need to devote effort to keeping others from poaching their committee assignments, that reduces the effort they can use to accomplish other ends. Rather than having to fight to keep their assignments, the seniority system offers them some guarantee that others will not be able to take them.[12]

It seems unlikely that the most competent person to chair a committee would be the most senior person, or that a newer committee member would necessarily be less qualified than the current chair, but the institution of seniority is not meant to choose the most qualified committee

---

[12] This idea is explained in Randall G. Holcombe, "A Note on Seniority and Political Competition," *Public Choice* 61, no. 3 (June 1989), pp. 285–288.

members or chairs. It is designed to create and protect a property right for the people currently in those positions. It is an example of an institutional structure created by the political elite for their own advantage.

Because all members of the legislature have equal voting power, one question is why junior members would not rebel against the seniority system. One answer is that eventually, they hope to have the privileges of seniority, but this assumes that, first, they will continue to be reelected (which is likely, because incumbents are very likely to win reelection) and that the seniority system will still be in place once they attain senior status. There is always the possibility that a coalition of junior people will form to eliminate the privileges of seniority. To be a stable institution, the system must provide benefits to junior members as well as senior members.

The benefit to junior members is that when they run for reelection, they will always have more seniority than their challengers, who will have none. Even the most junior incumbent has already acquired some seniority, and if seniority is valuable, this is an asset incumbents can use in their reelection campaigns against their challengers. The seniority system is another example of a political institution that has been designed by the political elite for their benefit. It also is an example of an institution that benefits the elite by creating a barrier to entry for their challengers.

The seniority system is an informal institution that was established around the beginning of the twentieth century along with the committee system. There is no formal enforcement of the seniority system, and it may be weakening in the twenty-first century, not because junior people are rebelling against it but because members in the top leadership positions are more willing to use their power to replace committee members and chairs who challenge those at the top of the legislative hierarchy. A contributing factor may be the high reelection rates of all incumbents. If incumbents are almost certain to be reelected, junior members may not value that benefit of always having more seniority than their challengers.

GERRYMANDERING

Gerrymandering is the drawing of legislative districts to give a particular party or candidate an electoral advantage. The boundaries of legislative districts typically are drawn up by legislatures, so it is not surprising that those in the legislature would want to draw them to their own advantage.[13] The way this can work is that the party that holds the advantage in the legislature can design districts to provide "safe" districts for their members by drawing the boundaries to include more voters who support that party, and exclude voters who tend not to support the party. For example, if Republicans are drawing the district boundaries, they can include Republican-leaning areas within a legislator's district, and exclude areas that tend to have Democratic voters. This makes the district more safe for the Republican incumbents.

Recognize, however, that by doing so, this also makes the Democratic districts more "safe" for Democratic legislators. If voters who tend to lean Democratic are drawn out of Republican-leaning districts, they must be drawn into Democratic-leaning ones. Gerrymandering makes all districts either more Republican or more Democratic, enhancing the reelection prospects for all incumbent legislators. While gerrymandering may benefit the majority party that is drawing district boundaries, it also benefits incumbent members of the minority party by making their districts more secure. Gerrymandering is another example of a political institution that benefits the political elite over those who would challenge them.

INCUMBENT ADVANTAGES

The above examples show how political institutions are designed by the political elite to give incumbents advantages over challengers. Incumbents start out with the advantage that the news media tends to cover their activities, keeping their names in front of the public. Challengers have to pay for advertising to get the same amount of media exposure. Incumbents also have office space provided to them, a paid staff, and state-provided transportation. Members of the US Congress are able to mail communications to their constituents at no charge through the franking privilege. Single-member districts mean they do not have to compete with other incumbents for office, and the seniority system gives them an advantage – more seniority – over their challengers. Many elected officials are elected from gerrymandered districts that give them a further advantage in elections.

In many ways, political institutions are designed to enable incumbents – the political elite – to retain their elite positions of power, and to prevent challengers from displacing them. As Chapter 5 noted, while political

---

[13] Some issues with gerrymandering are discussed in Bernard Grofman, ed., *Political Gerrymandering and the Courts* (New York: Agathon Press, 1990).

commentary tends to focus on competition between candidates and parties, the primary dimension of political competition is between members of the political elite and those who challenge them for their positions. Elites of different parties have more in common with each other than they do with challengers in their same party. The elite write the rules, so it is understandable that the rules tend to give them advantages.

THE CHARACTERISTICS OF POWER

Douglass North, John Joseph Wallis, and Barry Weingast divide the characteristics of individuals into personal characteristics and socially ascribed characteristics.[14] Personal characteristics, which exist independent of institutions, are those inherent in the individual and include things like a person's intelligence, physical abilities, race, and gender. Socially ascribed characteristics are those that go with the positions people hold in society. Some examples are member of parliament, bank teller, corporate manager, police officer, and Sunday school teacher.

The ruling elite gain and hold power based on a combination of personal and socially ascribed characteristics. Revolutionary leaders like Vladimir Lennin and Fidel Castro began their ascendency to the ruling elite based on their personal characteristics. They were charismatic individuals who were able to inspire others to follow them. By developing a critical mass of followers, they were able to overthrow the existing governments in Russia and Cuba and establish themselves as those countries' rulers. Having established themselves as rulers based on their personal characteristics, they designed political institutions that enabled them to remain in power indefinitely.

Power can be obtained, as with Lenin and Castro, as a result of the personal characteristics of the individual gaining power. That person then constructs institutions that enable the ruler to maintain that power. With institutional backing and the comparative advantage in the use of force, institutions reinforce the power that comes with the ruler's personal characteristics.

Within an existing institutional framework, individuals can obtain power by moving into positions that bring with them the socially ascribed characteristics of power. The president of the United States and

---

[14] Douglass C. North, John Joseph Wallis, and Barry R. Weingast, *Violence and Social Orders: A Conceptual Framework for Interpreting Recorded History* (Cambridge: Cambridge University Press, 2009).

the prime minister of Britain, for example, hold their power because of the socially ascribed characteristics of those positions. Presidents Jimmy Carter, George H. W. Bush, and Donald Trump wanted to retain the power that came with the presidency, but lost their reelection bids and, with it, lost that power. The power they had came not from their personal characteristics, but from the socially ascribed characteristics that went with the presidency.

Personal characteristics and socially ascribed characteristics have an interesting interrelationship in the acquisition of power. First, one can see that personal characteristics have a substantial influence over how much power one can accumulate, regardless of the institutions. Lenin and Castro ascended to their positions of power based solely on their personal characteristics, able to overthrow those who previously had the socially ascribed characteristics of political power. But those who compete for elective office also are differentiated by their personal characteristics. People who are good-looking, who are tall, and who have charismatic personalities tend to do better in elections than others. They use their personal characteristics to be voted into positions that carry the socially ascribed characteristic of power.

Once a position of power is acquired, the power the person holds is determined by institutions. The president of the United States has certain powers, for example, that are attached to the position. But the person holding that power has the incentive to modify those institutions to give the position more power, in keeping with the idea that members of the ruling class want to maximize their power. Franklin Roosevelt was able to increase the powers that went with the office of President of the United States, giving him more power, and also making that position more powerful for those presidents who followed him.

INSTITUTIONALIZING POWER

Institutions define the limits of the power of the ruling class. Thinking about political institutions in the early twenty-first-century United States and Europe, the powers that can be exercised by members of parliament, cabinet ministers, senators, and presidents are defined by institutions. Those who hold power do so because of the socially ascribed powers of their positions. Should they lose those positions, they lose the power that goes with them.

Once in those positions, those who hold them have the incentive to expand the socially ascribed powers that go with them. Again considering early twenty-first-century examples, both Vladimir Putin, as president of Russia, and Xi Jinping, president of China, were able to overturn term limits that came with their positions, allowing them to remain in power longer than they could have under the rules in place when they were elected. They have been able to alter institutions to shift some of the power they acquired through the socially ascribed characteristics of their positions toward their personal characteristics.

Vladimir Putin was elected as president of Russia in 2000 and acquired political power because of his socially ascribed position of president. Over time he was able to shift the source of his power toward his personal characteristics, so that more of his power came from the fact that he is Putin than that he is president.

One result has been a relaxing of the institutional constraints on Putin's power. His relaxing of the term limits that would have put him out of office is a formal example, but his ability to act unilaterally to jail and even kill his adversaries, his ability to dictate Russian military activity across the globe, and his ability to act independently of others in Russian government illustrate the shifting of the base of his power from the socially ascribed institutional characteristics as president to his personal characteristics. Kim Jong-un, who became Supreme Leader of North Korea in 2011, provides an even more dramatic example of someone who gained power based on his personal characteristics. He assumed that position upon the death of his father, the previous Supreme Leader, and has ruthlessly killed potential challengers to his power, including his brother and uncle.

In contrast with these examples in which political power is held by individuals by virtue of their personal characteristics, political leaders in the United States and Western Europe hold power because of the socially ascribed characteristics of their positions. If those political leaders lose their elections, they lose the power that went with their positions. Boris Johnson, former Prime Minister of the United Kingdom, was accused of holding parties during the COVID lockdowns in 2020 and 2021 and, as a result, was forced to resign from the position in 2022. Could anyone imagine Vladimir Putin being forced to resign as Russia's president because he held parties? The contrast between Johnson and Putin illustrates the difference between power being derived from socially ascribed characteristics versus personal characteristics.

One way to constrain the abuse of political power is to establish institutions in which political power comes from the socially ascribed characteristics of those who hold it rather than their personal characteristics.

This is easy to say but sometimes difficult to implement. Adolf Hitler, Hugo Chavez, and Vladimir Putin all were democratically elected political leaders. In markets for goods and services, formal institutional constraints are enforced by a third party – typically, government. The problem is that institutions in the political marketplace are enforced by the political elite that are constrained by them, opening the possibility that the elite will decide not to enforce them.

CONCLUSION

In markets for goods and services, institutions serve the role of lowering transaction costs to facilitate mutually advantageous exchanges. Political institutions are also designed to facilitate mutually advantageous exchanges. This chapter has reviewed a number of those institutions, finding that, first, they tend to be designed to facilitate exchange among the political elite, and second, that they are often designed to give advantages to the political elite over those who would challenge them for their positions of power. The specific examples are interesting in their own right, but even more, they conform with what one would expect from self-interested individuals who have chosen for themselves to seek power over others. The institutions they design help them do just that.

In societies with strong institutional foundations, people's political power comes from their socially ascribed characteristics. They are members of parliament, or presidents, or agency heads, and their power comes from the powers vested in those positions. People also gain power derived from their personal characteristics, and to the degree that their political power comes from their personal characteristics, the institutional constraints on the exercise of power are eroded. Adolf Hitler was democratically elected, but ultimately, the source of his power shifted to his personal characteristics. His power came because he was Hitler, not because he was elected. To a lesser degree, Franklin Roosevelt held the powers socially ascribed to the US presidency, but he was able to expand those powers while he held office because of his personal characteristics. The power of the office of the presidency was permanently enhanced as a result of Roosevelt's increasing its scope.

Political institutions are more effective constraints on the abuse of power when the power that comes with them is associated with the positions people hold rather than with the individuals who have power. Effective political institutions contain mechanisms that allow those who hold political power to be replaced, while retaining the power of those positions. This naturally points toward democratic institutions and elections, but one theme that extends throughout this volume is that transaction costs prevent the masses from having any meaningful oversight over the political elite. A division of power is necessary to constrain the power of the political elite. Effective checks and balances come from the ability of some members of the political elite to check and balance the power of others.

Enforcing institutional constraints in the political marketplace comes with a challenge that does not exist in the market for goods and services. Some institutions lower transaction costs to facilitate mutually advantageous exchanges, while others are necessary to enforce the institutional constraints that come with those institutions that lower transaction costs. In the market for goods and services, the institutions of authority and governance that enforce institutional constraints lie outside of those who are transacting in markets. In the political marketplace, the same people who are engaging in political exchange also have the power of enforcement. Again, this illustrates the importance of a division of power so that some members of the political elite can prevent others from abusing their power.

7

Political Transactions

The political marketplace, as with markets for goods and services, is structured by institutional constraints that facilitate some transactions and prevent others. The institutional structure lays out collective decision-making procedures, often requiring a collective agreement for government action to be taken. Legislative decisions, the prime example, require a majority of legislators to approve to enact legislation. Legislators can engage in bilateral exchanges – "I'll vote for your bill if you will vote for mine" – but those bills will pass only if a majority of legislators vote in favor. This adds a layer of complexity to the political marketplace. Only rarely can a political outcome be negotiated with a single transaction.

Those who want to buy access to legislative power cannot simply find and negotiate with a seller. Even if they have a single contact – they might just negotiate with one legislator – that contact will then have to negotiate with others in the political marketplace to transform that demander's desire for legislation into law. A simple rent-seeking model of the political marketplace has rent seekers bidding for a rent, with the rent going to the highest bidder. In the actual political marketplace, there are no rents that are up for bid, and in most cases there is no single contact point at which those bids can be submitted.

An exception arises in cases where rents can be granted to rent seekers through regulatory action. The head of a regulatory agency may be in a position to unilaterally grant a regulatory benefit to a rent seeker. Even there, the rent would come with tacit legislative approval and the risk that it could be legislatively undone. But legislators and regulators do not just have rents that they auction off to rent seekers. The rents are designed and proposed by the rent seekers, not the rent creators.

All government activity is initiated by some outside demand for that action. Expenditures, regulations, taxes – any actions – are a response to someone's demand for access to government power. Constituents, corporations, lobbyists, interest groups, and even those inside government want government to do something for them. But government is not a single entity that does anything. Individuals within government are the actors, and they negotiate with each other in the political marketplace to respond to the demands for their services – for access to government power.

DEMANDERS AND SUPPLIERS

The demands of those outside government for access to government power lay the foundation for the political marketplace. All that transpires within that marketplace is directly or indirectly motivated by those demands. The logrolling and vote trading that occur among legislators, discussed later in this chapter, take place because legislators are negotiating to pass legislation to benefit some constituency, almost always at the same time imposing costs on some other group. Legislation that benefits everyone should be an easy sell, because nobody will be against it. In general, however, negotiations are required when those exercising political power must weigh the benefits conveyed to some against the costs imposed on others.

Political entrepreneurs can profit by promoting legislation that improves the efficiency of resource allocation. Such an improvement would allow the same benefits to be produced at a lower cost, and the saving is a profit that the political entrepreneur can allocate elsewhere. Those efficiency gains are difficult to come by. They require the alertness to spot them, and the ability to convince others of their merits.[1] In addition, opposition to efficiency-enhancing legislation will appear when it enhances the ability of entrepreneurial individuals to compete with established interests. Monopolies are inefficient, for example, but monopolists will oppose legislation that opens them to competitive pressures. Efficiency-enhancing legislation often generates political opposition.

However, there is always a potential for political profit by redistributing resources. The simplest case is transferring resources to a majority

---

[1] Israel Kirzner, *Competition and Entrepreneurship* (Chicago, IL: University of Chicago Press, 1973) defines entrepreneurship as the noticing of a previously unnoticed profit opportunity. The fact that it has been previously unnoticed suggests the difficulty in spotting it.

to gain their support at the expense of a minority.[2] A cyclical majority example illustrates that point. Assume that three voters are all taxed a third of a dollar, leaving it to the legislature to decide how that dollar is distributed among the three taxpayers. A political entrepreneur could propose giving half a dollar each to two of the voters, providing a benefit to those two voters at the expense of the third. That outcome can be represented as

$$(1/2, 1/2, 0).$$

That proposal should get the political entrepreneur the support of two of the three voters, and therefore, a majority.

With that distribution as the status quo, another political entrepreneur can propose giving the second voter two-thirds of the dollar and the third voter one-third, making two of the three voters better off, again gaining majority support. That outcome is represented in the top row of Table 7.1. This opens the opportunity for a political entrepreneur to suggest giving the first voter one-third of the dollar and the third voter two-thirds, as shown in the second row of the table. Two of the three voters would prefer the distribution shown in the second row to the first, giving the entrepreneur the support of a majority. Following the same logic, the third row of the table, giving the first voter two-thirds and the second voter one-third, would gain the support of a majority. But the first row of the table shows an outcome that would be preferred by a majority to the third row.

TABLE 7.1 *A cyclical majority*

(0, 2/3, 1/3)
(1/3, 0, 2/3)
(2/3, 1/3, 0)

With majority rule voting, the first row of the table is dominated by the second, which is dominated by the third, which is dominated by the first. This well-known example of a cyclical majority illustrates that under majority rule politics, regardless of the status quo, a political entrepreneur can always find a distributive policy that would benefit a majority at

---

[2] This idea is developed in Randall G. Holcombe, "Political Entrepreneurship and the Democratic Allocation of Resources," *Review of Austrian Economics* 15, nos. 2/3 (June 2002), pp. 143–159.

the expense of a minority.³ Efficiency-enhancing opportunities for political profit are rare and difficult to identify, and may be difficult to pass even if they are identified, but distributive opportunities always exist for political entrepreneurs.

As straightforward as this analysis of the cyclical majority is, the recognition that transaction costs prevent large groups from effectively organizing, while concentrated interests face lower transaction costs and a greater ability to organize, means that in most cases, political entrepreneurs are more likely to propose policies that benefit a minority at the expense of a majority. The same principle holds. There is always a potential political profit to be gained by designing policies that impose costs on some for the benefit of others. This principle has not escaped the politically well-connected who are able to transact in the political marketplace. Indeed, the goal of much legislation is to create inefficiencies by erecting barriers to entry to benefit concentrated interests and raising transaction costs to prevent competitors from encroaching on politically created rents.

RENT CREATION

A major area of academic research interest within the public choice research program is rent-seeking. Rents refer to the benefits that well-connected demanders hope to obtain through their negotiations in the political marketplace. The suppliers of rents are those who have the ability to use the powers of government to create them. The literature on rent-seeking has, for the most part, presented a very unrealistic depiction of the process. Rent-seeking has been depicted as a contest which rent seekers can enter and bid to win the rent. As depicted in the literature, the high bidder wins the rent, while all of the money bid by all bidders is wasted.⁴ Typically, the conclusion is that the amount of resources wasted in seeking the rents is equal to the value of the rents.⁵

---

³ Kenneth J. Arrow, *Social Choice and Individual Values* (New York: John Wiley & Sons, 1951) lays the foundation for his work by demonstrating the problem of cyclical majorities in democratic politics.

⁴ Roger D. Congleton and Arye L. Hillman, eds., *Companion to the Political Economy of Rent-Seeking* (Cheltenham, UK: Edward Elgar, 2015) devote eight chapters of their volume to the theory of rent-seeking, and all eight depict rent-seeking as a contest. Five of the eight refer to rent-seeking as a contest in their titles.

⁵ This is the plainly stated conclusion of Anne O. Krueger, "The Political Economy of the Rent-Seeking Society," *American Economic Review* 64 (1974), pp. 291–303, who gave rent-seeking its name. The framework was earlier developed by Gordon Tullock, "The Welfare Cost of Tariffs, Monopoly, and Theft," *Western Economic Journal* 5, no. 3 (June 1967), pp. 224–232, who comes up with the same conclusion.

This literature raises a very important issue related to the political marketplace. Those who are trying to purchase access to government power expend substantial resources to do so, and those expended resources add no value to society. Indeed, they take value away in most instances by promoting incentive-sapping transfers. But the literature falls short because it depicts rents as a prize that contestants hope to win. It does not consider, first, that the rent must be created before it can be captured, and second, that in the actual political marketplace, rent seekers are all seeking different prizes; they are not contesting to win the same prize.

In 1983 the Reagan administration imposed a 45 percent tariff on the importation of motorcycles with engine displacements of 700cc or larger. The only domestic manufacturer of such motorcycles was Harley-Davidson. Obviously, the Reagan administration did not think up the idea of this tariff on their own. Harley-Davidson engaged in the lobbying that ultimately resulted in their access to government power – the power to enact a tariff that raised the costs of its competitors. Harley-Davidson got the rent, but nobody else was competing for it.

In 2002 President George Bush imposed tariffs of from 8 to 20 percent on the importation of steel. Those tariffs were targeted to benefit the domestic steel industry, and as with the motorcycle tariffs, nobody else was competing to gain those rents. The rent – the tariff on steel – was designed to target one rent seeker and to create a barrier to entry to prevent competition for the rent, in contrast to the academic literature that depicts rent-seeking as an open competition for a prize.

Domestic steel manufacturers had originally proposed tariffs of 40 percent, so they did not get everything they asked for in their seeking of rents, illustrating one aspect of the political marketplace. The steel industry wanted the tariffs, but downstream producers who used steel faced higher costs because of them. Competition between those who wanted the tariffs and those who did not resulted in a compromise. Legislators weighed the benefits they could get from steel producers against the costs they would incur from a loss of support by steel users. Nobody got everything they wanted.[6]

The ethanol mandate requiring that ethanol be included in motor fuels, passed in 2005, was used as an example in Chapter 1. In 2008 Congress approved a tax credit for those who purchased electric passenger vehicles.

---

[6] This weighing of political costs against political benefits to determine public policy is modeled by Gary S. Becker, "A Theory of Competition among Pressure Groups for Political Influence," *Quarterly Journal of Economics* 98, no. 3 (August 1983), pp. 371–400.

These few examples suffice to show that rent seekers are not all competing for the same rent. The rent is not some prize they are hoping to win. Rather, every rent seeker is seeking something different that differentially advantages themselves.

The rent does not exist prior to the rent-seeking process. It is proposed by the demander, the rent seeker, and is created by the supplier, the legislators, and regulators who have the ability to use government power to create it. Rent seekers decide for themselves what they are seeking and approach those with access to political power to ask them to create the rent. An exchange then takes place in the political marketplace in which the rent seeker offers something of value to the potential rent creator in exchange for creating the rent.

In rent-seeking theory, the entire value of the rent is dissipated in the form of costs incurred by rent seekers to acquire the rent. That dissipation occurs because of the way that rent-seeking is depicted as a contest. Within a political marketplace, nobody has an incentive to create a rent if the entire value of the rent will be dissipated through wasted rent-seeking expenditures. There is no benefit to the rent creator from creating such a rent. Rent creators will create rents when there is a benefit to them from doing so, and rent seekers will only seek rents if there is a benefit to them from their rent-seeking activity. If all the rents are dissipated, there is nothing left to benefit the rent seeker, and more significantly, the rent creator.

The benefits to rent seekers and rent creators are produced by barriers to entry built into the rent creation process. When the rent that is sought is a tariff on motorcycles with large displacement engines, the only possible beneficiary is Harley-Davidson. When the rent that is sought is a mandate to require that ethanol be included in motor fuels, the only possible beneficiaries are the producers of ethanol (and its inputs into the production process). Rents are targeted, with barriers to entry into seeking those rents, for the purpose of limiting competition for the rents. That generates a positive benefit to the rent seeker, out of which the rent seeker can compensate the rent supplier. This is how the political marketplace works.

Anne Krueger, the American economist who wrote the seminal article that gave rent-seeking its name, titled her article "The Political Economy of the Rent-Seeking Society." Krueger is a development economist, and her article drew upon her experience in India and Turkey, two less-developed economies at the time she wrote. She was not writing about her home country, the United States, or Europe, but rather was describing the distributional political institutions in less-developed economies that were preventing them from developing, as the United States and Europe had.[7]

An important element that has largely been missing from the academic literature on rent-seeking is a discussion of the incentives of rent creators to create rents. They have no reason to create rents unless there is some benefit to themselves, and for there to be a benefit to rent creators, all the rents cannot be dissipated, or there is nothing left out of which to provide those benefits. So, deals are struck to create barriers to entry into rent-seeking, which provides the surplus to rent seekers out of which they can compensate the rent creators as they negotiate in the political marketplace.[8]

Take an extreme example in which a rent seeker is willing to spend $99 to get a rent of $100. Some of that $99 must be channeled to the creators of the rent in the form of real benefits, or the potential rent creators have no incentive to create the rent. Only in the most dysfunctional cases, which are what Krueger intended to describe as rent-seeking societies, will all the rents be dissipated.

One factor that creates a barrier to entry is that transaction costs prevent most people from engaging in rent-seeking. Only an elite few are in the low-transaction cost group that can negotiate such bargains. Beyond that, rent creators will create rents only when the rent seekers demonstrate that the rent creators will benefit from doing so, and rent seekers will only seek rents when they anticipate that the rent they expect will be more valuable than the costs they will incur to get the rent.

Rent seekers typically negotiate deals in which both the suppliers and demanders of rents share in the gains from trade. In general, most of the rents are not dissipated, and those who design the rents – the rent seekers themselves – do so in a way that limits dissipation. Rents are not some prize that is out there for rent seekers to win, but are benefits targeted specifically to the rent seekers, and designed to provide a benefit to themselves as well as compensation to the rent creators in exchange for creating the rents.

---

[7] See Randall G. Holcombe, "The Transformative Impact of Rent-Seeking on the Study of Public Choice," *Public Choice* 196, nos. 1/2 (July 2023), pp. 157–167, for a discussion of the influence Krueger's article had on the development of public choice.

[8] This idea is developed in Randall G. Holcombe, "Political Incentives for Rent Creation," *Constitutional Political Economy* 28, no. 1 (March 2017), pp. 62–78.

LOGROLLING

Logrolling is the process by which politicians trade support on issues they care less about to gain support on those that are more important to them. It could be "I will vote for your bill if you vote for mine," but exchanges could also be more complex, as discussed in Chapter 1. Setting aside complexities, Table 7.2 presents a simple example to consider the efficiency of logrolling.

Assume that there are three voters, 1, 2, and 3, who place values on options A, B, and C given in the table. Voter 1 places a value of 100 on option A, 2 on option B, and 1 on option C, for example. This table presents an example of a cyclical majority, in that a majority of voters prefer A to B, but a majority prefers C to A, and a majority prefers B to C. No one option can secure a majority over the others, so voting by simple majority rule will lead to an uncertain outcome. If these voters face high transaction costs, the outcome of a majority rule decision process depends on the way alternatives are considered. If A is voted on against B, for example, and then the winner faces C, A defeats B, and C defeats A, so C is the collective choice if that is the choice mechanism. There is no guarantee that the highest-valued alternative will win under majority rule.

If these voters face low transaction costs – if these are legislators who are voting – they can negotiate with each other to affect the outcome. Because option A is very highly valued by voter 1, that legislator can offer to bargain with one of the other legislators to get a majority in favor of option A. Voter 1 could offer voter 3 a payment of 10 in exchange for favoring A, for example. The exact payment would be subject to negotiation, but there is a profitable exchange that can be made, and the assumption of low transaction costs implies that the exchange will be made.

TABLE 7.2 *Overcoming a cyclical majority*

	Voters		
	1	2	3
Options			
A	100	1	2
B	2	3	1
C	1	2	3

With high transaction costs, the outcome of democratic decision-making in the example in Table 7.2 is uncertain. With low transaction costs, option A, the highest-valued option, will be chosen. This suggests that logrolling is a mechanism that can lead to more efficient outcomes in the political marketplace.[9] In the absence of transaction costs, cyclical majorities will not occur, and the outcome of political decisions will be the one most highly valued by members of the decision-making group.

A strong caveat must be added to any suggestion that option A is economically efficient. The outcome is the highest-valued to the members of the bargaining group – voters 1, 2, and 3 in the example. But those in the low transaction cost group often approve public policies that impose costs on third parties. It may be that the reason option A has a high value to voter A is that option A creates large rents for an interest group that has lobbied for voter 1's support.

Voluntary exchange creates value for those who engage in the exchanges. Exchanges in the political marketplace can therefore be expected to create value for the elite few who trade in that marketplace, but because political exchanges typically impose costs on those excluded from the political marketplace, there is good reason to question the degree to which political exchanges are value-enhancing. Theories of rent-seeking, regulatory capture, and interest group politics provide an academic foundation for raising the question.

CENTRALIZED VOTE TRADING

Legislators can participate in logrolling because their small numbers mean they face low transaction costs. Recalling Dunbar's number, Dunbar suggests that people can only know personally about 150 other individuals, and legislatures often have more members than this. Thus, legislators have an incentive to develop institutions that facilitate political exchange.

The simplest type of political exchange is a straightforward quid pro quo: "I will vote for your bill if you will vote for mine." The larger the group becomes, the more difficult it will be for legislators to locate people who are willing to trade – and can be trusted to uphold their side of the bargain. The US House of Representatives has 435 members, for example, meaning that 218 votes are required to gain majority support. Legislators who are less well-connected, perhaps because they are newer

---

[9] The efficiency of logrolling is discussed by James M. Buchanan and Gordon Tullock, *The Calculus of Consent* (Ann Arbor, MI: University of Michigan Press, 1062).

members and have not had time to build personal relationships, could find transaction costs standing in their way as they try to promote legislation. Just as in markets for goods and services, political markets develop institutions that facilitate mutually beneficial exchanges.

Senior members and party leaders have had time to build connections, so they are better able to engage in political exchange. Those connections lower transaction costs so they have more opportunities to locate other members with whom to trade. Members who are seeking support for legislation but are unsure where to get it can approach those members with better connections for help. This makes those well-connected members natural market makers for political exchange.

Junior member A can approach the well-connected senior member seeking support for some legislation; meanwhile, junior member B does the same. The senior member tells A that he can get support for his legislation in exchange for supporting B's legislation, and tells B he can get support for his legislation if he supports A's legislation. The senior member acts as a middleman, facilitating support for A's legislation in exchange for support for B's legislation. As the middleman, both A and B incur a debt to the senior member. This institution of centralized vote trading increases the power of the senior legislator who acts as the middleman because both A and B are now indebted to the middleman for facilitating the exchange.

Over time, some members accumulate more IOUs from other members, which gives them more power. Those members find themselves in a position to make a market in political exchanges. Even though all members have equal votes, some members have more power because they have accumulated more IOUs from their colleagues. Although this is an informal institution, with no outside enforcement mechanism, those debts must be acknowledged and repaid if those who incurred the debts want to participate in the political marketplace.

To limit transaction costs – the costs involved in rounding up sufficient votes to pass legislation – parties will designate a well-connected party member as the party "whip." The role of the whip is to negotiate with other party members to pass legislation the party leaders want passed. The whip acts as a middleman in the negotiations, bargaining with legislators and, like middlemen in other markets, takes a cut of the profits. The whip accumulates IOUs from helping party members secure sufficient votes for legislative passage.

These exchanges are based on trust, and members will not trade with those who cannot be trusted to repay their debts. This provides an additional advantage to powerful legislators. In cases where legislator A might have second thoughts about repaying a favor from legislator B, who is less powerful, legislator A would be very reluctant not to repay the powerful market maker, who would be in a better position to levy informal sanctions against those who do not repay. Legislators can accumulate political power by helping out colleagues and accumulating IOUs from them. Powerful legislators can help colleagues get things done.

Those who hold the most power can lower transaction costs by facilitating political exchanges among the less powerful, and in the process can accumulate more power. Those are the power brokers who have reputations for getting things done, and those with less power can resist their requests only at the risk of being left out of future political exchanges.[10] When powerful politicians ask to call in their IOUs, those with less power must repay.

POLITICAL CAPITAL

Politicians acquire political capital by accumulating IOUs from their colleagues. Exchanges are informally enforced, and ultimately, the currency is votes. But all votes are not equal, and there are not clearly defined market prices in these political exchanges, as there are for goods and services. That leaves some ambiguity over exactly what constitutes repayment. If a legislator seeks support for some minor legislation, can the colleague holding the IOU ask for support on major legislation in exchange? If a legislator agrees to support some legislation if the sponsor adds funding for a project in the legislator's distract, what would constitute repayment? Perhaps that project constitutes full payment. "I gave you the project, you gave your vote. We are even."

As with any exchange, there are gains from trades that are made in the political marketplace, but without market prices, there is some ambiguity as to how those gains from trade will be divided. This can put those who already have power in a position to capture most of the gains from trade, increasing their power even more. Every legislator is, in one sense, equal. They all have the same voting power in the legislature. But in other ways, legislators who accumulate IOUs build their political capital. They can become party leaders and committee chairs, which further enhances their power. This facilitates their building connections, which

---

[10] A more formal presentation of this idea appears in Kenneth J. Koford, "Centralized Vote Trading," *Public Choice* 39, no. 2 (1982), pp. 245–268.

can lower transaction costs, providing them with power over their legislative colleagues.

One can imagine a powerful legislator asking a less powerful one for repayment, and the less powerful legislator hesitates, arguing that the repayment the powerful legislator is requesting is much more valuable than the original favor that incurred the IOU. If the powerful legislator disagrees, the imbalance of power suggests that the less powerful legislator must pay up, shifting most of the gains from trade from the less powerful to the more powerful. Power enables those who have it to accumulate more power.

Chapter 6 noted how political institutions are designed to preserve the political power of the politically powerful. Seniority, the committee system, and gerrymandering are among those institutions. The building of political capital by accumulating IOUs aids politicians in their quest for power. Much as in the market for goods and services, even if everyone starts out equal (although they do not, in either type of market), the market process enables some to engage in exchanges which, over time, enhance their power over others.

One mechanism legislators can use to enhance their power is to work together to form voting blocs. Their power is then multiplied by the number in the bloc. In the US Congress, groups like the Congressional Black Caucus and the Freedom Caucus are examples. These groups lower transaction costs, making it easier for members to bargain among themselves and giving the group more power within Congress than the individual members would have on their own.

The accumulation and use of power can occur in subtle ways that are difficult to detect. One interesting example comes from a reporter who was able to get a politician to boast too much. T. K. Wetherell chaired the Florida House of Representatives appropriations committee "when he confided to [the reporter] that he'd tucked $1 million into the 1990-91 budget for restoration of 'Silver Beach.' There is no such place. Wetherell used the budget line as a cash stash when House members asked him for favors, collecting IOUs from his colleagues by parceling out $50,000 here and $100,000 there for hometown projects."[11]

Had Wetherell not told the reporter about what he had done, it likely would have gone undetected. This type of activity occurs on a regular basis, but politicians are understandably reluctant to disclose their deceptive practices.

---

[11] Reported in the *Tallahassee Democrat*, September 22, 2023, p. 9A.

BUNDLED LEGISLATION

An overly simple depiction of the legislative process would envision a legislature voting, item by item, on government activities. Should government fund a particular health care program? Should government build this bridge? However, items in the legislative agenda often are bundled so that they are voted on together, rather than individually. Chapter 1 opened with a discussion on Alaska's bridge to nowhere. If that bridge, and many other similar programs, were voted on individually, they would not have the support to pass. So, they are bundled with popular programs. "If you will include my bridge in your legislation, I can support it." So the bridge goes in, and is approved because even though most legislators do not want the bridge, they want other items in the bill to pass.

The US Department of Defense has been trying to retire its fleet of A-10 aircraft, known as Warthogs, since 2010, but Congress continued to block the phaseout of the aircraft, bowing to interest groups that profit from the aircraft. Many of the A-10s need new wings, for example, which are manufactured by Boeing. Why put new wings on aircraft the Defense Department wants to retire? The A-10 program continues because it is not voted on separately; it is part of the Department of Defense budget. Members who want the budget passed must vote for all of it or none, which keeps the program alive. The A-10 program remains alive as this is being written. To some legislators, it seems desirable to put new wings on an aircraft that is being phased out of use.

Consider this analogy to shopping in a supermarket. Consumers push their shopping carts along the supermarket isles, selecting items they wish to purchase, and end up with the goods they want. In the legislature, a majority vote is required to make a purchase, so the legislation's sponsors seek out support for the legislation, giving other legislators the ability to say, "I'll support the legislation if you will include funding for a community center in my district." So, that item gets added to the shopping cart. After that happens a few times, legislators have the choice of voting for the whole shopping cart to get the items they want, or voting against, and not getting what they want. The legislation either passes, or fails.

In economic terms, legislators are being offered an "all-or-nothing" sale. They cannot take just what they want, they also must take some things they do not want. To use more economic jargon, this bundling of items in a bill is a way to extract consumer surplus from the legislators. They get a benefit from items they want, so they are willing to pay a cost, which reduces their net benefit, to vote for the bundled legislation. To continue with the supermarket analogy, legislation is like a shopping cart that contains items that have been put in it by other shoppers. To get the items legislators want, they have to vote for additional items they do not want.[12]

Legislatures often budget this way through omnibus bills that include many diverse and unrelated items. Different legislators have different priorities, and often will find that by themselves they cannot gain majority support for items they want. Those legislators can negotiate with each other, perhaps with the assistance of a middleman to facilitate the exchange, to include those potentially unpopular items in legislation that has more support. The political entrepreneurs who put together the components of omnibus legislation can, in this way, extract the consumer surplus their colleagues would get from their own projects, and in the process collect those IOUs from getting those projects passed.

The federal budget of the United States is drawn up by twelve separate subcommittees in the US House of Representatives, which in principle would produce twelve different appropriation bills to be voted on by Congress. It has, however, become common for these twelve appropriation bills to be bundled into an omnibus spending bill in which all twelve either pass or fail. This places legislators in the position of having to vote for all of them to get what they want, although they might oppose some if they were considered separately. A legislator might favor most of the twelve appropriations bills but be opposed to the Homeland Security budget, or the Agriculture budget. Instead of having the option of considering all twelve separately, legislators are more likely to approve them all rather than vote against all of them in an omnibus bill.

DELEGATED POWERS: THE ADMINISTRATIVE STATE

The concept behind separation of powers in government is that different branches of government have different powers that allow them to check and balance the powers of the other branches. With the growth of government, there has been a tendency over time for legislative and judicial powers to be delegated to government agencies within the executive branch. This weakens the checks and balances within government, and gives agencies the power to write the rules (legislate), administer the rules (execute), and adjudicate the rules.

---

[12] William A. Niskanen, *Bureaucracy and Representative Government* (Chicago, IL: Aldine-Atherton, 1971) presents a similar model of bureaucratic budgeting, in which government agencies are able to offer legislators all-or-nothing budgets.

Woodrow Wilson, the only American president to have earned a PhD, was an early promoter of the administrative state.[13] Wilson's idea, shared by many, was that principles of scientific management could increase the efficiency of government. Public policy can be better carried out by experts rather than being determined by politics. Those ideas led, in the late 1800s, to a professional civil service in which government employees were qualified professionals rather than political appointees – professionals whose tenures would last beyond the terms of elected officials. That would make government administration more independent of politics, and more in the service of constituents.

Noting the increasing democratization of government in English-speaking countries, President Wilson said, "The English race, consequently, has long and successfully studied the art of curbing executive power to the constant neglect of the art of perfecting executive methods."[14] Wilson thought citizens would be better served by a government administered by professional civil servants. Half a century later, Wilson's ideas were reinforced by an influential book by Dwight Waldo, promoting the administrative state for its service to the public.[15] It would take the politics out of government.

To the degree that this vision of the administrative state can be executed, it gives administrators dictatorial powers over the areas they administrate. As a result of its enabling legislation, the US Environmental Protection Agency (EPA), for example, has broad legislative, executive, and judicial powers given to it by congressional legislation. It can write rules that define what constitutes a wetland along with rules that dictate what owners of wetlands are allowed to do on their property, it can administer those rules, and in case of disputes with landowners, can adjudicate whether they are in violation of the rules. While those found in violation can appeal to the courts, they are appealing a decision made by those who have been empowered to write and enforce the rules.

This movement toward an administrative state has been produced in the political marketplace. It begins with vague legislation that gives broad powers to the bureaucracy. The purpose of the vagueness is to limit opposition to the legislation. As previously noted, legislation tends to impose costs on third parties who do not participate in the bargaining

---

[13] Woodrow Wilson, "The Study of Administration," *Political Science Quarterly* 2, no. 2 (June 1887), pp. 197–222.
[14] Wilson, "The Study of Administration," p. 206.
[15] Dwight Waldo, *The Administrative State: A Study of the Political Theory of American Public Administration* (New York: Ronald Press Co., 1948).

to create the legislation. Vague legislation obscures who will be paying those costs, lessening potential opposition. If legislators empower a regulatory agency to design the specifics of regulations, those who support the regulation get their foot in the door, and those who oppose have no specific regulation to campaign against.

Again, using the EPA as an example, nobody will mount an effective argument against protecting the environment. This applies to regulatory agencies in general. The Consumer Product Safety Commission regulates product safety. Does anyone advocate unsafe products? The Federal Aviation Administration regulates airline safety. Does anyone want unsafe airlines? Once empowered, the specific rules are written by the regulatory agencies, insulating legislators from complaints about their interpretation and enforcement.

Incentives in the political marketplace lean toward legislators giving broad powers to write and enforce the rules to regulatory agencies, rather than writing those rules themselves. Any public dissatisfaction with the specific rules then is aimed at appointed administrators rather than elected officials. Meanwhile, if legislators are dissatisfied with the actions of agencies, they can address that dissatisfaction with additional legislation.

Administrators then have broad discretion in writing and enforcing the rules. For those covered by the rules, this lowers transaction costs. Rather than requiring a majority of the legislature to approve regulatory changes they desire, they have a single point of contact. For those who deal with regulatory agencies on a regular basis, they are able to negotiate to design a regulatory structure that furthers their interests. George Stigler hypothesized that over time, negotiations produced in the political marketplace lead regulatory agencies increasingly to modify their regulations to favor those they regulate.[16]

Regulatory agencies are not always captured by those they regulate, however. They may be captured by those who demand regulation. The EPA, for example, is likely better viewed as being captured by environmental groups than by those who are subject to environmental regulations. The environmental lobby persists over time and has broad support, giving them a voice in the political marketplace. Meanwhile, regulations are enforced against one accused violator at a time. Those accused of violating regulations do not know each other and are not all accused at the

---

[16] George J. Stigler, "The Theory of Economic Regulation," *Bell Journal of Economics and Management Science* 2, no. 1 (1971), pp. 3–21.

same time, so the accused face high transaction costs that prevent them from organizing.

Regardless of which interests have more clout, the noble theory of the administrative state working to further the public interest is undermined once interest group politics is taken into account. The administrative state is more subject to interest group politics because it legislates, executes, and adjudicates the rules under its authority. Those administrators, as civil servants, are insulated from democratic accountability and typically have job security that further lessens their accountability to citizens.

THE DEEP STATE

A typical citizen's perception of the state conforms with the way it is constitutionally defined: legislative, executive, and judicial branches of government that check and balance each other. The administrative state short-circuits that process by enabling government agencies to make the rules, administer the rules, and adjudicate disputes that may arise between the agencies and those subject to the agencies' rules. This happens because the legislature writes legislation with broad goals, leaving the agencies to write and enforce the specific rules.

This opens the potential for agencies to operate without oversight. Armed with a general charge to protect wetlands, the EPA might, for example, rule that someone filling puddles on their land is destroying wetlands. The EPA writes the rules, enforces them, and adjudicates disputes. In cases like this, the landowner does have the option to sue in federal court.[17] Ultimate recourse to the courts can provide some protection against arbitrary government action when the activities of an agency are known to those affected, but the existence of the administrative state opens the possibility that agencies with broad mandates can undertake activities unknown to constituents, and unknown to legislators. This extension of the administrative state has been called the deep state.

The deep state refers to government activities that are not revealed to citizens and, because of the nature of their activities, have no oversight. The deep state is a part of government, is funded by the government, but acts independently. Even if the intention is to have legislative or executive oversight, oversight is not possible when an agency's activities are not revealed to anyone outside the agency. This is more likely to happen

---

[17] See, for example, SACKETT v. EPA 598 U.S. (2023) in which Sackett was doing just this.

within agencies that engage in covert activities: law enforcement agencies like the FBI or intelligence agencies like the CIA or NSA.

In 1976 the Church Committee, cochaired by Senators Frank Church and John Tower, found that "The country's most powerful law enforcement and intelligence agencies – the FBI and the CIA – had secretly and in some cases unilaterally, broke [sic] the law."[18] David Rohde reports that "the NSA had opened intelligence files on at least 75,000 Americans" and that "The IRS was also implicated, launching investigations 'on the basis of political rather than tax criteria,' and opening intelligence files on 11,000 Americans."[19] The FBI "broke into Americans' homes without warrants, stole incriminating material, or planted false information."[20]

Rohde reports that after Donald Trump was elected president in 2016, unbeknownst to him, and to the American public, "the FBI was still secretly investigating contacts between Russian operatives and Trump campaign officials."[21] Trump himself used the term deep state to refer to activities within the federal government that were designed to undermine his presidency. Although the deep state can work against those at the top of the political hierarchy, many of the examples Rohde reports are cases in which those at the top of the political hierarchy – presidents, senators, agency heads – employed the deep state for their own purposes, its activities kept secret and its power unchecked. As a well-known example, when J. Edgar Hoover was director of the FBI, he investigated and kept files on 500,000 people, compiling information that could be used against them if Hoover disapproved of their activities.[22]

Mike Lofgren links the military–industrial complex to the deep state, noting that much of what goes on in the Department of Defense, and between that department and defense contractors, is classified information, so shielded from public scrutiny.[23] Their activities are potentially open to legislative scrutiny, if legislators have an idea about what they would like to scrutinize. Often, they have no incentive to exert oversight. Why pick a fight if constituents are unaware of that government activity, especially if that activity enhances the power of the political elite?

---

[18] This quotation is from David Rohde, *In Deep: The FBI, CIA, and the Truth about America's "Deep State"* (New York: W. W. Norton, 2020), p. 7.
[19] Rohde, *In Deep*, p. 4.
[20] Rohde, *In Deep*, p. 7.
[21] Rohde, *In Deep*, p. 156.
[22] Rohde, *In Deep*, pp. 3–4.
[23] Mike Lofgren, *The Deep State: The Fall of the Constitution and the Rise of a Shadow Government* (New York: Penguin Random House, 2016).

The deep state is a fourth branch of government that acts outside the checks and balances that exist within the legislative, executive, and judicial branches. There is no transparency in the activities of the deep state.

The deep state is a slippery concept. There is no doubt that there is a deep state, in the sense that the FBI, CIA, NSA, and other government agencies undertake activities with no oversight, and with no legislative awareness of some of the actions of these agencies. But, that is the case to some degree with any agency in which employees have some degree of discretion in the decisions they make. A building inspector must use independent judgment, for example, to determine if new construction meets the building code, despite written guidelines. A contractor who has had long-time dealings with a building inspector might find it easier to get construction approved than one without those connections. The building inspector acts with discretion and little oversight.

As Richard Wagner has emphasized, organizations that are nominally organized hierarchically necessarily leave room for discretion in the behavior of those lower in the hierarchy.[24] Those at the top cannot possibly know every action of everyone below, and cannot possibly specify all of their actions. This gives the power to act with discretion to anyone who has even a small amount of government power. This creates the opportunity for the deep state.

The deep state is not a monolithic underground government. It is decentralized, with many elements of government acting independently of each other and without the knowledge of what other parts of the deep state are doing. One can imagine a small group in the CIA undertaking clandestine activity, limiting any knowledge of that activity to those who have "a need to know." Meanwhile, a group in the NSA might be undertaking their own clandestine project. Even if an agency's activities are not officially secret, bureaucrats can hide activities within their budgets that are unlikely to be discovered, because nobody knows to look for them.

Despite the existence of a deep state, the degree to which it threatens transparent governance is unclear, precisely because the deep state is difficult to observe. The deep state receives funding from the legislature and is part of the executive branch of government, so one concern is the interaction between the deep state and those branches of government. Could

---

[24] Richard E. Wagner, *Politics as Peculiar Business: Insights from a Theory of Entangled Political Economy* (Cheltenham, UK: Edward Elgar, 2016). Along the same lines, see Gordon Tullock, *The Politics of Bureaucracy* (Washington, DC: Public Affairs Press, 1965).

the NSA leak damaging information about the political opponents of incumbents? Could the FBI infiltrate and undermine groups that oppose incumbents? Could the deep state reinforce its power by influencing election outcomes to place those it prefers in power? Could the deep state blackmail elected officials? Regardless of the degree to which one views the deep state as a current threat to transparent government, it is prudent to recognize that potential.

PRINCIPLES AND POLITICS

People profit from their dealings in the political marketplace by making exchanges with others. Legislators trade with each other, and bargain with lobbyists and interest groups for their mutual benefit. Success in the political marketplace comes from the willingness to bargain. Politicians who always vote based on principle shut themselves out of potentially profitable political exchanges, which explains why principled politicians are a rare breed.[25]

Consider a hypothetical bill that is being considered by the legislature. A principled politician would decide whether to support it based on principle. Imagine that the politician opposes the bill in principle. No amount of bargaining could sway the principled politician to vote in favor of it. A less principled politician would consider voting in favor of the bill in exchange for the support on legislation that was more important to the legislator. "Even though I'm against it, I'll vote for your bill if you will vote for mine."

Now assume that the legislator would support the bill in principle. There would be no need to payoff the principled legislator to support the bill, because the principled politician will vote for the legislation on principle. In contrast, even if the less-principled legislator would favor the legislation in principle, that less-principled politician would be willing to sell his vote in exchange for some political payoff. Even if a less-principled politician would support some legislation in principle, the politician still might have to be paid off to actually vote for it, to prevent opponents from buying the less-principled politician's vote. The votes of less-principled politicians are always for sale.

Similarly, there would be no reason for lobbyists to try to buy the vote of the principled politician, but the unprincipled politician's vote is

---

[25] This idea is discussed further in Randall G. Holcombe, "Principles and Politics: Like Oil and Water," *Review of Austrian Economics* 22, no. 2 (June 2008), pp. 151–157.

always in play. Politicians will be more successful in the political marketplace the less principled they are. The unprincipled politician is always open to negotiation, always ready to trade if the trade looks profitable. The principled politician, whose vote cannot be bought, will be excluded from transacting in the political marketplace. There is nothing anyone could gain from attempting to negotiate with the principled politician.

What does the unprincipled politician hope to gain in the political marketplace? The primary goal is power over others. That is why Friedrich Hayek says that in politics, the worst get on top.[26]

CONCLUSION

Transactions in the political marketplace are structured by formal and informal institutions. The different branches of government have different formal powers, and within those branches there are formal procedures that structure political exchanges. Formal decision-making procedures require majorities to pass legislation, for example, which is a significant constraint, and one factor that differentiates political markets from markets for goods and services.

Within those formal institutions, informal norms and institutions arise to facilitate political exchange. While legislation must be approved by a majority, legislators themselves determine the contents of the bills they will vote on. Unlike citizens in general elections, who are able to choose only among alternatives that are offered to them on a ballot, legislators determine what they will vote on prior to any vote. They negotiate to get the terms they want in legislation before it comes up for a vote. Low transaction costs mean that they get the legislation that maximizes its value to the legislators themselves. Because formal institutions require a majority, this implies tradeoffs and negotiations in which legislators compromise on issues less important to them to get outcomes they value more highly.

Transactions in the political marketplace are not as inefficient as some academic analysis has implied. The academic literature on rent-seeking suggests that all of the surplus from political transactions could be consumed by resources used to enable the transaction, but those in the low transaction cost group who engage in political exchange have every incentive to minimize resource waste, so they can keep more

---

[26] See Friedrich A. Hayek, *The Road to Serfdom* (London: George Routledge & Sons, 1944), ch. 10, titled "Why the Worst Get on Top."

for themselves. The real costs are imposed on third parties. What the literature refers to as rents are really transfers from those who face high transaction costs to those who face low transaction costs – from the masses to the elite.

The political marketplace operates because those who face low transaction costs are willing to negotiate for their own advantage. On the demand side, interests negotiate for access to government power. On the supply side, those who have the ability to access government power negotiate with each other to determine how it will be used. The more one is willing to negotiate for personal advantage rather than on principle, the more successful that person will be in the political marketplace. Success translates into more political power, which is a primary goal in political exchange. Ultimately, what is being bought and sold in the political marketplace is access to government power.

8

Interest Groups

Elites and Masses

The institutions of authority and governance necessarily divide a society into two groups: the rulers and the ruled. Some people are in that group that makes and enforces the rules. Most people are in the group that is required to follow the rules. Democratic government accords considerable power to the masses as a group. The problem, from the standpoint of the typical individual, is that no one individual has any perceptible power. One way that individuals can participate in the political process to act on their policy preferences is to join with others who have similar preferences and participate in organized interest groups.

Even then, the individual members of organized interest groups have no power. The leaders of successful organized interest groups acquire the power to join the political elite and engage in the political bargaining process based on the strength of their membership. Those leaders can offer politicians financial contributions, campaign support, and potential voter support from their membership. This enables those interest group leaders to participate in the political marketplace because they have the support, both financial and otherwise, of their members.

Perhaps more significant than their direct support, interest group leaders can encourage their members to make their own financial contributions, and vote for candidates the interest group promotes. Leaders of organized interest groups are able to participate in the political marketplace because they have something to offer to those who design public policy.

ORGANIZED AND UNORGANIZED INTERESTS

Organized interest groups are sometimes referred to as special interests, but there is nothing special about them or their interests. Everyone has interests. Some who have interests in common are better able to organize than others. One factor that facilitates organization occurs when a small number of individuals share a common concentrated interest. An example discussed earlier in this volume is the corn farmers and processors who produce ethanol that is added to motor fuels in the United States. There are relatively few big firms who produce most of the ethanol used in motor fuels, and they were able to organize to get the US Congress to mandate that ethanol be added to motor fuels in 2005, and have been able to expand that mandate since. Buyers of motor fuels have no choice but to buy fuel with the mandated levels of ethanol.

This is a classic example of a small group with common interests being able to organize to effect a transfer to themselves from a larger and unorganized group. Every time a motorist buys fuel containing the mandated ethanol, a few cents of that purchase goes to ethanol producers. A few dollars over the course of a year from every consumer add up to millions of dollars going to the producers. The producers of ethanol were able to organize because there are relatively few of them, and a major ethanol processor, Archer Daniels Midland, has been able to take the lead in lobbying for ethanol in motor fuels. They face low transaction costs. Meanwhile, consumers are unorganized. Each pays only a small amount, so individual consumers have little incentive to oppose the mandate, even though they would prefer it not be there. The evidence is that if consumers wanted ethanol in their gasoline, there would be no need for a mandate that it be included in motor fuels.

Interests on either side of the issue are symmetrical, in the sense that the amount transferred from purchasers of motor fuels is the same as the amount received by the producers of ethanol. The difference is that the producers are an organized interest, whereas the consumers are not.

Mancur Olson explained that concentrated interests with smaller numbers are better able to organize than larger dispersed interests, for several reasons.[1] Because they are smaller in number, a small cost imposed on each member of an unorganized interest can add up to large revenues for each member of the concentrated group. If there are 10 million members of an unorganized group, each of whom pays $10 to a concentrated group of 100 members of an organized interest, each member of the organized interest receives on average $1 million. The unorganized members of the large group pay only $10 each, so they have little to gain

---

[1] Mancur Olson, Jr., *The Logic of Collective Action* (Cambridge, MA: Harvard University Press, 1965).

from opposing the transfer. The members of the small group gain $1 million, so they have a big incentive to lobby for the transfer.

If there are small numbers in an interest group, lower transaction costs can facilitate their being able to work together for their mutual benefit. Also, because members of a smaller group will be in a good position to monitor others in the group, that reduces the likelihood that some members will try to free ride off the efforts of others. Transaction costs, which separate the elite from the masses, have the same influence on separating organized interests from unorganized interests. Low transaction costs enable the ethanol lobby to organize; high transaction costs prevent the masses who bear the cost from organizing to oppose the mandate.

TRANSACTION COSTS AND ORGANIZED INTERESTS

While the number of individuals who share a common interest has a major effect on the group's ability to organize, ultimately, the ability of an interest group to organize comes down to transaction costs. In the earlier example, if one group has 10 million members who each pay $10 to another group with 100 members, each member of the smaller group receives $1 million. Now, assume that organizing either group would cost $20 per member. Each member of the large group would be reluctant to bear $20 in cost to prevent the $10 transfer, while each member of the small group would gladly bear the transaction cost of $20 to receive a transfer of $1 million.

Even that example understates the advantage the small group has, because it is more difficult to organize a large group than a small group, so the transaction cost per member will be lower for the small group than for the large. The incentive to free ride is greater in the large group, and the cost of organizing and finding a collective interest is greater when more people are involved in negotiations. This is yet another aspect of the political marketplace in which transaction costs play a crucial role. High transaction costs prevent large groups with interests in common from effectively organizing.

The same analysis applies when stakes are small. The ethanol mandate is an example in which the stakes are large, but imagine another example where a group of parents want a school playground to be chaperoned for two hours after school, so they can leave their children there in a supervised environment. Hiring a playground monitor would result in small and widely dispersed costs on others who would not use the supervised playground, but a small group of parents might find it worthwhile to organize and petition school officials.

Even if the gain to each parent were small – say, $30 – if the transaction cost involved in organizing the parents and petitioning school officials were less, the parents would find it in their interest to organize and ask for the playground supervision. In the absence of transaction costs, everybody has an incentive to ask for anything they would value, and everybody has an incentive to oppose everything that would impose net costs on them. Whether interest groups do form to pursue their common interests depends on whether the transaction costs involved in forming the group and pursuing their interests are lower than the expected gain from organizing.

Interest groups do not enter the political marketplace with the intention of persuading a majority to support their interests, but rather to enable a minority to prevail over the majority. E. E. Schattschneider says, "Pressure politics is a method of short-circuiting the majority."[2]

UNORGANIZED INTERESTS BEAR EXTERNAL COSTS

The examples in the previous section also illustrate the trilateral nature of the political marketplace. Two parties – legislators and industry lobbyists – are able to bargain for their mutual advantage because they face low transaction costs. A third party – motor fuel purchasers – bears the cost of that exchange, but is unable to engage in politics as exchange because high transaction costs prevent them from negotiating.[3] Two parties – school officials and parents who want supervised playgrounds – are able to organize to obtain that playground supervision. A third party – taxpayers who pay for that supervision – bear the cost of that exchange.

Members of the same industry, who nominally are competitors, can lobby for benefits for their industry. Oil companies want special depletion allowances for their wells, airlines want subsidies for air travel, and domestic steel manufacturers want protective tariffs to be placed on imported steel. The benefits are even more concentrated if a single firm is able to lobby for benefits. These activities fall under the heading of

---

[2] E. E. Schattschneider, *Party Government* (New York: Reinhart & Company, 1959), p. 189.

[3] The trilateral nature of the political marketplace is emphasized by Richard E. Wagner, *Politics as Peculiar Business: Insights from a Theory of Entangled Political Economy* (Cheltenham, UK: Edward Elgar, 2016).

rent-seeking, which more accurately should be called transfer seeking.[4] Organized interests enter the political process to try to get government to mandate that transfers be made from unorganized interests to their own organized interest group.

The costs borne by the unorganized group are external costs as economists define them. Some people engage in exchange in the political marketplace, and a third party, prevented from participating in the marketplace because of high transaction costs, bears an external cost as a result of the exchange. James Buchanan has noted that democratic decision-making leads to a built-in externality because a majority has the ability to impose costs on the minority,[5] but recognizing the role that transaction costs play in the political marketplace, the situation is worse than that. High transaction costs enable organized minorities to impose external costs on the majority.

Everybody has interests, so the idea of special interests is vague enough to be meaningless. No interests are more special than others, but some interest groups are better able to organize to use the political system for their benefit. There are organized interests and unorganized interests.

INTEREST GROUP ENTREPRENEURS

The examples in the previous section illustrate the advantage that concentrated interests with small numbers can have in the political process. In many cases, interests are shared by a large number of people who would find it difficult to organize to have their interests represented. This opens the opportunity for a political entrepreneur to organize that large group of people. If they can each be convinced to contribute a small amount to the interest (perhaps with some larger donors), the entrepreneur can profit from organizing the group and can gain sufficient political power to become a member of the political elite.

The National Rifle Association (NRA) is an example of such a group. Many people support the right to keep and bear arms, but most have other interests that are more important to them – their jobs, their families, their leisure time – so most members of the NRA would have little incentive to organize to support the right to bear arms themselves. Besides, what

---

[4] The idea was first articulated by Gordon Tullock, "The Welfare Cost of Tariffs, Monopolies, and Theft," *Western Economic Journal* 5 (1967), pp. 224–232. The name rent-seeking comes from Anne O. Krueger, "The Political Economy of the Rent-Seeking Society," *American Economic Review* 64 (1974), pp. 291–303.

[5] James M. Buchanan, "Politics, Policy, and the Pigouvian Margins," *Economica* n.s. 29, no. 113 (February 1962), pp. 17–28.

effect will one individual have anyway? This opens the opportunity for the organizers of the NRA to offer to support that right. If enough people are willing to contribute a small amount, their combined contributions can be sufficient to allow the group's entrepreneurs to buy their way into the political marketplace. To encourage people to join, the organization also offers other benefits to members, such as a monthly magazine and organized shooting events. Whenever there is a large, unorganized group with a common interest, that presents an entrepreneurial opportunity for someone to organize the group.

The NRA is supported by more than just its individual members. Firearm manufacturers also have a big stake in preserving the right of consumers to purchase their products. Firearm manufacturers can (and do) lobby on their own behalf, but they also support the NRA, giving that interest group's leaders more resources with which to bargain in the political marketplace. By accumulating a large membership that supports the group with financial contributions and who may vote as the group's leaders recommend, the entrepreneurs who lead interest groups can buy their way into the political elite. They are able to offer campaign contributions and the political support of their membership to legislators who further the group's interests.

Even as the group's leaders buy their way into the political marketplace, individual members of the group still have no political power as individuals. The organization's leadership decides on the group's activities. Individuals can choose either to join and contribute or not. Individual members have no influence over what the group does. Meanwhile, the entrepreneurs who run the organization gain political clout because they have the financial contributions of members and the potential political support of those members to offer legislators. Members of the group are part of the masses, whose actions have no effect on public policies, or even on the interest group's policies. By aggregating the contributions of a large number of individual members, the group's leaders are able to buy their way into the political elite.

Not everybody supports the right to bear arms, at least to the extent that it is protected in the United States. Everytown for Gun Safety is an interest group that lobbies in favor of restricting the right to bear arms. That group is financed primarily by billionaire and former New York City Mayor Michael Bloomberg. Having a single individual undertake the bulk of the group's financing overcomes the free rider problem, and Everytown is able to counter the efforts of the NRA with the same sources of power: money and membership.

The American Association of Retired Persons (AARP) is another example of an interest group made up of a large number of people with similar interests that has been organized by a political entrepreneur. Retirees have many interests in common, but have little incentive to work toward those common interests as individuals. One person will have little effect on influencing health care benefits for seniors or maintaining Social Security payments. The entrepreneurs who run the AARP have succeeded in organizing those seniors, enticing them with a magazine and discounts they have negotiated with businesses for their members. As with other large-membership interest groups, individual members of the AARP have no political influence themselves. They can choose to either join the group or not, but do not influence the group's activities. The members of groups with a large number of members face the same transaction cost issues as the masses in general politics. Their large numbers prevent them from being able to negotiate with the group's leaders. Meanwhile, the leaders of the group are able to buy their way into the political elite because of the funding they raise and the large numbers of members in the group.

The NRA and AARP engage in lobbying activities financed by their members, but these two groups illustrate that to attract members, they can offer those who join private benefits that free riders cannot enjoy. Those who share the group's goals but want to free ride on the lobbying efforts will be excluded from getting the group's magazine, enjoying discounts negotiated for members, and similar benefits. One can conjecture that people who do not share the group's goals will be reluctant to join, but also can just as easily conjecture that the excludable benefits that come with membership can push like-minded individuals to join and contribute to the group's common goals.

The political activities of interest groups are largely centered around attempts to shift public policy in a direction that is favored by the group's membership. Whenever there are unorganized groups with similar interests, there is a profit opportunity for a potential entrepreneur to organize the group. Gun owners and firearm enthusiasts are a large group that faces high transaction costs to organize. Older citizens are a large group with many common interests that face high transaction costs to organize. This presents the opportunity for an entrepreneur to create an organization and solicit members who will contribute to the group's common interests. The challenge is overcoming the free rider problem.

The existence of many interest groups that attract membership from the masses shows that this is possible. Individual members remain politically powerless because with a large membership, high transaction costs prevent individual members from negotiating to determine the group's activities. But with a large membership behind them, the entrepreneurs who head those interest groups are able to buy their way into the elite – they are able to participate in politics as exchange.

THE RECIPROCAL NATURE OF THE PROBLEM

The examples of the NRA and Everytown for Gun Safety clearly illustrate what Ronald Coase referred to as the reciprocal nature of the problem.[6] The NRA wants to loosen restrictions on the right to bear arms; Everytown wants to tighten those restrictions. Any gains for the NRA are losses for Everytown, and vice versa. To benefit one group harms the other. This is true with (almost) all interest group activity. Legislation that benefits ethanol producers imposes costs on motorists. Interest group activity imposes costs on unorganized interests to confer benefits to organized interests.

There may be cases in which public policy benefits some without harming others. Such policies should be easy to approve because they should engender no opposition. They merely need to be suggested. Transaction costs should be minimal in those cases, and policies should be rapidly approved. A possible example of such a policy is the "California rule" that allows motor vehicle traffic to make right turns at a red light if no conflicting traffic is present, after coming to a stop. California implemented that rule in 1939, and the California rule was mandated in all states of the United States by the Energy Policy and Conservation Act of 1975.

It would seem that the California rule imposes minimal costs on anyone, but benefits drivers who otherwise would have to wait at red lights before turning right, even if there was no conflicting traffic. If this is true, once the California rule was created (some innovator had to think of it), why was it not adopted everywhere immediately? One answer is that it does impose costs on pedestrians and bicyclists who risk being hit by a right turner, who likely is looking left to see if there is any oncoming traffic while turning right. Right turns on red remain prohibited in New York City for that reason. It appears that the rule was passed nationwide when the goal of energy conservation trumped the (poorly organized) interests of pedestrians.

---

[6] Ronald H. Coase, "The Problem of Social Cost," *Journal of Law & Economics* 3 (1960), pp. 1–44.

The motivation for transactions in the political marketplace is to use the power of government to provide benefits to some at the expense of others. Some benefit. Others pay the cost. Those groups are situated in a reciprocal position to each other. Which group benefits depend partly on the cost of organizing. If one group faces high transaction costs, the other group has an advantage in organizing and negotiating in the political marketplace to receive a benefit for itself.

RATIONAL IGNORANCE AND INTEREST GROUPS

A well-established idea in the social sciences is that voters tend to be rationally ignorant about candidates and issues because except when the number of voters is very small, their one vote will have no influence over the outcome of an election.[7] There is no material payoff from becoming informed about issues over which an individual can have no effect.

The choices people make in market settings are instrumental choices. People get what they choose. The choices people make at the ballot box are expressive choices. People express a preference for one party or candidate over another, but regardless of what they choose, the election outcome will be the same. The result is that people have little incentive to be well-informed about those expressive choices they make at the ballot box.

This same principle applies to interest group membership. Individuals can choose whether to join an interest group, but members have no influence over the group's activities, so they have little incentive to be informed about them. Much of the information they get regarding interest groups they belong to will come from the group itself. Interest groups like the NRA and AARP send out magazines and newsletters to their members, which provides them with information. Other sources of information on the activities of those groups will be few, so members get the information about the groups that their leaders want them to get.

Consider groups with opposing interests like the NRA and Everytown for Gun Safety. One group supports individual freedom and the right to bear arms. The other supports commonsense firearm regulations and offers a plan to end gun violence. While those groups have opposing goals, NRA members will get their information from the NRA, while Everytown members get their information from Everytown, reinforcing members' views on those issues. Both organizations supply information

---

[7] This idea was clearly articulated by Anthony Downs, *An Economic Theory of Democracy* (New York: Harper & Row, 1957).

about the other. The NRA vilifies Everytown while Everytown vilifies the NRA. The individual members of each organization want to minimize cognitive dissonance, so they are ready to accept the vilification their own organization casts on the organization's rival.

In 2020 the State of New York filed a lawsuit against the NRA claiming the organization was illegally misusing the funds contributed by its members. The lawsuit received minimal press coverage, but was discussed more extensively in the NRA's own publications, in which the lawsuit was characterized as an attempt by the State of New York to infringe upon citizens' rights to bear arms. Without taking sides on the merits of the lawsuit, what might appear as negative information about the group was spun by the NRA as a further reason to support the group.

Donald Wittman has suggested that interest groups provide a mechanism whereby individual citizens can participate and make their voices heard in the political marketplace.[8] This claim must come with caveats, because, first, individual members have no perceptible influence over an interest group's activities, and second, just as with politics in general, individual members have little incentive to become informed about the details of the organization's activities.

Interest group members may like the group's message, but most members will have little idea about the group's budget or the group's activities. How many members of the NRA know the size of the organization's budget, how it is allocated, or what specific activities the organization undertakes to promote the ownership and use of firearms? Just as with political issues in general, interest group members tend to be rationally ignorant. Individuals join those groups because they feel good by doing so, even if they are not well-informed about the details of those groups they support.

THE DECISION TO JOIN

Individuals may join interest groups for a number of reasons. One reason would be to receive the excludable benefits of membership, such as publications and participation in group activities that are limited to members. Interest group entrepreneurs have the incentive to look for ways to provide exclusive benefits for members. At the other extreme, individuals might join because they want to support the organization's goals. This

---

[8] See Donald A. Wittman, "Why Democracies Produce Efficient Results," *Journal of Political Economy* 97, no. 6 (1989), pp. 1395–1424, and *The Myth of Democratic Failure* (Chicago, IL: University of Chicago Press, 1995).

motivation is similar to contributing to a political party. The individual contributor gains no political power from doing so, but contributions strengthen the position of the party. Looking at this motivation, it may be easier to contribute to an interest group than to a political party, because interest groups tend to be narrowly focused on their goals. An individual might agree with some things a political party advocates but disagree with others. If there are interest groups that promote only goals the individual agrees with, the individual can contribute to those groups without provoking the cognitive dissonance that would come from donating to an organization with some goals the individual does not support.

Much like voting, supporting an interest group is an expressive act, because one individual's support and contributions will make only an imperceptible difference to the group's operation. All the supporters, taken together, enable the interest group to be effective. Any one contribution will have no noticeable effect. Outside of excludable benefits, people will contribute to and support interest groups because doing so has expressive value to them. They feel good about supporting a cause and get utility from contributing, much as people get utility from supporting their favorite sports teams.[9] People do not have to vote. They do not have to join interest groups. Why do they?

People's political preferences, whether for political parties or for interest groups, are influenced by the people individuals associate with. Family influences are strong. If a person's family is made up primarily of Democrats, the individual is likely to support Democratic candidates. If a person's family owns and uses firearms, the person is likely to be a Second Amendment supporter. An individual's peer group also will influence the individual's political preferences and interest group support. If an individual's peer group supports stronger government action to preserve the environment, the individual is more likely to support the Sierra Club and Nature Conservancy. The individual's contribution will have little effect, but the individual gains utility from expressing support for the values of those in the individual's peer group.[10]

Joining an interest group requires more commitment than voting in an election because joining the interest group typically means paying dues or

---

[9] This idea is developed by Geoffrey Brennan and Loren Lomasky, *Democracy and Decision: The Pure Theory of Electoral Preference* (Cambridge: Cambridge University Press, 1993).

[10] Support for this conclusion is found in Randall G. Holcombe, *Following Their Leaders: Political Preferences and Public Policy* (Cambridge: Cambridge University Press, 2023), ch. 5.

otherwise making financial contributions. Thus, the first step to commit is bigger than the first step toward voting rather than abstaining. Once that commitment is made, people want to minimize cognitive dissonance and believe they did the right thing, rather than wasting their money or, worse, contributing toward an organization that they come to see as not congruent with their interests. Thus, once they commit support, they have an additional reason to continue that support – to minimize cognitive dissonance that would come from thinking they made a mistake. For this reason, the act of joining, by itself, will strengthen the member's support.

Because the individual's contribution will have no perceptible effect on public policy, the cost the individual would bear from making a mistake is purely expressive. If the individual makes a bad choice about what to have for lunch, the individual gets a bad lunch. If the individual makes a bad choice about supporting or contributing to an interest group, that choice has no perceptible impact on the interest group's success. If the individual has chosen to join an interest group because members of the individual's peer group have also joined, continuing to be a member increases the individual's utility, as long as the individual sees no reason to question whether the group's goals are consistent with the individual's. Individuals will look for reasons to perceive that the organization's goals are consistent with their own to minimize cognitive dissonance. People support interest groups because it makes them feel good, not because their support has any perceptible impact.

Analyzing the political marketplace, there are important differences between making choices in the market for goods and services and making choices in the voting booth, and those differences carry over to the decision to join and support interest groups. Voting and interest group participation are expressive activities, and one individual's actions have no perceptible impact on public policy. Thus, individuals may join and support interest groups even when the activities of those groups are not in the individual's interest.

Once they are members, individuals tend to anchor on the group's policies, supporting them using the reasoning offered them by the group's entrepreneurs.[11] The only incentive they have to question their membership is the money they could save by no longer contributing, but this would come at the cost of questioning the values of their peer group and the wisdom of their previous choice to support. Because

---

[11] Holcombe, *Following Their Leaders*, ch. 6 explains the idea of anchor preferences in more detail.

membership buys members nothing more than good feelings (and possible excludable benefits), members may be "rationally irrational" in their decisions to join.[12]

BIG PLAYERS

Roger Koppl makes the observation that there are big players in markets whose actions can disrupt markets and create uncertainty.[13] Central bankers are examples of big players given by Koppl. They can act with discretion and their actions are not subject to the discipline of profit and loss. The political marketplace contains more than its share of big players in this sense because the costs of actions undertaken by the political elite often are borne by third parties.

Legislators would seem to be high on the list of big players, in that they do not bear the consequences of the policies they create. Often, public policies have unintended negative consequences, and when they do, rather than being punished for them, the masses often push for additional policy actions to address the negative unintended consequences of earlier actions.[14] Businesses take losses when they undertake projects that cost more than the value they return, but politicians often profit from imposing policies that have a net cost on society.

A straightforward example is the imposition of a protective tariff. Free trade produces net benefits, as demonstrated by the fact that the traders themselves voluntarily agree to trade and view themselves as better off as a result. Politicians impose tariffs because the economic elite bargain with the political elite to get them, with the costs being borne by the masses in the form of higher prices for those goods that are being "protected." The politicians are not the only big players here. The lobbyists who transact in the political marketplace to have tariffs imposed for the benefit of their clients are also big players: participants in the political marketplace who do not bear the costs of their actions.

As Chapter 7 noted, in 1983 Harley Davidson, the US motorcycle manufacturer, was able to convince the Reagan administration to impose a 40 percent tariff on motorcycles with engines larger than 700cc. Harley

---

[12] See Bryan Caplan, *The Myth of the Rational Voter: Why Democracies Choose Bad Policies* (Princeton, NJ: Princeton University Press, 2007).
[13] Roger Koppl, *Big Players and the Economic Theory of Expectations* (Houndmills, Basingstoke, Hampshire, UK: Palgrave Macmillan, 2002).
[14] This idea is explored by Sanford Ikeda, *Dynamics of the Mixed Economy: Toward a Theory of Interventionism* (London: Routledge, 1997).

was the only US manufacturer that made such motorcycles. The big players, transacting in the political marketplace, were able to impose costs on the buyers of motorcycles for their own benefit. Big players have the clout to lobby for their own interests, a power that individuals within the masses lack. The masses, however, can contribute to interest groups, giving the leaders of those interest groups that clout, making those interest group entrepreneurs big players.

In the Harley example, one might cite the jobs that would be lost if Harley Davidson lost market share, or even went out of business, as a benefit of the tariff. One can debate whether protecting those jobs is worth the cost of a protective tariff – most economists would argue no – but that is not relevant in the political marketplace. Those workers are not the ones who negotiated in the political marketplace. The firm's owners and managers lobbied for the tariffs to protect their own interests. Other costs or benefits were external to the political marketplace.

The masses remain outside the political marketplace because they face high transaction costs, but their contributions to interest groups enable the leaders of those groups to bargain in the political marketplace, making those interest group leaders big players. In the same way that lobbyists in general can be big players, those who lead interest groups are big players. Based on the strength of their memberships, they can lobby for policies that further their groups' interests without bearing the costs of the policies they promote. Their "profits" (most are nonprofit groups) come from the contributions of their members, not from the consequences of the policies they produce.

INTEREST GROUPS AND POLITICAL EXTORTION

Successful rent-seeking by interest groups creates policies that benefit the group. The ethanol mandate that motor fuels again provides a good example. The benefit to corn farmers and processors continues as long as the mandate remains in place. The mandate benefits members of a concentrated interest group by imposing a cost on a larger, unorganized group. That concentrated interest group then has been put in the position of relying on the political elite to retain that benefit and must continue to support those who have the power to repeal it – or it could be repealed.

The rent-seeking process opens the possibility for the rent creators in the political elite to extort the interest group receiving the rent. The rent creators can threaten to repeal the policy that creates the rent unless they continue to pay up.¹⁵ Threats do not have to be explicit because interest groups know what is at stake. A simple reminder from a legislator or regulator that they have always had a good relationship with the interest, and they hope it will continue, should be enough for the protected interest group to keep paying up to maintain their legislated benefits.

Gordon Tullock has analyzed these types of political exchanges and suggested that they are policy traps. There is a short-run benefit to the rent-seeker, which results in a long-run inefficiency. He says, "The moral of this, on the whole, depressing tale is that we should try to avoid getting into this kind of trap in the future. Our predecessors have made mistakes and we are stuck with them, but we can at least make efforts to prevent our descendants from having even more such dead-weight losses inflicted on them."¹⁶

Tullock understands the problem – that big players are able to create inefficient policies that impose costs on third parties – but these policies are not designed by mistake. They are designed so that the political elite who create these interest group benefits can continue to extort payment from the beneficiaries year after year. The existence of these policies alone contains the implicit threat that if payment for the policies does not continue, the policies can be repealed.

Organized interest groups make an easy target for political extortion because they offer the political elite a single point of contact to negotiate payment. The fact that they are organized makes them an easy target. The representative of the interest group who lobbied for the rent has at the same time identified himself or herself as the person to ask for continuing payment to keep the rent-producing policy in place. The rent creator does not have to search for someone to extort. The act of rent-seeking has identified that person as the point of contact to demand ongoing payments in exchange for not repealing the policy. That negotiation is a bilateral bargaining process, and with two parties, the transaction costs are low.

Unorganized interests, in contrast, are difficult to extort because there is no single point of contact. Imagine trying to extract payment of a few dollars from thousands or millions of autonomous individuals who may be rationally ignorant of the policy in question, and may be inclined to

---

[15] This idea is developed by Fred S. McChesney, "Rent Extraction and Rent Creation in the Economic Theory of Regulation," *Journal of Legal Studies* 16, no. 1 (January 1987), pp. 101–118, and *Money for Nothing: Politicians, Rent Extraction, and Political Extortion* (Cambridge, MA: Harvard University Press, 1997).

[16] Gordon Tullock, "The Transitional Gains Trap," *Bell Journal of Economics* 6, no. 2 (Autumn 1975), p. 678.

free ride off the actions of others. Transaction costs would be prohibitively high. It is relatively easy to extort the ethanol lobby, a concentrated interest group that, through their lobbying, has established a single point of contact between the rent-seeker and the rent creator. It would be difficult to demand compensation from motor fuel purchasers to repeal the mandate.

The act of organizing an interest group, by itself, makes that group susceptible to political extortion because it opens the opportunity for those with political power to negotiate with the interest group's representative. The same person who transacts in the political marketplace to receive the interest group benefit is the person to contact to demand payment for it. The purpose of organizing the interest group is to lower transaction costs to facilitate political exchange, and the by-product of that organization is that it creates an easy target for political extortion.

When Gordon Tullock wrote about this problem in 1975, one group he singled out as receiving rents from a government policy was the airlines, who were regulated by the Civil Aeronautics Board (CAB).[17] Tullock explained that the CAB effectively organized the airlines into a cartel by restricting output – limiting the routes they were allowed to fly – and keeping regulated airfares high. Its explicit purpose was to support the airlines and maintain their profitability. It is an interesting case because a few years after Tullock wrote, in 1978, this regulation was eliminated and the CAB was eventually disbanded.[18] One illustration of the value of those rents is that after deregulation, many of the major air carriers from the 1970s went out of business, including Eastern Airlines, Trans World Airways, Braniff, and Continental Airlines.

Once policies are created that generate ongoing rents to rent-seekers, those rent-seekers become easy targets for political extortion in exchange for maintaining those rent-generating policies. If transaction costs are low enough to create the rent, they are also low enough for the suppliers of the rent to extort the demanders. Organized interests are relatively easy to extort; unorganized interests are not.

CONCLUSION

Most individuals have no influence over public policy because high transaction costs keep them from participating in the political marketplace.

---

[17] Tullock, "The Transitional Gains Trap."
[18] It is worth a footnote to remark that although the CAB's regulation of airlines ended in 1978, the agency itself was not disbanded until 1985.

Each individual's one vote will not affect political outcomes, and most individuals are not in a position to negotiate directly with the members of the political elite who make public policy. Another avenue through which individuals might have an effect on public policy is to join interest groups that represent public policy preferences similar to their own. This avenue has the same issues as voting. Individuals can participate, as expressive acts that show support for an interest, but one individual member has no perceptible influence over the actions or success of the interest group. When individuals join, they gain no political power, even though their participation, along with all other members, gives political power to the group's entrepreneurs. The group's leaders can use the resources provided by their membership to buy their way into the political elite and participate in political exchange.

The public policy gains that interest groups receive as a result of negotiating in the political marketplace make the interest group dependent on policymakers to continue providing them with that benefit. This makes the interest group subject to political extortion. Legislators can threaten to undo the benefit unless the interest group continues to pay up. The mere creation of an interest group lowers the transaction costs of this political extortion because it creates a single point of contact between legislators and the interest group. The people who ask for the benefit are the people legislators approach to ask for payment. Unorganized interests have no similar point of contact, making it more difficult to extort payment from them.

Joining an interest group is an expressive activity. Individual members have no influence over the group's activities or over public policy. The collective action of all members gives the group's leaders the power to negotiate in the political marketplace – to become members of the political elite – but individual members remain powerless. They can only choose to participate or abstain. Ultimately, transaction costs determine who can participate in the political marketplace.

9

Welfare Maximization, Redistribution, and Governance

Using the Pareto optimal general equilibrium framework as a benchmark, Chapter 2 discussed two economic functions of institutions that facilitate moving toward that benchmark. Institutions of organization reduce transaction costs. Institutions of governance define and enforce rights and contracts. That discussion noted a third economic function of institutions – redistribution – which is the subject of this chapter.

The first economic function of institutions, reducing transaction costs, enables suppliers and demanders to locate each other so they are able to engage in mutually advantageous exchange. The second economic function of institutions is to define and enforce property rights and contracts so that resources only change hands through mutually agreeable exchanges. Those institutions that define and enforce rights – the institutions of authority and governance – are effective only to the degree that they display sufficient power behind them that citizens choose to comply rather than suffer the government-imposed consequences. Government redistribution is dependent on those institutions of authority and governance. Without the ability to force people to comply with its mandates, the government could not forcibly transfer income from some to others.

If an individual were to forcibly take resources from a fellow citizen to give it to a third party, that first individual would be viewed as a thief. Governments generally outlaw theft and punish those who engage in it. Yet governments do this same thing, labeling it redistribution, and not only do the political elite claim this is a legitimate activity of government, citizens also generally view government redistribution as within

9 Redistribution and Welfare Maximization

its legitimate powers.[1] Say that a poor individual's mother has run out of food, so that individual forcibly takes resources from someone else to provide food for the poor individual's hungry mother. Despite any need, most people would say that the individual is guilty of theft. If the government taxes some to fund a program to provide food for others (who may be needy), that redistribution is seen as legitimate because it is undertaken by government.

A partial answer to the question of why governments are able to take from some to give to others lies in the necessity of those institutions of authority and governance to enable an orderly and productive society. Individuals must accept those institutions that compel compliance, or, as Hobbes described it, descend into a situation of anarchy, where life is a war of all against all. As a consequence, most individuals not only accept those institutions of authority and governance but they also support them. Once the political elite have that power to enforce their mandates, they can use that power to mandate the forcible transfer of resources from some to others. But that is only a partial answer because not only does the government have this power, but those who are subject to it – people who are having resources taken from them – commonly view that forced transfer as a legitimate power of government.

Chapters 2, 3, and 6 focused on two economic functions of institutions: they lower transaction costs, and they enforce governance. The social benefits these institutions provide are fairly obvious. Redistribution may provide social benefits too, but the case is not so clear. Even under ideal circumstances, it is not clear that taking from some to give to others is a benefit to society as a whole. That may not even be its objective. Those who have the power to redistribute resources may have motives other than furthering the general public interest.

This chapter begins by discussing economic arguments in support of the claim that redistribution provides social benefits. Aside from considering whether these arguments apply to redistribution in the real world, they are relevant because they contribute toward the general view that redistribution falls within the legitimate powers of government. The fact that reputable economists – including many Nobel laureates – argue the social benefits of redistribution lends legitimacy to the claim. The appearance of legitimacy lowers popular resistance and even provides popular

---

[1] Murray N. Rothbard, *The Ethics of Liberty* (Atlantic Highlands, NJ: Humanities Press, 1982) is among the many individuals who have pointed out the parallels between government redistribution and theft.

support, facilitating the ability of the political elite to use its power to take from some to give to others.

WELFARE MAXIMIZATION

For most of human history, the masses viewed themselves as subjects of the ruling class and accepted the fact that part of their obligation as subjects was to pay tribute to the ruling class. Justification, to the extent that any was needed, was that of the obligation the ruled had to the ruling class. Social contract theorists from Hobbes to Rousseau and on up to twentieth-century contractarians like Rawls broadened that justification to explain that the obligation was not just to the ruling class, but to their fellow citizens. Redistribution is a part of the social contract. Moving into the second half of the twentieth century, the general equilibrium framework that earlier chapters used to explain the functions of institutions of organization and institutions of authority was further applied to explain the desirability of institutions of redistribution.

The same framework that explained why a competitive general equilibrium would result in an efficient allocation of resources was used as a foundation for explaining why the resulting allocation of resources was unlikely to be socially optimal. The tribute that had been demanded of the masses throughout human history was, in twentieth-century welfare economics, depicted as an essential ingredient for maximizing welfare.

Nobel laureate Kenneth Arrow says, "It was, of course, recognized, most explicitly perhaps by Bergson, that Pareto efficiency in no way implied distributive justice. An allocation of resources could be efficient in a Pareto sense and yet yield enormous riches to some and dire poverty to others."[2] Referring to the conclusions from his article with fellow Nobel laureate Gerard Debreu,[3] Arrow goes on to say, "We are assured indeed that not only can an allocation be achieved, but the result will be Pareto efficient. But, as has been stressed, there is nothing in the process which guaranteed that the distribution will be just."[4]

---

[2] Kenneth J. Arrow, "General Economic Equilibrium: Purpose, Analytic Techniques, Collective Choice," *American Economic Review* 64, no. 3 (June 1974), p. 255. See also, Abram Bergson, "A Reformulation of Certain Aspects of Welfare Economics," *Quarterly Journal of Economics* 52, no. 2 (February 1938), pp. 310–334, and Bergson, "On the Concept of Social Welfare," *Quarterly Journal of Economics* 68, no. 2 (May 1954), pp. 233–252.

[3] Kenneth J. Arrow and Gerard Debreu, "Existence of an Equilibrium for a Competitive Economy," *Econometrica* 27, no. 3 (1954), pp. 265–290.

[4] Arrow, "General Equilibrium," p. 269.

9 Redistribution and Welfare Maximization

That concept of a just distribution is problematic for two reasons. First, there is no good way to discover it. Second, even if it were identified, there is no reason to think that the ruling class would implement it.

The first issue can be summarized with some notation. Representing social welfare as W, it is assumed to be a function f of the utilities of all individuals, $u1, u2, u3 \ldots un$, such that

$$W = f(u1, u2, u3, \ldots un).$$

To maximize social welfare, that is, to find the maximum W, requires that income or wealth be taken away from some individuals and redistributed to others. For example, taking some resources from individual 1 to give to individual 2 would decrease the utility of 1 and increase the utility of 2. If individual 2 gains more utility than individual 1 loses, aggregate welfare W is increased as a result, and the society would be closer to a social welfare maximum. If W decreased, it would be further away. The idea is to adjust the resources going to all individuals to find the maximum W.

There is no reliable way to do this because there is no way to compare the utility gain to 2 with the loss to 1. There is no way, even in theory, to actually measure and compare the utility gain of one individual against the utility loss of another. In the real world, there is not sufficient information to solve this problem. If person 2 claims that she would gain more utility from taking a dollar from person 1 than person 1 would lose in utility, how would one demonstrate this claim to be false?

In practice, the assumption has often been made that income has a diminishing marginal utility, so that taking a dollar from a rich person to give to a poor person results in a utility gain to the poor person larger than the utility loss to the rich person. Even if that is true for each individual – a person's first dollar of income gives the person more utility than the person's last dollar – it is not necessarily true across individuals. One reason a rich person may be rich is that the person derives much utility from wealth and works hard to make a lot of money. Another person may work little and take more leisure because that person receives less utility from income and more from leisure time.

The second reason this idea is problematic is more straightforward. Even if there was some way to redistribute income to increase social welfare, those who have the power to redistribute income have incentives to redistribute based on other criteria. Most obviously, they may choose to redistribute income from others to themselves. How did it happen that the kings of centuries past amassed so much wealth even though they, as individuals, produced no goods or services? Even in twenty-first-century democratic governments, the political elite seem to amass fortunes disproportionate to their economic productivity and disproportionate to the official salaries they are paid.[5]

Furthermore, if they want to maximize their power, they have an incentive to redistribute income to buy political support, a motive that likely is at odds with maximizing social welfare. Political leaders are not shy about telling their constituents about government spending they are undertaking on their behalf. The money they spend for the benefit of some constituents comes from money taken from others.

While there are many possible reasons to think that the political elite might abuse the power to forcibly take income from some individuals to give it to others, this section has explained that, in theory, such redistribution can maximize welfare only by assuming that there is some mechanism to measure and compare utilities among individuals. However, there is no such mechanism, so no real-world public policy can redistribute income to maximize social welfare.

The argument for forced redistribution of income is that without that redistribution, resources might be allocated efficiently, but unjustly. If so, redistribution can increase social welfare. The idea conforms with popular sentiment, in that many people will see it as self-evident that if income were taken from a rich person and given to a poor person, the poor person would gain more in utility than the rich person would lose. Proving such a proposition may not be possible, but in political matters an emotionally appealing argument can often trump a scientific one. If people believe it, it is politically powerful even if scientifically dubious.

When analyzing the actual policies produced in the political marketplace, scientific proof takes a back seat to the desires of those who engage in politics as exchange. Whether the argument holds up to scientific scrutiny is beside the point when analyzing the way that public policy is actually negotiated in the political marketplace. What matters is whether the masses find it persuasive. The fact that reputable Nobel laureate economists have made the argument gives it that much more legitimacy.

THE ROLE OF GOVERNMENT

If people accept the idea that redistributing income and/or wealth is socially desirable, that by itself does not demonstrate that it is socially

---

[5] Peter Schweizer, *Secret Empires: How the American Political Class Hides Corruption and Enriches Family and Friends* (New York: Harper, 2018) gives many examples.

desirable to use the authority of government to mandate that redistribution. Many charitable organizations engage in activities that help the less fortunate. Let individuals decide for themselves how charitable they want to be. Why should government be involved? Several arguments have been put forward.

One argument is that those who are well-off care about the welfare of those less fortunate, but a free rider problem exists that may prevent the well-off from doing anything to help those who are less fortunate. Any one individual, even if relatively well-off, would be able to make only a small contribution that would hardly be noticeable. So, even if everyone wants to help the less fortunate, everyone has an incentive to let others contribute to the less fortunate and free ride on the contributions of others. But because everyone has the same incentive, less is redistributed to those less fortunate than would be optimal, even in the views of the potential donors – those who are well-off. Those who are well-off would agree to contribute themselves, the argument goes, if others would also agree to contribute. A government redistribution program is a mechanism to enforce such an agreement.[6]

A related argument is that taking care of the less fortunate in a society is a social responsibility, not an individual one. Individuals have no obligation to take care of other individuals, but they do have a responsibility to contribute to the social good. So, those who can afford it pay government, and government looks after the less fortunate. James Buchanan suggests that some people favor government redistribution because they want a "safety net" that allows them to avoid the responsibility of looking after their own well-being.[7]

An objection to this line of reasoning, explained in Chapter 5, is that these justifications for government redistribution make it appear that the government's activity is the result of some implied agreement, but there was no agreement. There is no social contract, and these justifications make it appear that the product of coercion is the product of agreement. No matter how much someone approves of government redistribution programs, people are forced to pay into them.

One manifestation of this social contract view of redistribution is that the money taken from those who are forced to pay is often

---

[6] This idea is developed in Harold M. Hochman and James D. Rodgers, "Pareto Optimal Redistribution," *American Economic Review* 59, no. 4, Part 1 (1969), pp. 542–557.

[7] James M. Buchanan, "Afraid to be Free: Dependency as Desideratum," *Public Choice* 124, nos. 1/2 (July 2005), pp. 19–31.

referred to as a contribution. Despite this misuse of language – calling money forcibly taken from someone a contribution – the terminology is accepted without question by most citizens. That is a component of the propaganda that enhances the political acceptability of government redistribution.

Government redistribution would not be possible in the absence of institutions of governance. Without those institutions that give the political elite the ability to coerce the masses, the political elite would not have the power to force people to give up some of their income to be redistributed to others. Because those institutions of authority and governance are necessary components of an orderly and productive society, the masses are not in a position to eliminate them. That means that they are not in a position to eliminate those institutions that enable governments to take from some to give to others.

This does not imply that people would want to eliminate government redistribution; only that if they did want to, they would be unable. Governance institutions are based on the threat of force. Once those institutions are in place to enforce the institutional constraints that come with voluntary arrangements – those institutions that lower transaction costs – the force behind them can then be used to take resources from some individuals to give to others. Institutions of governance lay the foundation for institutions of redistribution.

THE DISTRIBUTIVE IMPACT OF ECONOMIC INSTITUTIONS

The competitive general equilibrium model that has served as a benchmark throughout this volume implicitly assumes a set of institutions that define and enforce property rights, but those institutions are designed by the ruling class, and different institutional structures can affect the distributions of outcomes among individuals in a society. As Chapter 4 noted, this was the emphasis of the old institutionalists, dating back to the early twentieth century. John R. Commons, a leading institutionalist, argued that the distribution of income and wealth was overwhelmingly determined by institutions, and supported institutional reforms to create a more equal distribution of income.[8]

---

[8] See, for example, John R. Commons, *The Legal Foundations of Capitalism* (Madison, WI: University of Wisconsin Press, 1924) and Commons, *Institutional Economics: Its Place in Political Economy* (New York: Macmillan, 1934).

One example noted by the old institutionalists is the impact of bargaining rights for labor unions. As they saw it, firms had a disproportionate advantage in bargaining with potential employees, which could be lessened if employees were able to organize into labor unions and bargain collectively for employment conditions rather than individually. The transaction cost framework used as a foundation for this volume's analysis supports that idea. Without collective bargaining, one firm deals individually with each of its employees. It can tell employees that if they do not like the terms of their jobs, the firm will hire someone else. Each individual employee becomes inessential to the firm. Collective bargaining enables employees to bargain as a group – one employer bargains with one group of employees. Employees gain bargaining power as a result.

Labor law is not unique. Patent and copyright law affects the incomes of those who own intellectual property. The length of patents and copyrights can be extended or reduced, and coverage can be broadened or narrowed. Legal institutions are not somehow exogenously imposed on a society, as would appear to be the case in the general equilibrium model of the economy. They are designed and implemented by the ruling class. Analysts ranging from Karl Marx to Thomas Piketty join Commons in the thought that capitalist institutions have a strong influence on the distribution of income.[9] And they all went beyond just this observation to advocate that the force behind institutions of governance be extended to another economic role: redistribution.

Redistribution commonly is thought of as taxing some to give to others. Economists have developed models of "optimal taxation" to describe how this can be done in theory.[10] But if other institutions have a substantial effect on distributive outcomes, redistribution does not have to be limited to money transfers. By altering institutions, the political elite can convey benefits to some by imposing costs on others. The general equilibrium model shows the ultimate end result that is approached from that propensity to truck, barter, and exchange described by

---

[9] This was the theme of Karl Marx, *Capital: A Critique of Political Economy* (Chicago, IL: Charles H. Kerr & Company, 1906). See also Thomas Piketty, *Capital in the Twenty-First Century* (Cambridge, MA: Harvard University Press, 2014).

[10] See, for examples, James A. Mirrlees, "An Exploration in the Theory of Optimum Income Taxation," *Review of Economic Studies* 38 (1971), pp. 175–208, Mirlees, "Optimal Tax Theory – A Synthesis," *Journal of Public Economics* 6, no. 4 (1976), pp. 327–358, and Peter A. Diamond and James A. Mirlees, "Optimal Taxation and Public Production: I and II," *American Economic Review* 81 (March), pp. 8–27, and (June 1971), pp. 261–278.

Adam Smith, but it assumes a set of property rights and legal rights as a starting point from which the process begins. Institutions determine that starting point, and in so doing influence the ending point – the general equilibrium.

Different sets of institutions will produce different general equilibrium outcomes. The institutional structure is determined in the political marketplace, and the political elite have the power to design institutions to favor some over others. Institutional design has, by itself, distributional impacts. In this sense, redistributional impacts of public policy cannot be escaped. The way that rights are defined and enforced determines the status quo from which that propensity to truck, barter, and exchange begins, and the starting point determines the ending point.

Beyond any academic arguments in support of government redistribution, there is general public support for redistribution programs, perhaps bolstered by the academic arguments. This extends to institutions explicitly designed to benefit some at the expense of others. Affirmative action policies give preference to some groups over others, homestead exemption tax policies benefit homeowners over renters, and as previously noted, labor laws give bargaining advantages to employees that are not extended to employers.

Whether these advantages are justified is beside the point. The point is that institutional design, implemented in the political marketplace, has distributional consequences. Those who design those institutions through negotiations in the political marketplace are well aware of those distributional consequences and take them into account when they negotiate with each other to produce public policy.

REDISTRIBUTION AND GOVERNANCE

Institutions of authority inevitably bring with them the creation of benefits to some by imposing costs on others. Those institutions, which have the threat of force behind them for those who do not comply, are necessary only because without the threat of force, people would not choose to comply. Those who are forced to comply bear a cost, presumably to provide a benefit to others. There would be little point in creating policies that imposed costs on some without benefiting others – recognizing that the political elite must always be among the beneficiaries. They are unlikely to be inclined to impose costs on themselves.

The most common benefit the political elite produce for themselves through redistribution is support from the recipients of benefits. When they take from Peter to pay Paul, they receive no direct benefit or cost, but must believe that they will gain more political support from Paul than they will lose from Peter. The political marketplace enables those who trade in it to see those benefits and costs, as various interests weigh in as they lobby for and against various policies.[11]

In many cases, the beneficiaries mount a strong case for receiving benefits, while various factors weigh against accounting for the costs. If redistributive policies are viewed as just, those who bear the costs may not only choose not to oppose those policies but even to actively support them. The rich should pay their fair share is a sentiment often expressed by the rich.

In other cases, the beneficiaries may be more clearly identified than those who bear the costs. For example, in 1998 the United States Congress extended copyright protection from the life of the author plus 50 years to the life of the author plus 70 years, deliberately providing a distributional benefit to copyright holders. It is clear that the beneficiaries are the copyright holders and their heirs, but it is unclear who might bear the cost decades down the road. One justification often given for protection of intellectual property is that it gives people an incentive to create it, but it would appear that this incentive would be little affected by transfers like this, more than half a century after the creator's death. The intention of this extension was purely redistributional.

The perceived legitimacy of government-enforced redistribution comes from the idea that redistribution is designed to make society more just. In a theoretically ideal world where public policy is made by an omniscient benevolent social planner, redistribution may be able to enhance social welfare and create a more just society, measured in some way. Even this idea is problematic. In the real world, where institutions of governance are controlled by a political elite who act on their own interests, redistribution offers another tool that the elite can use to their advantage. Recognizing that public policies, generally, have distributive impacts, it becomes apparent that there is no escape from the fact that the institutions designed in the political marketplace will benefit some by imposing costs on others. It is then a small step to make redistribution explicit by directly taking from some to give to others.

---

[11] A model of the political marketplace along these lines is developed by Gary S. Becker, "A Theory of Competition among Pressure Groups for Political Influence," *Quarterly Journal of Economics* 98, no. 3 (August 1983), pp. 371–400.

REGULATORY TRANSFERS

Redistribution is often thought of in idealistic terms as providing benefits to the most disadvantaged members of a society. Rent-seeking, regulatory capture, and interest group politics are also redistributive. They are by-products of government that has the power to take from some to transfer to others. Discussing government redistribution to the politically well-connected rather than to the needy, Oliver Williamson says, "A somewhat backhanded way of ascribing legitimacy to redistribution is to view this as an unavoidable cost of democratic government."[12]

The interest group politics discussed in Chapter 8 is purely distributive in nature. Some groups organize to lobby for policies that transfer benefits from others to themselves. Those benefits sometimes come in the form of cash transfers, but are often conveyed through beneficial regulation. George Stigler explains that "the fact that an industry with power to obtain governmental favors usually does not use this power to get money: unless the list of beneficiaries can be limited by an acceptable device, whatever amount of subsidies the industry can obtain will be dissipated among a growing number of rivals."[13] Public policy is motivated by many factors, but all policies have distributive implications, and when both supporters and opponents of particular policy proposals choose sides, distributional impacts often take precedence over any efficiency or equity concerns.

TAX THE RICH

Government redistribution is often justified by two different motivations which, at first glance, appear to be two sides of the same coin but, upon closer inspection, are substantially different. One motivation is to help those in society who are less fortunate. The other is to reduce inequality. Without thinking through it, people often believe that if they reduce inequality, they will be helping the less fortunate. A simple example is taking a dollar from a rich person and giving it to a poor person. But it is much easier to redesign institutions to make the rich worse off than it is to redesign them to make the poor better off.

---

[12] Oliver E. Williamson, *The Mechanisms of Governance* (New York: Oxford University Press, 1996), p. 198.
[13] George J. Stigler, "The Theory of Economic Regulation," *Bell Journal of Economics and Management Science* 2, no. t (Spring 1971), p. 5.

9 Redistribution and Welfare Maximization

The issue of poverty is often addressed by trying to understand why some people are poor, but poverty is the natural state of things. As Thomas Robert Malthus explained more than two centuries ago, population tends to grow more rapidly than the increases in resources to support the population, so most people will always be struggling to obtain enough to survive.[14] Wealth must be produced. If one is really concerned about poverty, a better line of analysis is to ask why some people are rich, and then attempt to duplicate that outcome for everyone. Looking at the issue this way, inequality is not a problem but is the first step toward increasing everybody's welfare.[15] Why should anyone care if some people are extremely wealthy if the well-being of the least fortunate is the real concern?

The market mechanism works by enabling people to engage in mutually advantageous exchanges, and wealthy individuals like John D. Rockefeller, Henry Ford, Bill Gates, and Jeff Bezos made their fortunes by engaging in economic activities that made others better off. They received their incomes because their customers believed they were better off buying their products. The inequality represented by their wealth is the result of their improving the well-being of the masses.

The logic behind this argument suggests that people who are concerned about improving social welfare should focus on the well-being of the least well-off and not be concerned about inequality. Indeed, the arguments made earlier in this chapter all have that focus. However, the focus of redistribution increasingly is on inequality, not poverty.

Thomas Piketty's well-received book, *Capital in the Twenty-First Century*, focuses entirely on the inequality that exists in capitalism and never considers the well-being of the least well-off.[16] He looks at the distribution of income by measuring the income shares of the top 1 percent, the top 5 percent, the top 10 percent, and the bottom 50 percent, without ever considering their absolute levels of income. His argument is that capitalism naturally leads to growing inequality, a problem that should be remedied through public policy. He never considers that the standard of living of those at the bottom end of the income distribution has continually been rising. His concern is inequality, not poverty.

---

[14] Thomas Robert Malthus, *An Essay on the Principle of Population* (London: J. Johnson, 1798).

[15] Edgar K. Browning, "Inequality and Poverty," *Southern Economic Journal* 55, no. 4 (April 1989), pp. 819–830, emphasizes the distinction between policies intended to reduce inequality and policies intended to alleviate poverty.

[16] Thomas Piketty, *Capital in the Twenty-First Century* (Cambridge, MA: Harvard University Press, 2014).

One can question Piketty's findings,[17] but Piketty is not alone in viewing inequality itself as a problem that should be addressed through government intervention. The academic arguments coupled with popular opinion lend legitimacy to the redistributive activities of the ruling class. Because reducing inequality is depicted as an end in itself, the motivation behind the push to reduce inequality is unclear.

Some people equate reducing inequality with helping the least fortunate, although the connection is far from clear. Others may be motivated by envy. Still others actively want to reduce the material well-being of the wealthy and everyone else. Thinking along green political lines, reducing everyone's income by reducing production is desirable because (1) people already have enough stuff, and (2) producing more stuff negatively impacts the environment. As noted earlier, it is easier to reduce inequality by reducing the well-being of the rich than by increasing the well-being of the poor, and some who push to reduce inequality actively want to reduce the well-being of the rich, regardless of its effect on the poor.

One argument for government redistribution is that people evaluate their well-being not so much by what they have, but by what they have relative to others.[18] Those who have income taxed away will feel no worse off if their relative positions in society remain unchanged. The argument has a ring of plausibility, but it depends on public policies that retain or reduce positional inequality, and as earlier noted, transactions in the political marketplace often are designed to increase positional inequality – to benefit the elite who design those policies.

The push to reduce inequality through the application of the institutions of governance gives power and legitimacy to those in the ruling class – those who are being petitioned to implement policies that reduce inequality. The argument is that without forced redistribution, undesirable inequality will continue to grow. One reason the ruling class is willing to implement policies to reduce inequality is that it helps them to preserve their hold on power. If the political elite's power to redistribute is viewed as serving a legitimate public purpose, that only solidifies the elite's hold on power.

One of the challenges to the power of the political elite is the power that is held by the economic elite. Money can fund political opposition.

---

[17] See, for example, Jean-Philippe Delsol, Nicolas Lecaussin, and Emmanuel Martin, eds., *Anti-Piketty: Capital for the 21st Century* (Washington, DC: Cato Institute, 2017).

[18] See, for example, Robert H. Frank, *Luxury Fever: Weighing the Cost of Excess* (Princeton, NJ: Princeton University Press, 2000).

Government's power to redistribute brings with it the power to confiscate resources the economic elite could use against the political elite. One reason the economic elite cooperate with the political elite is that the political elite have the power to transfer income and wealth, and those with a lot of income and wealth make good targets.

"Tax the rich" is a sensible policy threat for the political elite to consider because it is a mechanism that can check the power of a group that can use their resources to undermine the ruling class. If individuals in the economic elite choose to oppose the political elite, they must see that their wealth could be subject to confiscation. The rich realize this, which is why they tend to use their wealth to support the political elite, and in exchange are supported by them.[19]

In some countries the political elite are more constrained than in others in their ability to use government power against their critics. In the United States, members of the economic elite may be able to speak out against the political elite with minimal consequences.[20] In Russia, oligarchs who do not support President Putin can lose their fortunes and end up in prison, or dead. The idea that the political elite use the power of government to impose costs on those who oppose them is not just a theory.

GOVERNMENT LOTTERIES

While one might think that government programs should lessen inequality, government lotteries are an obvious example in which the opposite is true. A lottery takes a small amount of money from lots of people to redistribute a large amount to a few. In this process, government typically skims half of the proceeds for its own purposes. Governments set themselves up as monopolists, preventing private lotteries, to enhance its ability to skim the proceeds. Lotteries sell the hope that ticket purchasers might improve their financial well-being, increasing inequality in the process.

---

[19] This idea is developed further in Randall G. Holcombe, *Political Capitalism: How Economic and Political Power Is Made and Maintained* (Cambridge: Cambridge University Press, 2018).

[20] In Florida, the Walt Disney company publicly criticized legislation proposed by Governor Ron DeSantis, prompting DeSantis, in 2022, to abolish the Reedy Creek Improvement District that was run by the company. Even in the United States, the political elite will impose costs on the economic elite who oppose them. This is discussed further in Chapter 10.

The real winners in this particular government redistribution program are obvious. The government takes a few dollars from lots of people to give lots of dollars to a few, while keeping much for itself. The arguments above suggest that this characterizes much government redistribution. A frequent criticism of lotteries is that lottery tickets are disproportionately purchased by the poor who can least afford them, further increasing inequality. This digression on lotteries is, perhaps, a minor point, but if one of the legitimate functions of government is to reduce inequality, how would one justify government-run lotteries, which do the opposite?

OTHER INEQUITIES

The arguments in support of government redistribution would seem to apply to other inequities at least as much as to income inequality. Intelligent people do better than the less intelligent; good-looking people have advantages not available to the ugly; tall people tend to do better than short people. There is little in the way of public policy designed to address these inequities. The same is not true of differences in race and gender. Those differences are addressed with specific policies. Specific policies are also designed to assist the physically handicapped.

One might question whether these characteristics are really inequities. Is it really unjust that some people are taller than others, or that some are better looking than others? Is Oprah Winfrey, a Black woman, really disadvantaged compared to White men? But those questions are of secondary importance in the political marketplace. Some groups have been more successful at organizing than others. Race and gender are defining characteristics, made more so by government policies that require people to identify themselves by race and gender. Rarely are people asked whether they identify as ugly. This categorization of people, treating them as members of groups rather than as individuals, encouraged by government, provides an opportunity for political entrepreneurs to organize people to lobby for special treatment.

Representatives of women and Blacks have been able to organize support and bargain in the political marketplace because people identify as members of those groups. Representatives of Asians have been less successful.

Whether special treatment is merited is (almost) beside the point. Nobody claims they are lobbying to ask for special advantages over others. They always argue that the policies they advocate are just, merited to overcome the unfair disadvantages they face. The merit argument comes into play because minorities must get the support of a majority to score a victory in a democratic system. But merit does not, by itself, provide benefits to anyone. There is still the question of how the groups that received benefits were able to organize.

Affirmative action aids racial minorities. Why have ugly people not been able to organize to get similar programs? One reason is that there is not a clear dividing line that identifies someone as ugly; another is that many who might fall into that category would not want to acknowledge it. But, there is not a clear dividing line for race either, and societies are becoming increasingly interracial. The role of government must be acknowledged. Government requires people to identify their races and genders, enhancing people's ability to identify with those groups. This lowers the transaction costs of organizing, which enables some groups to organize based on their common characteristics while others cannot.

Perhaps an increasingly interracial society will erode the ability to organize racial groups, and in a society where gender was once binary, the increasing visibility of LGBTQ+ individuals is blurring the political distinction between, or among, genders, which may erode the ability of women to organize. Arguments based on merit do have rhetorical value, but the ability to negotiate in the political marketplace for favorable treatment requires that the petitioning group be able to organize to gain support.

Much income inequality is the result of differences in productivity. If one thinks that the market mechanism compensates people in proportion to the value they create for others, those who create more value for others receive more income. Henry Ford, for example, made a fortune because he created affordable automobiles for the masses. Sam Walton made a fortune because his Wal-Mart stores brought affordable goods to the masses. One could argue that there was an element of luck in cases like these, but even if luck played a role, their compensation still came from something they actively chose to do – as a result of voluntary exchanges that created value for millions of people.

Should lucky people be forced to transfer some income to the less fortunate? Should the rich be forced to transfer to the poor? Should the beautiful be forced to transfer to the ugly? There are arguments on both sides of these questions, but if popular opinion answers yes, groups that can claim to be disadvantaged have an advantage in their negotiations in the political marketplace. Success in the political marketplace requires that those who seek benefits make a case that they further some social purpose.

Some people have the bad fortune of health problems that were no part of their making. Is there any justice to making someone who gets cancer at an early age bear the costs of treatment in addition to suffering the disease, while someone in good health both enjoys the health and avoids the health care costs? This is the type of case that must be made for redistributive policies to succeed in the political marketplace.

One might like to imagine a government that enacts policies to address these inequalities based on some notion of fairness, but public policies are the result of political exchange. Interests must organize and gain sufficient support to demonstrate to the ruling elite that policies to benefit the interest group will also be in the interest of those who design the policies.

THE BENEFICIARIES OF GOVERNMENT REDISTRIBUTION

Because their prime motivation is to hold onto, and possibly increase, their political power, a primary motivation for the ruling elite to enact redistribution programs is to buy the support of the recipients. If programs like Social Security and Medicare – the largest redistribution programs in the United States – were meant to help the needy, they would be means-tested. The goal of the program is not to reduce inequality or alleviate poverty. It is to buy the support of older voters, who turn out to vote at higher rates than younger citizens. Government provides child care services and education for the benefit of young families, rent subsidies and funds to buy food, health care programs, and more. Redistribution is targeted to the masses to buy their support – to make as large a share of the population recipients as they can.[21]

Redistribution is often targeted toward the well-off in the form of corporate subsidies and tax breaks. The larger the share of the population that receives government transfers, the more the masses view government as their benefactor and want the political elite to have the power to continue to support them.

Redistribution tends to be viewed narrowly, as the transfer of resources from one group to another, but as John R. Commons emphasized, the institutional structure of governance has distributional impacts

---

[21] George J. Stigler, "Director's Law of Public Income Redistribution," *Journal of Law & Economics* 13, no. 1 (April 1970), pp. 1–10, argues that most redistribution comes from the middle class and is distributed to the middle class. That is where the votes are.

well beyond direct transfers, as examples earlier in the chapter show. Following the common assumption made by economists that people act to further their own interests, one would expect that government institutions, which are designed by the political elite, would work to the advantage of the elite. An extensive literature supports this conclusion.

Nobel laureate Joseph Stiglitz argues that the rules of the game are biased to favor a small elite over the general public.[22] David Stockman offers a similar observation, saying that those who propose to use government to fix market failures "fail to recognize that the state bears an inherent flaw that dwarfs the imperfections purported to afflict the free market; namely, that policies undertaken in the name of the public good inexorably become captured by special interests and crony capitalists who appropriate resources from society's commons for their own private ends."[23]

Thomas Piketty has characterized capitalism as a system inherently biased toward the rich,[24] and Emmanuel Saez and Gabriel Zucman describe the institutional structure of capitalist economies as designed to favor the elite over the masses.[25] Anne Case and Angus Deaton argue that the inherent inequities that have been introduced into market institutions have led those not privileged by the system toward personally destructive behavior.[26] They blame increases in drug addiction, alcoholism, and suicides on the increasing inequities in modern capitalist economies.

Cooperation between the economic and political elite for their mutual benefit leads to a system of political capitalism in which economic success increasingly is the result of political connections rather than the production of value for others.[27] The observation that the distributional impact of institutions of governance benefits the elite over the masses has been made many times before, by observers ranging from left to right on the political spectrum. Some, going back at least to Karl Marx, have

---

[22] Joseph E. Stiglitz, *The Price of Inequality: How Today's Divided Society Endangers the Future* (New York: W. W. Norton, 2012), p. 59.
[23] David A. Stockman, *The Great Deformation: The Corruption of Capitalism in America* (New York: Public Affairs Press, 2013), p. 169.
[24] Thomas Piketty, *Capital in the Twenty-First Century* (Cambridge, MA: Harvard University Press, 2014).
[25] Emmanuel Saez and Gabriel Zucman, *Triumph of Injustice: How the Rich Dodge Taxes and How to Make Them Pay* (New York: W. W. Norton, 2019).
[26] Anne Case and Angus Deaton, *Deaths of Despair and the Future of Capitalism* (Princeton, NJ: Princeton University Press, 2020).
[27] Mancur Olson, Jr., *The Rise and Decline of Nations* (New Haven, CT: Yale University Press, 1982). See also Randall G. Holcombe. *Political Capitalism: How Economic and Political Power Is Made and Maintained* (Cambridge: Cambridge University Press, 2018).

drawn the conclusion that capitalism is a flawed institutional structure that should be replaced. Others, such as Milton Friedman, celebrate the benefits capitalism has brought throughout the world and describe government intervention as the problem.

When institutions of governance have the flexibility to use the threat of force to transfer income from some to others, there is good reason to think that this flexibility will be used to the advantage of those who have the power to employ it. Institutions of governance enforce institutional constraints. The power the political elite require to enforce those constraints also gives them the power to transfer resources from some to others. Those who design the transfers should be expected to do so in a manner that benefits the designers. Thinking otherwise is naïve.[28]

Conclusions either way are insufficient without an understanding of how the institutions of the political marketplace operate. If an elite few design and control those institutions, the challenge is to find ways that the power of the elite can be constrained so that it is not abused for their benefit.

CONCLUSION

The human propensity to truck, barter, and exchange pulls an economy toward a competitive general equilibrium with the assistance of institutions that lower transaction costs, and that enforce institutional constraints through authority and governance. The market economy represented in that competitive general equilibrium model cannot operate without these two categories of institutions. Because institutions of governance give the ruling elite the power to force the masses to comply with their mandates, those same institutions of governance enable the ruling elite to engage in redistribution – to forcibly take from some to give to others.

The redistributive powers of the political elite do not begin with the explicit taking from some to give to others, but with the definition and enforcement of rights. All exchanges within the political marketplace have distributive consequences, and explicit transfers of resources from some to others add to the distributive impacts of political exchange.

---

[28] Steven Kelman, "'Public Choice' and Public Spirit," *The Public Interest* 87 (Spring 1987), pp. 80–94 argues that reasoning along these lines undermines the public spirit and makes people act more selfishly rather than in the public interest. Kelman's argument has little force if those who hold political power are already using it for their own benefit.

9 Redistribution and Welfare Maximization

One might think that this organized plunder would be met with resistance by those who are forced to surrender their assets to a predatory government, but while there is some opposition, redistribution is typically seen as a legitimate function of the state. Supported by abstract academic models and the wishful thinking of the masses, government redistribution is often viewed as one mechanism to further social justice – to correct inequities that arise through economic activity in the marketplace. Setting aside wishful thinking, government is not an omniscient benevolent dictator who can identify and implement redistribution programs to maximize social welfare.

The political elite are prone to consider their own interests when designing redistributive institutions. Support from academics and the masses for forced redistribution legitimizes the actions of the elite that take from some to give to others. The line of reasoning in this chapter is not meant to pass judgment on the merits of government redistribution, but rather to understand how this institutionalized transfer of resources can be supported by the masses, and why it is a product of the political marketplace.

Direct transfers of income are relatively visible, and it is apparent that whatever the other effects of the transfers, they serve the function of buying political support for the elite who facilitate them. Supported by theoretical arguments about welfare maximization and social justice, redistribution gains public support as the masses willingly cede this power to the elite. The greater the share of a society's resources that are transferred through government redistribution, the more important it becomes for citizens to petition for a share of those resources, which gives more power to the political elite. Those resources are allocated through the political marketplace, and as with markets in general, those who are engaged in the transactions undertake them because they believe they have something to gain.

The argument is not a normative one either supporting or opposing government redistribution. It is a positive one that analyzes the institutional foundations of government redistribution to show the tendency for government redistribution to favor the elite who design it. Part of the benefit comes directly, as the elite are recipients. Part comes indirectly as an increase in the power that the masses convey to the elite.

10

The Scope of Authority

Participants in the political marketplace engage in transactions with the intention of accessing government power to further their ends. Their ability to do so can be enhanced by enlarging the scope of authority of government. The broader the government's scope of authority, the more power those in the political marketplace can exercise over others. In that sense, expanding the scope of authority of government is analogous to increasing productivity in the market for goods. A larger scope of authority means more for the political elite to buy and sell, which increases their potential for gains from trade.

In their pursuit of power, from the vantage point of those who make the laws, an increased scope of authority can increase the range of activities individuals undertake that fall under the authority of the political elite. This gives lawmakers more power over ordinary citizens. From the vantage point of the government's subjects, an increased scope of authority makes them more dependent on favorable treatment by the political elite, and also imposes more costs on them. Recalling the trilateral nature of the political marketplace, exchanges made by members of the political elite tend to be paid for by the masses, who are excluded from the bargaining process because of high transaction costs.

Benefits given to some typically come at a cost to others. Even when public policies produce efficiency gains, often those gains go to a concentrated interest and the masses can still bear costs. But people tend to focus on the concentrated benefits that can be targeted toward them rather than the dispersed costs they bear from policies that benefit other interests. Rather than mobilizing for lower overall tax rates, less regulation, and a reduction in the scope of government, they lobby for regulatory protections, subsidies, and targeted tax reductions that increase the scope of government. Interest groups do not lobby for policies that produce widespread benefits for most members of society, but for policies that produce benefits narrowly targeted to themselves, often imposing costs on others. Those narrowly targeted benefits increase the scope of government.

The American Founders recognized the potential problems that could arise from a government with an expanding scope of authority, and Article I, Section 8 of the Constitution of the United States gives the federal government limited and enumerated powers. The Tenth Amendment to the Constitution reaffirms that concept of limited and enumerated powers, stating, "The powers not delegated to the United States by the Constitution, nor prohibited by it to the states, are reserved to the states respectively, or to the people." But constitutional rules are not constraining unless they are enforced, and by a plain reading of the Constitution, it would appear that the scope of authority of the federal government has expanded well beyond those powers enumerated in the Constitution.

Which of the enumerated powers in the Constitution gives the federal government the power to force people to pay into a compulsory retirement program? The Social Security program does just that. Which of the enumerated powers gives the federal government the power to mandate that motor fuels must contain ethanol? One might refer to the (much abused) commerce clause giving Congress the power "to regulate commerce with foreign nations, and among the several states, and with Indian tribes," but it is surely an abuse of the language to interpret a motorist buying fuel at a gas station to be "commerce ... among the several states." Interpreted that way, any economic activity is subject to government regulation, and that is the way the clause has been interpreted.

The Supreme Court case of *Wickard v. Filburn*, 317 U.S. 111 (1942), affirmed the broad reach of the commerce clause. The Court ruled that Ohio farmer Roscoe Filburn was not allowed to grow wheat on his own land to feed his own chickens because of a restriction the federal government had created limiting the amount of wheat a farmer was allowed to grow. There was no commerce involved in Filburn's actions, let alone interstate commerce. The logic behind the Court's decision was that had Filburn not grown that wheat to feed his own chickens, he would have purchased wheat for that purpose, and wheat is a commodity traded across state lines.

The case remains significant in essentially defining interstate commerce as any productive activity, even if no products enter the marketplace or cross state lines. If Filburn's growing wheat on his own land to feed his own chickens is interstate commerce, because otherwise he would have had to have bought the wheat, by that logic it would appear that people growing food in their own gardens for their own consumption is interstate commerce. They would have to buy food if they did not grow their own. The case is interesting in its own right, but it also illustrates the importance the American Founders placed on limiting the scope of government, and how, nevertheless, the scope of government has increased over the centuries.

When the political elite use their authority to convey benefits to a specific group, that group then becomes dependent on the elite, lest those benefits be withdrawn. If ethanol producers annoy the political elite, they might lose the ethanol mandate that benefits them. If Social Security recipients ceased to be a reliable voting bloc, or as a group appear hostile to the political elite, they could find their benefits reduced or eliminated.

Social Security is an interesting case because for decades the Social Security Administration has projected that the system will go bankrupt, which causes some uneasiness among recipients. This provides an opportunity for the political elite. Rather than implement any reforms, politicians reaffirm their support for the program, assuring seniors that if they remain in office, Social Security benefits will not be cut. This is an example of how members of the political elite negotiate to gain the support of the masses.

In 1967 the state of Florida established the Reedy Creek Development District to give the Walt Disney Company the power to govern its own development of Disney World. Disney was able to access the power of government for its benefit, which in turn made it dependent on the political elite for its continuance. In 2022 the company angered Florida Governor Ron DeSantis by vocally opposing legislation the governor was promoting, prompting Governor DeSantis to push through legislation to remove that power of self-governance from Disney. This provides an example of what can happen when the beneficiaries of government power fail to support the political elite who can take those benefits away. The governor's action also sets an example for other businesses that might be inclined to challenge the political elite. The transfer of government authority to Disney increased the authority Florida's government had over the company, and the political elite in Florida's government used that authority against Disney when the company vocally opposed the political elite.

The situation is even more perilous than that for those who oppose the political elite. If they do not have targeted benefits that can be taken

10 The Scope of Authority

away, the ruling class can target them with special taxes, or impose regulatory costs on them.[1] The broader the scope of government, the more power the political elite has to threaten to impose costs on their challengers, which pressures those challengers to realign with the authority of the ruling class.

The idea that the primary objective of the political elite is to maintain and increase their power is not difficult to defend. The quest for power is descriptive of the activities of the political elite since the beginning of recorded history. Only recently, within the past few centuries, have those who held political power suggested that their power was justified based on its benefit to the masses. Prior to the Enlightenment, citizens viewed themselves as subjects of their governments, obligated to serve the interests of the state, as articulated by the ruling class. There was no question that government was under the control of an elite few, and that the masses were obligated to abide by the mandates of the elite.

ENLIGHTENMENT AND THE IDEOLOGY OF DEMOCRACY

This perceived relationship between the state and its subjects was reversed with the popularization of Enlightenment ideas, which made the case that the state should serve its citizens, rather than citizens serving the state. John Locke asserted in 1690 that individuals naturally have rights, and that the role of the state is to protect the rights of its citizens. Locke's ideas, along with other Enlightenment writers offered a clear challenge to the idea of elite rule.[2]

The ideas of Locke and other Enlightenment writers were literally revolutionary. Bernard Bailyn describes how those ideas laid the ideological foundation for the American Revolution in 1776.[3] Those ideas also generated support for the French Revolution less than two decades later and continued to spread around the world for the next two centuries.

---

[1] This has been labeled rent extraction by Fred S. McChesney, "Rent Extraction and Rent Creation in the Economic Theory of Regulation," *Journal of Legal Studies* 16, no. 1 (January 1987), pp. 101–118, and *Money for Nothing: Politicians, Rent Extraction, and Political Extortion* (Cambridge, MA: Harvard University Press, 1997). On this same subject, see Peter Schweizer, *Extortion: How Politicians Extract Your Money, Buy Votes, and Line Their Own Pockets* (Boston: Houghton Mifflin, 2013).

[2] John Locke, *Two Treatises of Government* (Cambridge: Cambridge University Press, 1960 [orig. 1690]).

[3] Bernard Bailyn, *The Ideological Origins of the American Revolution* (Cambridge: Cambridge University Press, 1967).

Enlightenment ideas created an ideology of democracy: that romantic notion that democratic governments should be both accountable to their citizens and act in the interests of their citizens. If they did not, Locke argued, citizens have a right to overthrow and replace their governments with ones that did.

Enlightenment ideas threaten to undermine the power of the ruling class. The political philosophy of the Enlightenment depicted the political elite as servants of the public rather than their rulers. The undermining of the power of the old elite was the intent of a new rising political elite that aspired to replace the old. Gaetano Mosca says, "The modern democratic conception ... spread like wildfire because, first in France and soon after throughout western Europe, the new ruling class at once made use of it in order to oust the nobility and clergy from their privileges and in large part to supplant them."[4]

As Mosca notes, one set of elites was replaced by another. The impediment to eliminating the elite altogether and creating a completely egalitarian society is that institutions of authority and governance are necessary foundation for an orderly and productive society, and transaction costs limit the size of those who control those institutions to a small number – an elite few who make up the ruling class.

THE SCOPE OF AUTHORITY

Using the general equilibrium framework to understand the functions of institutions, the institutions of authority play the role of defining people's rights and enforcing the institutional constraints that lower transaction costs. Doing so requires that those in authority have a comparative advantage in the use of force, so their threats to sanction those who violate the rules produce compliance and an orderly society. Ideally, those in authority would rarely resort to the actual use of force because the threat of its use is a sufficient deterrent. People comply with authority because, first, they fear the consequences if they do not, and second, because they view the power of those in authority as legitimate and believe they should comply.

An orderly and productive society requires institutions that give some people authority over others, and people understand that they are better off because rules are enforced against assault, theft, and other rights violations. While people may have some conception of the rights they should

---

[4] Gaetano Mosca, *The Ruling Class* (New York: McGraw Hill, 1939), p. 334.

have, they also must see that the rights they actually are able to exercise are enforced by those in authority. The authority of some over the actions of others takes on an air of legitimacy.

When that authority is vested in a democratic government, Rousseau argued that its actions reflect the general will. This view of democracy gives those in authority the license to expand the scope of their authority. Chapter 9 offered one example: government redistribution. One would normally think that if someone forcibly takes the property of another person to give it to a third person, that forced transfer would have violated the rights of the person whose property was taken. Yet, when governments do this, people (often) believe that those in authority have the legitimate right to force the transfer. The scope of government is then increased to include forcibly taking from some to give to others.

The ruling elite can increase their scope of authority because they control government and its comparative advantage in the use of force. Those whose property is taken realize it would be futile to resist (although some do engage in tax evasion if they believe they can get away with it). Because the actions of the ruling class are widely viewed as legitimate, those in authority are able to expand the scope of their authority. If Rousseau's vision of democratic government is to be taken literally, the legitimate scope of a democratic government is, in principle, unlimited. Whatever those in authority do conforms to the general will.

Combining the quest for power with the legitimacy of actions by those in authority, what limits are there to the actual scope of government? Looking at Stalin's Soviet Union or Castro's Cuba, the ultimate limit may be the ability to monitor and detect violators. Underground markets tend to develop in command economies because of that propensity to truck, barter, and exchange. Those in power can use fear and intimidation to control the masses, but the perception of legitimacy produces the consent of the governed. Those in authority claim that the expansion of their scope of authority is in the public interest.

MARKET FAILURE AND THE SCOPE OF AUTHORITY

Chapter 3 discussed the concept of market failure in the context of the benchmark of general equilibrium. Having established the desirable properties of a competitive general equilibrium and having described that outcome in a mathematical framework, that same framework was then used to demonstrate with mathematical precision many conditions under which actual markets would fail to arrive at that benchmark of competitive general equilibrium.[5] Monopolies, public goods, externalities, macroeconomic instability, informational asymmetries, and more could be listed, and one presumption that often arises from this line of reasoning is that one role of government is to correct for market failures.

Just because markets are not perfect does not imply that government can improve them.[6] Governments are not perfect either, so a better way to design public policy to deal with "market failures" is to compare actual governments to real-world markets to see which would yield better results. While plausible in theory, such a comparison is problematic in practice. One reason is that there is no good evidence on the alternatives not taken. If government acts to expand its scope of authority, one can only conjecture about what would have happened had the government not acted. One can see that Roosevelt's New Deal programs did not end the Great Depression, but one cannot see what would have happened in the absence of those programs. New Deal supporters say that had those programs not been implemented, things would have been even worse. One cannot know what would have happened had different policies (or no policies) been implemented.

A second issue is that if a "market failure" becomes apparent, it may take some time for market entrepreneurs to respond. Market failures imply an inefficient allocation of resources, and when resources are allocated inefficiently, entrepreneurs have the incentive to look for ways to allocate them more efficiently. Market failures are profit opportunities. But entrepreneurial innovations take time to implement. Meanwhile, the masses demand that government do something. Government legislation preempts private entrepreneurship.

In 1906, Upton Sinclair published his book *The Jungle*, about unsanitary, dangerous, and deplorable conditions in the meat-packing industry.[7] Prior to the publication of Sinclair's book, people did not perceive a problem. That same year, in response to Sinclair's book, Congress passed the Pure Food and Drug Act to address the newly perceived problem. Had government not acted, it is easy to conjecture that meat-packing businesses would have instituted their own reforms, and publicized them, to retain their customers. But again, this is just a conjecture, because

---

[5] See, for example, Francis M. Bator, "The Anatomy of Market Failure," *Quarterly Journal of Economics* 72, no. 3 (August 1958), pp. 351–379.
[6] This was emphasized by James M. Buchanan, "Public Finance and Public Choice," *National Tax Journal* 28, no. 4 (December 1975), pp. 383–394.
[7] Upton Sinclair, *The Jungle* (New York: Doubleday, Page & Co., 1906).

government did act, so one cannot observe what would have happened had the market been left to respond.

The academic concept of market failure lends scholarly credibility to the idea that left to their own devices, markets will produce undesirable results. That opens the door for the political elite to expand the scope of government to respond to those market failures. It legitimizes the concept. But most citizens and voters do not push for government interventions based on academic arguments. They perceive problems and argue that the government should do something to address those problems. The political elite, in their quest for more power, are happy to respond, so little by little, the scope of government increases. Academic arguments about market failure merely lend credibility to the popular call for those in authority to address perceived problems.

MARKET FAILURE, ACADEMIA, AND THE MEDIA

The political process that leads to an expanding scope of government begins with the masses, who perceive problems they do not have the power to address – so they ask the powerful to address them. The demands of the masses are supported by the academic concept of market failure. The intellectual class is not motivated to support the interests of the masses, however. They support the interests of the political elite in their own quest for more power. By aligning themselves with the powerful, the intellectual class can increase their own power, by putting themselves in a position to negotiate with the political elite. They can enter the group with low transaction costs.

Journalists are looking for a story, and the political elite can provide them with information or withhold information. Those who have that information are more likely to provide it to a friendly source, which provides an incentive for those in mass media to support those in power. Likewise, academics can provide the political elite with ways to address the problems perceived by the masses and become political advisors and political appointees, entering the low-transaction cost group.

When the masses perceive a problem, the political elite are ready to address it by implementing a program that increases the scope of government. If the public perceives a problem with unsanitary conditions in food processing, or ineffective or dangerous medications, the political elite creates the Food and Drug Administration. If the public perceives a terrorist threat to the transportation network, the political elite create the Transportation Security Administration. If the public perceives a threat to the banking system, the political elite create banking institutions and regulation, from the Federal Reserve System (1913) to the Federal Deposit Insurance Corporation (1933) to the Dodd-Frank banking legislation (2009), and many other banking institutions and regulations between those.

If legislators, perceiving these demands from the masses and seeing an opportunity to increase their scope of authority, have a choice between two advisors, one who says "this is a temporary problem and private sector action will effectively deal with it," and "here's a plan for a government program to address the problem," it should be apparent that the political elite will choose the second advisor. There is a bias in favor of top-down solutions that increase the scope of government, partly because the incentives of those in power lean this way and partly because most people have little understanding of the spontaneous order of markets and social structures. They want action from the top, not a hope that a solution will work its way up from the bottom.

In many cases, government-imposed top-down solutions produce unintended negative consequences, prompting the masses to demand even more government intervention to address those unintended consequences, further increasing the scope of government.[8] Academicians who offer the political elite a plan in which they can increase the scope of government to address problems become advisors to the ruling class. Academicians who argue that decentralized markets more effectively address inefficiencies remain outside the sphere of political influence.

PUBLICLY PROVIDED GOODS

The theory of market failure includes public goods as one of the sources of market failure. The theory of public goods offers several definitions of a public good, with the assertion that markets fail to produce the optimal quantity of them. It is a short step to then recommend that public goods be provided by government. Public goods are often defined as goods that are joint consumption goods and/or are nonexcludable.

Paul Samuelson provided a rigorous mathematical definition of a public good as one that, once produced, could be consumed by everyone.[9]

---

[8] This idea is developed by Sanford Ikeda, *Dynamics of the Mixed Economy: Toward a Theory of Interventionism* (London: Routledge, 1997).
[9] See Paul A. Samuelson, "The Pure Theory of Public Expenditure," *Review of Economics and Statistics* 36 (November 1954), pp. 387–389, and "A Diagrammatic Exposition of a Theory of Public Expenditure," *Review of Economics and Statistics* 37 (November 1955), pp. 350–356.

If another consumer were to consume the good, it would not detract from the consumption of any existing consumer. A radio broadcast provides a good example. Once the radio station sends the signal over the air, an additional person can tune in and listen to the station without reducing the consumption of any existing listener. According to this theory, the market fails to provide an optimal amount of the public good.

The cost of adding an additional user is zero, so the good should be made available to everyone. But if the producer charges for access to the public good, that will inefficiently exclude some potential consumers, because it would cost nothing to allow them to consume. If everyone is allowed to consume at no cost, the producer could not recover the cost of providing the public good. So, government should produce it and make it freely available to everyone. The problems with this theory could be discussed at length, but one observation is that if a radio broadcast signal is a good example, the private sector does a good job of producing radio stations.[10]

Nonexcludable goods are goods that, once produced, the producer cannot prevent consumers from consuming. A radio broadcast might again offer an example. There are ways of encrypting a broadcast signal to exclude consumers, as is done with satellite radio, but doing so is costly. Local roads might be another example, although some cities have found ways to exclude drivers unless they pay a toll.

Using those definitions of public goods, perhaps the best examples of joint consumption nonexcludable goods are computer programs and digital music. Once written, a computer program can be endlessly copied and used by everyone without reducing its availability to anyone. In the early days of personal computing, software companies complained heavily about users pirating their programs without paying for them, indicating the nonexcludable nature of the programs. Yet some of the richest people in the world at the beginning of the twenty-first century made their fortunes selling microcomputer software, a nonexcludable joint consumption good that fits the definition of a public good as well as anything else.

The same is true of digital music files. Once recorded, the music can be endlessly copied and listened to by everyone, and producers complain about people pirating their music. Yet the private sector does a good job

---

[10] Jora R. Minasian, "Television Pricing and the Theory of Public Goods," *Journal of Law & Economics* 7 (October 1964), pp. 71–80, offers an explanation for why excluding consumers enhances the efficiency of the production of the public good.

of producing music despite what, in theory, is a "market failure." Does anyone think that people would have better computer programs if the government produced them, or that music would be better if government took over the production of music?[11]

The theory of public goods, often used to justify government production, does not do a good job of explaining why government production is beneficial. The market does a good job of producing goods that fit the definition well. Meanwhile, most of what government produces does not fit the economist's definition of public goods. A large percentage of government budgets go toward redistribution, discussed in Chapter 9. Health care is primarily a private good. Education is successfully produced by private schools, notwithstanding heavily subsidized government competitors. Users can be excluded from roads and parks, and those goods become congested with too many users, so they are not joint consumption goods. Theories of market failure do not correspond to the actual publicly provided goods produced by government.

Murray Rothbard and David Friedman have argued that private markets could produce everything government now produces and do so more efficiently.[12] That is an easy argument to make for most of what government produces because markets already provide education, health care, roads, parks, garbage collection, and more. Rothbard and Friedman cover the more difficult and controversial issues of privatizing law enforcement, courts, and national defense, but there is no need to delve into those issues here.[13] Suffice it to say that the scope of government has expanded substantially into producing things the private sector could provide, and often does, alongside government production.

Institutions of authority and governance are necessary for the functioning of a productive and orderly society. Once they are in place, with the institutions of coercion that necessarily comprise them, the political elite who control the institutions of authority and governance can use their coercive ability to expand the scope of government beyond just enforcing institutional constraints. They produce publicly provided goods – most

---

[11] This observation is made by Randall G. Holcombe, "Why Does Government Produce National Defense?" *Public Choice* 137, nos. 1/2 (October 2008), pp. 11–19.

[12] Murray N. Rothbard, *For a New Liberty: A Libertarian Manifesto* (New York: Macmillan, 1973), and David D. Friedman, *The Machinery of Freedom: Guide to Radical Capitalism* (Chicago, IL: Open Court Publishing Company, 1973).

[13] I discuss some of these issues in Randall G. Holcombe, "Government: Unnecessary but Inevitable," *The Independent Review* 8, no. 3 (Winter 2004), pp. 325–342.

of which do not come close to conforming to the economist's definition of public goods – financed by tax revenues, exempting them from having to face the market test that private sector producers would face.

Meanwhile, academic economists expound on a theory of market failure to legitimize enlarging the scope of government. Theories of market failure are used to justify government intervention, even when they address issues that do not fit the theories. The expanding scope of government is a consequence of the political elite's quest for power.

EDUCATION AND PROPAGANDA

Among publicly provided goods, education deserves special mention because it provides a vehicle for indoctrinating students to conform with the mandates of the state. As with other government-provided goods, education is produced in the private sector, and private sector schools are often thought to provide higher quality education than government schools. One justification sometimes given for government schools is that they do a better job of socializing their students. Socialization, in this context, might be taken to mean conformance with government-mandated institutions.

The political elite could mandate that schools teach students to comply with government authority, and sometimes they do, but educational institutions are designed to reinforce adherence to authority. For starters, teachers at government schools are government employees, giving them the inclination to support government. Higher taxes can mean more education funding, and higher teacher salaries; tax cuts could have the opposite effect. The regimentation of the education system pushes students to conform, and success for students is measured by the extent to which they are able to perform tasks assigned to them by their teachers, who have the authority to judge their performance. The ultimate goal is to produce compliant citizens who respect authority.

Ideally, students master academic subjects like math, science, language arts, and history. At the same time, the education system teaches students to conform to mandates issued by those in authority, and to mold their thinking to conform with those in authority. Schools teach students to show up to class on time, to behave in an orderly fashion, and through assignments and tests, to give teachers back the answers those in authority want. These skills, a by-product of the academic environment, are not only valuable in hierarchical work settings but also guide students to conform with the mandates issued by political authority.

Those messages do not end when students leave the formal education system. Government continues with its propaganda in sometimes subtle ways. Sporting events often begin with the national anthem and frequently with a display of military personnel and equipment. One cannot fail but to be impressed with the military flybys that occur at major sporting events.[14] More subtly, the political elite continually emphasize threats to the well-being of citizens, which are being addressed by their governments. Terrorist attacks, plagues and pandemics, and severe weather emergencies ranging from hurricanes to tornados to droughts are continual threats which the government stands ready to mitigate. When people fall on hard times, the political elite tell them that their government is there to help.

REGULATORY AUTHORITY

The activities of government might be divided into two categories, comprising the budgetary state and the regulatory state. Often, the budgetary state is the focus of analysis when discussing the size of government, but the regulatory state is more significant in at least one way: It conveys more discretionary power to the political elite. Many budgetary items are general. They convey benefits to a broad contingent of beneficiaries, including the masses as well as the elite. One reason the political elite will support such programs is that it can buy them votes and support from the masses. Even when expenditures are targeted to specific beneficiaries as a result of political exchange, it opens the opportunity for others to compete for those benefits. Once benefits are produced for one group, it is easy for other groups to argue that they should have similar benefits.

Regulation allows the political elite to target benefits to specific beneficiaries, partly as a result of the way regulations are written, and partly as a result of the way they are enforced. Because every case is different, it may be difficult for those who are not well-connected to see any evidence that regulations have been enforced unevenly, and the effects of regulation are often less visible to the masses than the effects of spending. For those seeking power, regulatory authority conveys more of it than budgetary authority. Thus, the scope of the regulatory state tends to

---

[14] See Christopher J. Coyne and Abigail R. Hall, *Manufacturing Militarism: U.S. Government Propaganda in the War on Terror* (Stanford, CA: Stanford University Press, 2021) for a good discussion.

increase, often barely noticed by the masses, as more rules are created but few are repealed.

Because of the discretionary nature of regulation, both as it is passed and as it is enforced, government regulation tends to lead to corruption.[15] Legislators and regulators can use it to benefit well-connected interests in the political marketplace, where its discretionary nature often goes unnoticed. Even when it is recognized, the masses find themselves powerless to act against it.

CENTRALIZATION

The scope of government expands as it takes on more functions, but its scope might also be measured in geographic terms. A more decentralized system of government can allow residents feasible alternatives to their current government. A federal system of government, as in the United States, consists of national, state, and local governments. If the functions of government are decentralized to the local level, citizens would have more options to "vote with their feet" and move to jurisdictions that more closely satisfy their preferences for governance.[16]

Even if moving to a new jurisdiction is infeasible, residents of one jurisdiction can compare the performance of their government with that of their neighbors in what has sometimes been called yardstick competition. If one's government does not measure up, those who run it can be voted out and replaced. Perhaps the most noteworthy example in which yardstick competition was effective came with the fall of the Berlin Wall. Residents in the Eastern bloc countries in Europe looked across the Berlin Wall and decided they preferred the institutions of the Western bloc countries, resulting in the rapid overthrow of those Eastern bloc governments.

If public policy is initiated at lower level governments, different governments can enact different policies, so citizens can compare the effects of the policies implemented by their governments with the policies implemented elsewhere. Centralization eliminates this possibility. With a central government, one can see the result of a government policy,

---

[15] Some evidence is offered by Randall G. Holcombe and Christopher J. Boudreaux, "Regulation and Corruption," *Public Choice* 164, no. 1 (July 2015), pp. 75–85.
[16] This idea was developed by Charles M. Tiebout, "A Pure Theory of Local Expenditures," *Journal of Political Economy* 64, no. 5 (October 1956), pp. 416–424.

but cannot see what would have happened had a different policy been implemented. Even if a policy turns out badly, without an alternative to observe directly, one can always conjecture that things would have been even worse without that policy. Centralization contains this mechanism that can lead to an increase in the scope of government.

Federal systems of government often use a system of revenue sharing in which revenue is raised by higher levels of government and then shared with lower levels through grants that come with strings attached. For example, in 1984 the federal government of the United States passed legislation that required states to mandate a minimum age for alcohol consumption of 21 years to receive federal highway funds. Tax revenues are collected from residents of the states, and then sent back to them only if they comply with federal mandates. This is a visible and well-known example, but federal grants to state governments and state grants to local governments typically come with mandated requirements.

This system of grants effectively cartelizes lower-level governments.[17] Rather than competing with each other by offering a variety of policies, they are required by the higher-level government to homogenize their policies. The political elite in lower-level governments often cooperate in the efforts of higher-level governments to limit their power because it lessens intergovernmental competition, and therefore constituent pressure, on lower-level governments.

Lower-level governments seek intergovernmental grants from higher-level governments. Localities get funding from states and states get funding from the federal government, which makes those lower-level governments more homogeneous and thus less competitive with each other. This gives higher-level governments more power even as it makes lower-level governments more homogeneous. Decentralization and intergovernmental competition can work to the advantage of the masses, and can constrain the power of the political elite, which is why it is often difficult to implement, and why governments tend to become more centralized rather than more decentralized.

A federal system tends toward centralization because a more centralized system insulates the political elite in lower-level governments from intergovernmental competition, while it conveys more power to those in higher-level governments.

---

[17] See Randall G. Holcombe and DeEdgra W. Williams, "The Cartelization of Local Governments," *Public Choice* 149, nos. 1/2 (October 2011), pp. 65–74.

THE FOUNDATIONS OF AUTHORITY

George Stigler says,

The state has one basic resource which in pure principle is not shared with even the mightiest of its citizens: the power to coerce. The state can seize money by the only method which is permitted by the laws of a civilized society, by taxation. The state can ordain physical movements of resources and the economic decisions of households and firms without their consent.[18]

How can the state do this? The ruling class is necessarily small and does not possess the physical power themselves to compel others to obey them. They employ armies, police, and courts to do that work for them. This means they must convince those who work for them to continue to do so. They have the power to tax, so they can use resources taken from the masses to pay their enforcers. Even then, the forces the ruling class has at their disposal are insufficient to actually use force to gain the compliance of everyone under their authority.

The ruling class is able to maintain their authority because, except in rare instances, most people under their authority comply, so actual force is not required. The threat of force to be used against those who violate the rules is almost always sufficient to create a compliant and orderly society. In the rare instances in which people do violate the rules, the use of force serves as an example to others of the negative consequences from noncompliance.

The ruling class never has sufficient power to force everyone to comply, but it does not need this much force when most people choose to comply. Even if most people are opposed to their existing rulers, it is difficult for a large group to coordinate their actions to rise up in opposition. As Gaetano Mosca says, "the larger the political community, the smaller will the proportion of the governing minority to the governed majority be, and the more difficult will it be for the majority to organize for reaction against the minority."[19]

While Mosca did not have the advantage of reading Coase, his reasoning follows along Coasian lines. Anticipating Mancur Olson,[20] Mosca says, "In reality the dominion of an organized minority, obeying a single impulse, over the unorganized majority is inevitable. The power of

---

[18] Stigler, "The Theory of Economic Regulation," p. 4.
[19] Mosca, *The Ruling Class*, p. 53.
[20] Mancur Olson, Jr., *The Logic of Collective Action* (Cambridge, MA: Harvard University Press, 1965).

any minority is irresistible as against each single individual in the majority, who stands alone before the totality of the organized minority. At the same time, the minority is organized for the very reason that it is a minority."[21]

The ruling class has the power to govern because they do not have to use actual force against an entire population to gain compliance. The threat of force is sufficient to convince most people it would be too costly to resist. The masses face high transaction costs that prevent them from organizing to oppose their rulers, so they comply. When revolutions occur (which is rare), they typically are led by a charismatic individual who hopes to be the new ruler. Lenin and Castro are examples. Popular uprisings almost never succeed because they can be dispersed by the force commanded by the ruling class. The fall of the Berlin Wall, followed by popular uprisings in other Eastern bloc nations, offers a rare counterexample, sufficiently at odds with the conventional wisdom in social science that few social scientists foresaw it.

CONCLUSION

The scope of authority tends to expand because those in authority seek more power, and the masses often perceive problems and demand that those in power do something to address those problems. The demands of the masses are supported by the academic concept of market failure. Viewing the competitive general equilibrium model as a mathematical description of an optimal allocation of resources, economists have used that same mathematical framework to describe a number of ways in which a real-world economy might fall short of the ideal. They then have taken the short step of saying that government should do something, supporting the demands of the masses to make things better.

What the demands of the masses have in common with the theoretical arguments of economists is that both tend to view government as an omniscient benevolent dictator, knowing the best course of action and taking the best course of action. That vision of government falls short because, first, those in power often do not know the best course of action. The theoretical models of economists would require policymakers to know things they have no way of discovering, so there are no real-world policies that could arrive at the optimal results those models derive. Second, even if the political elite could know the optimal public

---

[21] Mosca, *The Ruling Class*, p. 53.

policies described by those models, they do not have the incentive to implement them. They are seeking more power for themselves, not optimal public policies for the masses.

Exchanges in the political marketplace tend to undermine the economic outcome described by the general equilibrium model, because those in the low transaction cost group bargain to channel benefits their way – subsidies, tax breaks, regulatory protections – which often impose costs on the masses. An increasing flow of targeted benefits toward the elite makes economic success increasingly the result of political connections rather than satisfying the desires of consumers. The increasing scope of government leads to what Mancur Olson described as the decline of nations.[22]

---

[22] Mancur Olson, Jr., *The Rise and Decline of Nations* (New Haven, CT: Yale University Press, 1982). See also Randall G. Holcombe, *Political Capitalism: How Economic and Political Power Is Made and Maintained* (Cambridge: Cambridge University Press, 2018).

11

Mobility and Authority

The first ten chapters of this volume have emphasized the division between the political elite – those who transact in the political marketplace and design public policy – and the masses who are excluded from the political marketplace. That analysis paints a bleak picture for the masses, who have no option but to conform to the mandates of the elite. The elite make the rules; the masses are obligated to follow them. This division between the rulers and the ruled, which sounds descriptive of societies centuries ago, necessarily remains, because transaction costs necessarily give the powers of authority and governance to an elite few.

This would seem to place the masses at a substantial disadvantage with respect to their rulers, and for most of recorded human history, that has been the case. Yet in twenty-first-century postindustrial societies, the masses enjoy high and rising standards of living, and governments often do engage in activities that benefit the masses. The masses are not on par with the elite, either in terms of opportunities or outcomes, but the gap in both opportunities and outcomes has been narrowing for centuries. Many of the wealthiest individuals in the twenty-first century are not members of the political class – a recent development in human history.

The themes developed in the first ten chapters are based on old ideas, supported by more contemporary developments in economics, political theory, and political philosophy. Thomas Paine, in 1776, observed that "Government, even in its best state, is but a necessary evil; in its worst state an intolerable one,"[1] with an explanation along the lines of the

---

[1] Thomas Paine, "Common Sense," in Moncure Daniel Conway, ed., *The Writings of Thomas Paine*, vol. 1 (New York: G. P. Putnam's Sone, 1894 [orig. 1776]), p. 69.

preceding analysis. Man, he says, "finds it necessary to surrender up a part of his property to furnish means for the protection of the rest; and this he is induced to do by the same prudence which in every other case advises him, out of two evils to choose the least."[2]

The necessary part of government, this volume has emphasized, is its role in defining and protecting people's rights – creating an orderly society in which people can peacefully and productively interact with each other. The positive results from this aspect of government in the past several centuries have the potential to lead people into overlooking the possibility that, unconstrained, those who hold the power of government can abuse that power to the point where, as Paine says, government is intolerable. The exercise of power by the political elite has been relatively benign in many nations since the Enlightenment because it has been constrained by several factors.

In contrast to the ten chapters that have preceded it, this chapter and Chapters 12 and 13 consider factors that constrain the elite to prevent, or at least mitigate, their ability to abuse their power. The primary factor that has constrained the abuse of political power over the past several centuries has been the increased ability of the masses to move away from those who abuse it. That ability to move away from the abuse of power has been enhanced as a result of economic changes that have occurred since the beginning of the Industrial Revolution.

The improvement in the economic welfare of the masses is partly the result of increases in economically productive activity that has produced more for everyone, but for most of recorded human history, the ruling class was able to use its power to confiscate for itself any income produced by the masses beyond a bare subsistence level. This change in the balance of power between the elite and the masses has come largely from an evolution in economic conditions that has increased people's geographical mobility.

The masses as a group have limited power to constrain the elite; as individuals, they have none. But they may have the ability to move away from an exercise of authority they view as abusive. The ruling class, which produces no goods and services, depends on a productive citizenry for their well-being, so to the degree that those under their rule are mobile, the ruling class must make its subjects content to stay, rather than migrate to another jurisdiction.

---

[2] Paine, "Common Sense," p. 69.

When people have the ability to escape authority, and when those in authority rely on the productivity of those subject to their authority, abuse of authority erodes the ability of those who have it to benefit from it. People have become less oppressed by authority since the beginning of the Industrial Revolution because they have become more mobile. Mobility gives people the ability to limit the abuse of authority.

An optimistic vision of the benefits of mobility was described by Charles Tiebout, who depicted a political landscape with many local jurisdictions competing for residents by providing benefits to them.[3] In Tiebout's vision, people would sort themselves into government jurisdictions that satisfied their preferences for government goods and services. In Tiebout's world, the governments themselves have the incentive to produce what citizens want as governments compete for residents. This vision of intergovernmental competition would be descriptive if people had the option of choosing to locate in one of a large number of political jurisdictions, if mobility were costless, and if the only factor people considered in their relocation decisions was the quality of government. Still, Tiebout's optimistic vision points out that citizen mobility can act as a constraint on those in authority.

FACTORS OF PRODUCTION AND MOBILITY

The masses are the source of income for the ruling class. A ruling class can exist only if the masses produce surplus income beyond what is required for their own subsistence. The production of that surplus is necessary to support a ruling class that produces no goods or services for consumption. The more productive the masses, the larger the share of their productivity that can be taxed away and placed under the control of the ruling class. If the ruling class wants to control those they rule, their first task is to keep those they rule from moving away.

Over the course of human history, the ability of people to relocate to more favorable institutions of governance has undergone two major transformations, one associated with the agricultural revolution that occurred around 10,000 BC, and the other associated with the Industrial Revolution that picked up steam – literally! – in the mid 1700s. These economic transformations brought with them significant implications for the institutions of governance. The ability to relocate depends heavily on the ability of

---

[3] This idea was developed by Charles M. Tiebout, "A Pure Theory of Local Expenditures," *Journal of Political Economy* 64, no. 5 (October 1956), pp. 416–424.

people to take their productive capacity with them. Thus, the mobility of factors of production has a strong influence on personal mobility.

In preagricultural societies, labor was the most important factor of production. People could leave those societies and take their labor with them, giving individuals substantial options to relocate. After the agricultural revolution, land became the most important factor of production, and land is the least mobile factor of production. The agricultural revolution tied people to the land, reducing their mobility. Should people try to move, they would have to leave their land – the source of their productivity – behind. Capital became the most important factor of production as a result of the Industrial Revolution, and capital is more mobile than land. The Industrial Revolution increased the mobility of the masses, and thus lessened the monopoly power of the ruling class.

The evolution of political institutions, and the power of the ruling class, has been heavily influenced by the evolution of economic institutions. Different types of societies have different requirements for their institutions of governance and impose different types of constraints on those who rule. Economic institutions and political institutions are closely linked. Those who have power do not voluntarily give it up. Constraints on the power of the ruling class have evolved as a result of a bargaining process – a process of exchange – that has been the result of an improved bargaining position of the masses. The improved bargaining position of the masses has been the result of changes in the economy that have made factors of production more mobile.

INSTITUTIONS IN PREAGRICULTURAL SOCIETIES

The distinction between formal institutions, that have third-party enforcement, and informal institutions that are enforced by those who interact within those institutions, has been discussed previously. Preagricultural societies offer an excellent example of informal institutions because all institutions in those societies are informal. Interesting in their own right, understanding institutions in preagricultural societies also sheds light on the operation and limitations of informal institutions in contemporary industrial and postindustrial societies.

Preagricultural societies, sometimes called clan-based societies or hunter-gatherer societies, consist of people who live off the land by hunting and gathering but do not cultivate the land, keep livestock, or recognize the private ownership of land. That makes these societies as a whole mobile. If resources become depleted in an area, or if competing clans threaten a society, they can move to another location. These societies had been referred to as primitive societies, a term that has fallen out of favor, partly because members of those societies prefer that way of life to the agricultural or industrial societies that have displaced most preagricultural societies.[4] But that displacement has been slow. The agricultural revolution began around 10,000 BC, but preagricultural societies were common even as the Industrial Revolution began more than 11,000 years later, and a few preagricultural societies have remained even into the twenty-first century.

Because these societies have been in existence for such a long time and have existed in so many different physical environments, there have been many differences among them, as David Graeber and David Wengrow have noted.[5] Still, there is enough commonality among them – and equally important, enough of a difference between them and the agricultural societies that have gradually replaced them – that valuable insights on the evolution of authority and governance can be gained by analyzing characteristics of their institutional structures common to most of them.

Clan-based societies do not have sharp distinctions among social, political, and economic institutions.[6] These societies do not have fixed capital, which prevents them from storing excess provisions to consume in the future. If a hunter kills an animal, it must be consumed quickly or the meat will spoil. Hunters who kill more than they can consume themselves share the excess with others in the group. There is little cost to doing so, because otherwise the meat would spoil. This also acts as a social safety net. A hunter may have more than he can consume this week, but next week come up dry, in which case the individual can consume any excess from other hunters.

Marshall Sahlins describes hunter-gatherer societies as the original affluent society,[7] saying that people can be affluent either by producing

---

[4] Jared Diamond, *The World until Yesterday: What Can We Learn from Traditional Societies?* (New York: Viking, 2012) is an anthropologist who has lived among those in clan-based societies, and discusses their advantages to those who live within them.

[5] David Graeber and David Wengrow, *The Down of Everything: A New History of Humanity* (New York: Aarrar, Straus and Giroux, 2021).

[6] Randall G. Holcombe, *Coordination, Cooperation, and Control: The Evolution of Economic and Political Power* (Cham, Switzerland: Palgrave Macmillan, 2020), ch. 5, discusses institutions in preagricultural societies in detail.

[7] Marshall Sahlins, "Notes on the Original Affluent Society," In Richard B. Lee and Irven DeVore, eds., *Man the Hunter: The First Intensive Survey of a Single, Crucial Stage of Human Development – Man's Once Universal Hunting Way of Life* (Chicago, IL: Aldine Publishing Company, 1968), pp. 85–99.

much or wanting little. Along the same lines as Sahlins, James Suzman describes the Namibia bushman society as enjoying affluence without abundance.[8] People in preagricultural societies work little, have much leisure time, and produce just enough to support themselves.

While life in clan-based societies is mostly easy and pleasant, it is subject to sudden swings. Daryll Forde and Mary Doublas observe that "Preoccupation with the daily or seasonal food supply, the frequency of hardship, and the risks of hunger are obvious characteristics of a primitive economy."[9] In an economy that has no way to store food, even a slight interruption in the flow of food can be disastrous for the group.

One reason people do not have to work hard in preagricultural economies is that the sustainable population of such a group is limited to the number that can survive the occasional famine. Most of the time there is enough for all, but with a high variance, so that some of the time people are pushed to starvation. Members of the society take care of each other, and relationships are relatively egalitarian. Rabindra Chakraborty says, "Sharing rules prescribe that the prey is redistributed eventually to all members of the community while everybody receives an (approximately) equal share."[10]

A potential problem in these societies is shirking. When norms of sharing give people the right to consume what is produced by others, opportunistic individuals might let others do the work. Another problem in societies that have institutions based on reciprocity is keeping track of debts. Clan-based societies address these problems by remaining small enough that everyone knows everyone else. If someone is a shirker, or does not recognize a debt, everyone will know. Nobody can be anonymous in clan-based societies.

Dunbar's number – the number of people anyone can know personally, about 150 – was noted in Chapter 3.[11] It is particularly relevant to clan-based societies because their institutions rely on everyone knowing

---

[8] James Suzman, *Affluence without Abundance: The Disappearing World of the Bushmen* (New York: Bloomsbury, 2017).
[9] Daryll Forde and Mary Douglas, "Primitive Economies," ch. 2 in George Dalton, ed., *Tribal and Peasant Economies: Readings in Economic Anthropology* (Garden City, NY: Natural History Press, 1967), p. 13.
[10] Rabindra Nath Chakraborty, "Sharing Culture and Resource Conservation in Hunter-Gatherer Societies," *Oxford Economic Papers* 59, no. 1 (January 2007), p. 63.
[11] Robin L. M. Dunbar, "Neocortex Size as a Constraint on Group Size in Primates," *Journal of Human Evolution* 22, no. 6 (1992), pp. 469–493.

everyone else. The result is that clan-based societies tend to divide once they reach or exceed Dunbar's number. A society of 200 individuals can split into two groups of 100. Dividing a group this way is not difficult because people have no fixed assets. A subset of the larger group can decide to split off, not only with little cost to themselves but also producing the benefit that it will be easier to monitor the actions of group members in smaller groups.

Economic institutions in these societies tend to be one of two general types. Some societies share goods based on pooling. All goods are shared in common. If someone kills an animal and brings it back to the group, all individuals in the group have an equal right to consume. Other societies share goods based on reciprocity. If someone consumes something that was brought to the group by another individual, the consumer incurs a debt to the person who brought the good.[12]

Pooling societies tend to be more egalitarian than those based on reciprocity. Everybody has the same rights to goods in a pooling society, whereas in a society based on reciprocity, productive individuals can accumulate power by sharing what they produce and receiving IOUs in return. By accumulating IOUs, people accumulate power and become group leaders. Transaction costs create a political elite in larger societies, but the small numbers in preagricultural societies mean that nobody is prevented from negotiating with anyone else, creating a more egalitarian society. Some people have more power than others, just as, for example, some legislators have more power than others, but power differences do not stand in the way of political exchange, as they do in larger societies where transaction costs limit the size of the political marketplace.

Agricultural societies have obvious advantages over preagricultural societies. People who cultivate land and raise livestock are more productive than hunter-gatherers, and agricultural economies have mechanisms for storing food from their growing seasons to make them more immune to fluctuations in output. This enables agricultural societies to support larger populations, but with longer workdays and, because people are

---

[12] These descriptions of institutions are supported by the anthropological literature, and are intended to illustrate the way that institutions in hunter-gatherer societies are designed. David Graeber and David Wengrow, *The Down of Everything: A New History of Humanity* (New York: Aarrar, Straus and Giroux, 2021) argue that there was more variety in preindustrial institutions than the literature commonly recognizes. The purpose here is not to recount the history of such societies, but to analyze the operation of specific institutions within them.

tied to the land, less mobility, which brings with it more authoritarian institutions of governance.

AUTHORITY AND MOBILITY IN PREAGRICULTURAL SOCIETIES

Referring to the hunter-gatherer society as the original affluent society, Marshall Sahlins says that if people wanted more, they could work to get more. But this is not quite true because of the way resources are shared in such societies. Those who produce more must share it with the group, taking away the incentive to be productive. People have a limited incentive to be productive when they cannot keep what they produce.

In societies that share resources based on reciprocity rather than pooling, individuals have the opportunity to accumulate more power. More productive individuals accumulate more IOUs, which gives them power over others. However, there are several factors that limit the ability of those who have accumulated power to abuse it.

First, the low transaction costs among members of the group allow those who feel abused to directly confront the accused abuser, and to make any grievances known to everyone else in the group. The ability to communicate with everyone in the group can facilitate group resistance if those with power abuse it. Low transaction costs remove the sharp division between the rulers and the ruled that exists in larger societies.

Second, because these societies live close to the subsistence level of income, they do not produce enough to support a separate ruling class. A separate ruling class requires that the masses produce more than enough to support themselves, so they can also support a ruling class that produces no goods or services for consumption. This also prevents clan-based societies from having a separate warrior class. Societies that live close to subsistence cannot afford to support rulers, or warriors, who do not produce goods and services for the group to consume.

Threats from outsiders can be a factor in clan-based societies. In these societies, people view those in their clan as their allies and cooperate with them, while those outside the clan are potential adversaries. Jared Diamond notes that clan-based societies tend to occupy exclusive territories because strangers are viewed as threats to members of the group.[13]

---

[13] Diamond, *The World until Yesterday*.

At the same time, strangers could be the possible source of resources to be taken from them to enrich one's own group, so strangers are viewed as both potential predators and potential prey. Larry Neal and Rondo Cameron say, "The logic was to seize the assets of strangers while eliminating any threat of future reprisals."[14]

Third, individuals in preagricultural societies are mobile, so if those in positions of authority abuse that authority, people can leave. Members of preagricultural societies are mobile because the primary factor of production in those societies is labor, and when individuals leave the society, they take their labor with them. While it is unlikely that a single individual would leave the group, it is very feasible and likely that a subset of the group could choose to leave. Indeed, that happens regularly in clan-based societies when they approach Dunbar's number. There are advantages from being group members, both in sharing resources and for purposes of protection should they run into hostile individuals from another clan. The mobility of that key factor of production – labor – constrains the abuse of power by those who have it, because it is easy to leave an abusive situation. The ability to "vote with your feet" provides a check on any abuse of power by those in the group who hold it.

Eric Alden Smith and Brian F. Codding note that variation in geographic conditions can also have an effect on the accumulation of power.[15] They note that when resources are "highly clumped," such as when a group relies on a particularly productive fishing area for food, the group's social organization tends to be more hierarchical. This makes sense because while discontented individuals can leave and take their labor with them, they must leave the highly clumped resource base behind. This restricts mobility, relaxing constraints on the ability of those with more power to use it.

Low transaction costs and informal institutions that are enforced by members of the group mean that all individuals in clan-based societies share in the activities of governance. There is no separate ruling class. The mobility of individuals in these societies, which arises because labor is the most significant factor of production, creates a relatively egalitarian society which checks the abuse of authority.

---

[14] Larry Neal and Rondo Cameron, *A Concise Economic History of the World: From Paleolithic Times to the Present*, 5th ed. (New York: Oxford University Press, 2016), p. 24.

[15] Eric Alden Smith and Brian F. Codding, "Ecological Variation and Institutionalized Inequality in Hunter-Gatherer Societies," *PNAS* 118, no. 13 (2021) e2016134118.

INSTITUTIONS OF AUTHORITY IN AGRICULTURAL SOCIETIES

The Agricultural Revolution began about 10,000 BC and gradually transformed economic, political, and social institutions. It began in isolated locations around the globe and spread slowly. Agriculture brings with it several economic advantages. By cultivating the land and domesticating livestock, each individual can produce more than when a society relies on hunting and gathering. This offers the potential for increases in the material standard of living. A second big advantage is that agricultural produce can be stored for later consumption, lessening the risk a society would face if conditions turned against them. A small harvest might require more meager portions consumed until the next harvest, but would not necessarily lead to starvation. The Agricultural Revolution offered the possibility to make consumption over time smoother than production over time.

These advantages allow agricultural societies to support larger populations over a given area of land than preagricultural societies. The rise in population density then makes the society dependent on maintaining its agricultural economy. Should those in an agricultural society decide they want to migrate to preagricultural economic institutions, the land they occupied would not support them, because preagricultural societies are less productive per acre than agricultural societies.

The Agricultural Revolution required that legal, economic, and political institutions evolved together. Unlike preagricultural societies that are more mobile, agricultural societies are tied to the land they cultivate. Thus, they must develop mechanisms to protect that land from predators. Agricultural societies invest in capital and store crops and livestock for later consumption. They must develop mechanisms to protect their stored wealth.

Because workers in agricultural societies are more productive than those in preagricultural societies, they can produce a surplus over their own subsistence, which provides resources to support a separate class of people who oversee institutions of governance that protect individuals and their assets from potential predators. That surplus also provides an incentive for predators to attack and conquer agricultural societies, so the conquerors can appropriate the surplus. Agricultural societies cannot migrate away from conflict, as preagricultural societies can, so some of their production must be devoted to protecting their wealth.

Individuals in agricultural societies are not in a good position to protect themselves from predation. Individuals and groups with a comparative advantage in the use of violence will be able to take over and conquer those who have a comparative advantage in agriculture. Agricultural societies will be easy targets for predators because they are tied to their land and cannot run away from conflict. Unable to protect themselves, the masses will have to use some of their resources to employ a ruling class, and a warrior class, to protect them. To be effective, the ruling class will need the characteristics described in the Chapters 4 and 5 – a comparative advantage in the use of force and the ability to display sufficient power that people will perceive that it would be futile to try to oppose them. For this reason, rulers have often been those who are the most effective warriors.

For better or worse, the masses do not need to search for people to fulfill the role of the ruling class. History shows that, in fact, the rulers seek out and conquer those they rule. Governments have been formed throughout history as some people have conquered and taken over others by force and declared themselves to be rulers. The ruled have little alternative but to comply. Until very recently in human history, there was no illusion that the ruling class ruled as the result of some social contract – some agreement among the ruled to subject themselves to the mandates of a ruling class. The rulers took over and ruled their subjects by force.

The evolution from preagricultural societies to agricultural societies has necessarily been slow. Agricultural societies require institutions of governance with sufficient coercive power to protect them, and to pay for those institutions requires that societies produce a surplus above a subsistence level of production. Because an agricultural economy can invest in tools, in structures, and in developing more productive farming techniques, its productivity grows over time, providing more resources to the ruling class. Because the ruling class wants to rule over more resources so it can increase the tribute it can collect, greater productivity of the masses is directly beneficial to the ruling class, but also provides a source of resources the ruling class can use for further conquest, to enlarge its rule and its revenue.

The development of political institutions of authority and governance requires economic institutions with the productivity to support those political institutions. At the same time, the development of productive economic institutions requires institutions of authority and governance to protect that productivity. This bidirectional dependency has meant that institutional development has necessarily been slow. Economic institutions cannot develop beyond the ability of political institutions to protect them, and political institutions cannot develop beyond the ability of economic institutions to support them.

The ruling class provides order to the society it oversees and, at the same time, must protect its citizens from foreign invaders to retain its power. The essential exchange between the rulers and the ruled is an exchange of protection for tribute.[16] The ruling class also looks for weak targets it could conquer to enlarge its territory. Conquest benefits the ruling class both from the tribute it can collect from the conquered and because its conquests eliminate potential rivals.

COMPLEXITY AND HIERARCHY

David Graeber and David Wengrow question whether a larger society necessarily brings with it a more hierarchical society, saying

> It does seem to be received wisdom in many quarters, academic and otherwise, that structures of domination are the inevitable result of populations scaling up by orders of magnitude; that is, that a necessary correspondence exists between social and spatial hierarchies. Time and again we found ourselves confronted with writing which simply assumes that the larger and more densely populated the social group, the more 'complex' the system needed to keep it organized.... Complex systems don't have to be organized top-down, either in the natural or social world.[17]

That last sentence is certainly true. A market economy is a perfect example of a decentralized complex spontaneous order organized from the bottom-up. The hierarchy that divides elites from the masses does not come from the complexity of the system, but from the necessity to have institutions of authority and governance once societies grow larger than Dunbar's number. Societies can be very egalitarian when everyone knows everyone else, and when institutional constraints can be enforced informally, based on individual reputations that are known to the whole group. When societies become too large for informal governance to be effective, transaction costs prevent everyone from participating in the design and enforcement of governance.

Those institutions of authority and governance are imposed on the masses by those who have a comparative advantage in the use of force. Even if the masses benefit from those institutions, they have little choice

---

[16] This is the economic foundation of government, according to Randall G. Holcombe, *The Economic Foundations of Government* (New York: New York University Press, 1994).
[17] David Graeber and David Wengrow, *The Dawn of Everything*, p. 515.

but to accept them. Resistance is costly. But, as already noted, an agricultural society requires institutions of authority and governance to protect the society's assets from predation. Jean-Jacques Rousseau argued that inequality among members of a society arises because of the establishment of private ownership of property.[18] The preceding analysis supports Rousseau's conclusion. Someone claiming an ownership right over an immobile asset must have a way to enforce that claim against others who may be able to take that property by force, giving rise to an elite group with the power to protect claims to property. In many cases, those ownership claims were made by those who took the property by force as agricultural societies spread and gradually displaced hunter-gatherers.

GOVERNANCE AND THE DIVISION OF LABOR

One advantage that strong institutions of governance bring to agricultural societies is a third-party enforcement mechanism to punish those who violate institutional constraints. If someone commits fraud or theft, the victim can appeal to government law enforcement to act against the perpetrator. The ruling class wants to create an orderly society. Independent institutions of governance enable societies to grow beyond Dunbar's number. People can interact directly with others they do not know because those interactions are structured within institutions and protected by the ruling class.

A larger society gives rise to a greater division of labor, which leads to a more productive society. Adam Smith began his great book, *The Wealth of Nations*, by saying, "The greatest improvement in the productive powers of labour, and the greater part of the skill, dexterity, and judgment with which it is any where directed, or applied, seem to have been the effects of the division of labour."[19] But, as Smith later noted, the division of labor is limited by the extent of the market. The larger the society, the greater the potential for specialization and division of labor, and as a result, the greater will be the productivity of the society.

Agriculture, by itself, is more productive than hunting and gathering. But agriculture brings with it the requirement to have strong institutions of governance to protect the immobile assets of an agricultural population. These institutions of governance, in turn, enable a larger society, and

---

[18] Jean-Jacques Rousseau, *Discourse on the Origin of Inequality* (Indianapolis, IN: Hackett Publishing Company, 1992 [orig. 1755]).

[19] Adam Smith, *The Wealth of Nations* (New York: Modern Library, 1937 [orig. 1776]), p. 3.

because of the greater division of labor, a more productive one. A more productive society creates a greater surplus that can be appropriated by the ruling class, which in turn gives the ruling class more resources to maintain and enlarge the territory over which it rules.

MOBILITY AND AUTHORITY IN AGRICULTURAL SOCIETIES

The ruling class holds more power over those it rules in an agricultural society than does anyone with power in a preagricultural society because the masses are less mobile. The key factor of production in an agricultural society is land, and the masses are tied to the land they work. In a preagricultural society, where the key factor of production is labor, individuals can leave and take their labor with them. In an agricultural society, where the key factor of production is land, people who leave must leave the land they work behind. As a result, the masses in agricultural societies are relatively immobile, and therefore unable to escape the authority of the ruling class. This gives the ruling class in an agricultural society the ability to be more oppressive and more authoritarian than leaders in preagricultural societies.

Preagricultural societies tend to be relatively egalitarian. Agricultural societies tend to be very hierarchical, because the masses have no good way to escape the authority of the ruling class. While the increased productivity of an agricultural society offers the potential to increase the standard of living of the masses, the power of the ruling class prevents this from happening. Rather, any surplus above a subsistence income is taken by the ruling class. Rising productivity enabled some population growth, which gives the ruling class more labor under their control, but the historical fact that most people were relegated to living on a subsistence level income was obvious enough that when Thomas Robert Malthus published his *Essay on Population* in 1798 to explain that fact, his explanation that population tended to grow faster than resources available to support the population became conventional wisdom.[20]

Competition for power means that the ruling class must devote resources to maintaining and increasing its power. Some of the surplus production above subsistence is devoted to building armies that can protect the rulers' territory and perhaps enlarge it. Roman legions took over

---

[20] Thomas Robert Malthus, *An Essay on the Principle of Population* (London: J. Johnson, 1798).

Europe, medieval lords had armies of knights to fight their battles, and the British army and navy were able to give the King of England control over much of the world. Rulers who do not use resources at their command to defend and enlarge their power will find themselves forcibly displaced by those who do.

In preagricultural societies, authority comes from one's authority over people. In agricultural societies, authority comes from control over land. By controlling the land, rulers gain control over the immobile people who occupy the land. Thus, from the beginning of the Agricultural Revolution up through the twenty-first century, the ruling class has acted to maintain control of the land it rules and to enlarge its territory. In agricultural societies, control of land means control over an economy's productive assets.

The relative equality and limited authority of those with power in preagricultural societies came from the mobility of the key factor of production in that type of economy – labor. The substantial power and unquestioned authority of the ruling class in agricultural societies came from the immobility of the key factor of production in that type of economy – land. Comparing agricultural with preagricultural societies, one can see why those in the relatively egalitarian preagricultural societies which allowed individuals more freedom and more autonomy would prefer that lifestyle to the hierarchical agricultural societies and the more oppressive institutions of authority and governance that came with them. Despite the increased productivity of agricultural societies, one can make good arguments that they lowered the quality of life of the masses when compared to preagricultural societies.

STABILITY OR PROGRESS?

Political stability is always an objective of the ruling class. The ruling class wants to prevent any challenges to their rule. Progress is a challenge to stability, because progress can upset the status quo. Economic progress could bring more resources under the control of the ruling class, but it also could bring more power to the entrepreneurs who create that progress – power that could be used to challenge the existing elite. Throughout most of history, the ruling class has worked to preserve the status quo and to stifle progress.

Indeed, progress is a modern concept. Prior to the 1700s, nobody would have noticed any economic progress in their lifetimes. The economic world into which they were born would be the same one in which they died. They would produce and consume the same goods, using the same production methods, their entire lives, and most would remain at a subsistence level of income. Someone living in the Roman Empire around 500 AD who was magically transferred to Britain in 1500 AD, a thousand years later, would notice little difference in the types of goods consumed, the average standard of living, or production methods. Fields were being plowed by animal-drawn plows, and manual labor was the source of most productive power.

Civilization in ancient Rome was considerably more advanced than in preagricultural societies, but those advances had come gradually over the centuries, to the point that progress was too slow for individuals to perceive as it occurred. The ruling class had no reason to support any type of change. They were at the top of the social hierarchy and enjoyed wealth well beyond that of the masses. Their subjects viewed it as an obligation to obey the mandates of their rulers and were unable to escape their rule. The immobility of labor increased the scope of authority of the ruling class, resulting in more authoritarian government. The power of the ruling class in agricultural societies comes from the immobility of land, which prevents the mobility of the masses.

The relative immobility of people in agricultural societies creates more of a hierarchical society, and stifles progress. Joseph Schumpeter described the progress that took place in capitalist economies as creative destruction, and those at the top of the power hierarchy act to stifle creativity, to lessen the threat that they end up victims of the resulting destruction.[21] In light of the remarkable progress that has occurred since the beginning of the Industrial Revolution, the almost imperceptible progress that characterizes agricultural societies is noteworthy.

THE EMERGENCE OF CAPITALISM

Well-established markets have existed for thousands of years, and small numbers of people have made their living through commerce. But market economies, in which people produced goods and services to be sold in the market and bought the goods and services they consumed in the market, are relatively recent. The shift was not abrupt. Over time more and more people relied on the market for more and more of what they consumed until, in the twenty-first century, almost everything most people consume is produced by someone else and acquired through market transactions.

---

[21] Joseph A. Schumpeter, *Capitalism, Socialism, and Democracy*, 2nd ed. (London: George Allen & Unwin, 1947).

As an economic system, capitalism can be thought of as an institutional setting in which there are markets for factors of production, and in particular, markets for capital.[22] Markets for factors of production are only a few hundred years old and emerged along with the Industrial Revolution. In Europe, and elsewhere around the world, feudalism was the dominant economic system prior to the emergence of capitalism. In place of a market for labor, serfs produced goods for everyone, and rulers and their armies were obligated to provide security to those serfs. The economic system was not simply a process of bartering the services of the rulers for the services of the ruled. There were mutual obligations each group had to the other.

As medieval cities arose, labor was organized through a guild system in which guild masters and their apprentices had mutual obligations toward each other. Even with slave labor, slave owners had obligations – although not necessarily legal obligations – toward their slaves, if for no other reason than to preserve the value of the assets they owned.

The Industrial Revolution brought with it widespread markets for labor as a commodity. As serfs migrated from the countryside to cities, factory owners exchanged wages for labor with their employees. The labor market incurred no further obligations on either party. As long as the exchange was mutually agreeable, workers and employers exchanged labor for wages, treating labor as a commodity. The commodification of labor was one of the objections Karl Marx raised about capitalism.[23]

A similar phenomenon occurred with land. In agricultural societies, where control over land conveyed power to landowners, people would not voluntarily choose to give up their ownership of land. As commerce became more widespread, landholders began shifting the way they were compensated for the land they controlled. Rather than the mutual obligations of serfdom, sharecropping and tenant farming became increasingly common. Land, once considered a permanent part of one's estate, which would be given up only under duress, also became a potential source of revenue as markets for land developed.

Most significant for the development of capitalism, markets for capital emerged in which people with more resources than they could

---

[22] Robert L. Heilbroner, *The Making of Economic Society* (Englewood Cliffs, NJ: Prentice-Hall, 1962) identifies market economies as those economies that have markets for factors of production.

[23] Karl Marx, *Capital: A Critique of Political Economy* (Chicago, IL: Charles H. Kerr & Company, 1906).

immediately use could lend them, or invest them, with people who had productive ways to use those resources. The wealthy had other options rather than just building ever-grander homes on their estates – options that offered them ways to build their wealth.

THE DEVELOPMENT OF CAPITAL MARKETS

Capital markets developed as people created institutions to lower transaction costs, to facilitate mutually advantageous exchange. Early financial markets developed in Amsterdam, a city that generated a large share of its income through commerce. One way wealthy people could enhance their wealth was to buy and provision a sailing ship, which would be loaded with goods in Amsterdam to set sail for foreign ports, as far away as India, where those goods could be traded with the locals. Trade was very profitable, as long as the ships came back with foreign goods, but sometimes those ships did not come back. They could be destroyed by storms at sea, raided by pirates, or overtaken by mutiny. The phrase "when my ship comes in" to represent good fortune goes back to those days when all ships that set sail did not come back.

The Dutch East India Company was formed in 1594 to mitigate the risk involved in sending out these ships. Most of the ships came back, but rather than individuals bearing the risk that their ship would not return, a group of investors pooled their money to send out many ships, agreeing to share the profits and losses. The expense of provisioning and sending out the ships was shared up front, and then the profits would be shared as the ships returned. Some would not, but most did, making the Dutch East India Company very profitable. Seeing the profit, the owners decided to reinvest those profits rather than pay them out, to bring in even more profits.

Should investors want to get their money out, they would have to find someone willing to buy their shares. Similarly, those who wanted the opportunity to invest would need to find an owner willing to sell. The transaction costs involved in searching for mutually advantageous exchanges presented a profit opportunity that was seized by brokers who created a market in which anyone could buy or sell their shares. Brokers made a market in shares by agreeing to purchase the shares of anyone who wanted to sell and agreeing to sell shares to anyone who wanted to buy. Prices of shares were set by the market so that the quantity supplied equaled the quantity demanded. The system worked well enough for the

Dutch East India Company that other companies began issuing publicly traded stock in their businesses.[24]

Nobody set out to design a stock market from the ground up. Rather, when transaction costs stood in the way of potential sellers locating potential buyers, financial institutions emerged to make those matches. At first, someone saw a profit opportunity in operating as a central clearing house for Dutch East India stock, which opened opportunities to do the same for other companies, eventually developing into very sophisticated global financial markets. Nobody planned out the final result. It emerged, little by little, as people found new ways to lower transaction costs.[25]

CAPITAL IS MOBILE

As capitalism emerged to spark the Industrial Revolution, the key factor of production shifted from land to capital. An acre of land devoted to manufacturing will generate much more income than an acre of land devoted to agriculture, and factories can be built in almost any jurisdiction. A big difference between land and capital is that capital is mobile.

The sailing ships owned by the Dutch East India Company obviously are mobile, but even something like a factory or a warehouse can be built in many locations. Once built, a factory may be relatively immobile, but another characteristic that facilitates the mobility of capital is that it depreciates. Land stays where it is and maintains its productivity. Capital must be maintained and eventually replaced. If the ruling class decided to appropriate someone's land and had the power to do so, the appropriated land would retain its value. If the ruling class decided to appropriate a factory, without also maintaining the factory, its value would quickly depreciate down to nothing. Meanwhile, factory owners have the option of maintaining their existing factories or instead investing in new factories in different locations.

The clear implication for institutions of governance is that the political elite who control those institutions will have less power and authority in an industrial economy than in an agricultural economy. Capital can migrate to those jurisdictions that provide capitalists with the greatest advantages. It is no coincidence that the Agricultural Revolution, which

---

[24] See Catia Antunes and Jos Gommans, *Exploring the Dutch Empire: Agents, Networks, and Institutions, 1600–2000* (London: Bloomsbury, 2015) for some historical background.

[25] This idea is explained by Friedrich A. Hayek, "The Use of Knowledge in Society," *American Economic Review* 35 (1945), pp. 519–530.

shifted the key factor of production from labor to land, also brought with it an increase in power and authority for the ruling class. And it is no coincidence that the Industrial Revolution, which shifted the key factor of production from land to capital, brought with it a reduction in power and authority for the ruling class. The economic institutions that identify an economy as industrial came along with political institutions that weakened the power of the ruling elite, and necessarily so, because the economic changes that come with industrialization create more mobility for the key factor of production.

ECONOMIC ANALYSIS OF FACTORS OF PRODUCTION

The importance of this shift in the significance of factors of production can be seen in the way economists have depicted them. David Ricardo, in his *Principles of Political Economy and Taxation*, published in 1817, depicted an economy in which output is a function of land, labor, and capital. He envisioned wages being pushed to a subsistence level because as population expanded, the fixed supply of land would continue to push food prices higher. A rise in labor costs would squeeze profits until, Ricardo said, "the very low rate of profits will have arrested all accumulation, and almost the whole produce of the country, after paying the labourers, will be the property of the owners of land and the receivers of tithes and taxes."[26]

Ricardo was offering readers the same message expressed by his friend and contemporary, Thomas Robert Malthus.[27] The trajectory of the economy is heavily determined by the scarcity of that key factor of production – land. Contrast that with the economic theory of the twentieth and twenty-first centuries, in which economists depict output as a function of capital and labor, which they symbolically depict as $Q = f(K, L)$. Land, the crucial factor of production when Ricardo wrote in 1817, does not even enter the production function of twenty-first-century economists.

Along the same lines, Karl Marx wrote about how capitalists exploit labor, noting that in feudal times, at least serfs could grow their own food on land they worked themselves. When the Industrial Revolution turned those serfs into factory workers, they were separated from the

---

[26] David Ricardo, *Principles of Political Economy and Taxation*, 3rd ed. (London: John Murray, 1821), p. 79.
[27] Malthus, *An Essay on the Principle of Population*.

land and dependent on the jobs capitalists offered for their survival.[28] In contrast to capitalism as described by Marx, Thomas Piketty's *Capital in the Twenty-First Century*, which offers Marx's same message of exploitation, does not even include land as a separate factor of production, instead lumping it together with capital.[29] As economists have depicted it in their theories, land has gone from the key factor of production in the early 1800s to, at best, an afterthought by the mid twentieth century, as capital has taken that position.

The implication for institutions of governance is that the Industrial Revolution weakened the power and authority of the ruling class because economic activity can more easily migrate away from the abuses of power. Governments assert their authority within a given geographic area. Land cannot escape that boundary of authority, but capital can.[30] If the ruling class does not entice the entrepreneurial class to remain within their jurisdictions, entrepreneurs will leave and take with them the resources that otherwise might be appropriated by the rulers.

THE RESOURCE CURSE

Many individuals have noted that nations with abundant natural resources tend to be relatively poor.[31] The analysis of this chapter offers a clear explanation. Natural resources are in a fixed location, like land, which gives the ruling elite more power and authority over economies that rely on them. If the ruling elite can rely on mineral revenues, for example, it can cement its authority by reducing the autonomy of its citizens. This creates the stability that preserves the status quo, including the existing political leadership. Preserving their authority is a primary objective of the ruling elite. Resource-rich nations, in this regard, are like the agricultural societies described earlier. Citizens can leave, but they cannot take their country's natural resources with them, which enables an oppressive government and fosters economic stagnation.

---

[28] Karl Marx and Friedrich Engels, *The Communist Manifesto* (New York: International Publishers, 1948 [orig. 1848]).

[29] Thomas Piketty, *Capital in the Twenty-First Century* (Cambridge, MA: Harvard University Press, 2014).

[30] This is explained by Richard B. McKenzie and Dwight R. Lee, *Quicksilver Capital: How the Rapid Movement of Wealth Has Changed the World* (New York: Free Press, 1991).

[31] Jeffrey D. Sachs and Andrew M. Warner, "Natural Resources and Economic Development: The Curse of Natural Resources," *European Economic Review* 45 (2001), pp. 827–838 give evidence that this is the case.

INTERGOVERNMENTAL COMPETITION

In agricultural societies, where the key factor of production is land, the only way to gain more land is to acquire more territory, which in practice has meant taking it from someone else. One can see how the competition for power among ruling elites would lead to wars, and to those with more power conquering and ruling over those with less. When capital is the key factor of production, the ruling elite does not need to enlarge its territory to increase the amount of capital that is subject to its authority.

Capital is attracted to locations where it can be used most profitably, so the ruling elite have an incentive to design institutions that do not stand in the way of its profitability. This places constraints on rulers and reduces their power and scope of authority. The ruling class in the United States has increased its share of global power not by conquering more territory, but by encouraging investment and enlarging the nation's capital stock.

Intergovernmental competition for productive resources is much stronger in an industrial world than in an agricultural one. Competing rulers do not have to physically battle each other in a competition for territory when capital is the primary factor of production. They cannot expand their authority over capital by winning wars. They compete with each other by making their jurisdictions more profitable for investors.[32]

Polycentric political organizations that are composed of competing and overlapping jurisdictions can act as a constraint on the power of the political elites in all jurisdictions. Polycentricity also brings with it diversity that enables residents to compare the performance of their jurisdictions with others. When factors of production are mobile, this provides an advantage to political elites who establish more productive institutions and a constraint on the abuse of political power.[33]

In preindustrial times, military conquest increased the power of the ruling elite by giving them control over more land. In that context, it is notable that the victors in World Wars I and II did not take over the territories of those they defeated, and in the second half of the twentieth century, nations that had colonized others granted their colonies independence. The value in controlling that land in preindustrial times no longer remained in an industrialized world.

---

[32] See McKenzie and Lee, *Quicksilver Capital*.
[33] These ideas are developed in Chandran Kukathas, *The Liberal Archipelago: A Theory of Diversity and Freedom* (Oxford: Oxford University Press, 2007) and Paul Dragos Aligica, Peter J. Boettke, and Vlad Tarko, *Public Governance and the Classical-Liberal Perspective: Political Economy Foundations* (Oxford: Oxford University Press, 2019).

In 1960 South Korea was one of the poorest countries in the world, and four decades later was among the wealthiest. Capital-friendly policies can work relatively rapidly, but they do constrain the ruling class. Meanwhile, its adversary, North Korea, has maintained its authoritarian institutions and has fallen further behind the South. The gains that South Korea has experienced over North Korea have come from controlling more capital, not more land. In the same vein, the rapid decline in the Venezuelan economy in the twenty-first century, after the election of Hugo Chavez, shows that capital-unfriendly policies can damage an economy in short order.

Poor economic performance may be something the political elite are willing to tolerate if they perceive that it gives them more power. Dictators can use oppressive tactics to maintain their power, as long as they can keep the support of their underlings who actually deploy the force that enables the political elite to maintain their power. But the rapid collapse of many Eastern European dictatorships after the fall of the Berlin Wall in 1989 shows the risks involved in ruling a discontented population through oppression.

One advantage economic growth brings to the ruling class is the opportunity to collect more in revenues from their citizens, but intergovernmental competition puts a check on how much revenue can be collected before capital moves to more tax-friendly jurisdictions. International tax competition has sometimes been described by government leaders as a race to the bottom, as nations compete with each other by offering continually lower taxes on mobile capital.

Nations with higher taxes depict those with lower taxes as stealing their tax bases. The rhetoric parallels what one might expect if one nation was taking over the territory of another – but there is less of a parallel when capital displaces land as the key factor of production. Whereas taking land from one jurisdiction to enlarge another necessarily reduces the amount of land in the first jurisdiction, investment in one jurisdiction does not necessarily lessen investment in others. Capital, unlike land area, can increase in every jurisdiction.

This intergovernmental competition has driven nations to try to craft tax treaties in which all agree not to cut their tax rates below a certain amount. Essentially, governments cartelize themselves by agreeing not to compete based on offering their subjects a more favorable tax climate. This has obvious benefits for the ruling class, because it reduces the threat to the revenue they control, but it reduces the mobility of capital. Indeed, that is the intention. These treaties are designed to lessen constraints on the ruling class, giving them more power and authority. This is the mindset of the ruling class. Rather than designing rules that make people want to move into their jurisdictions, they prefer rules that make it more difficult for the masses to escape.

To limit intergovernmental competition, governments form cartel arrangements to prevent competition among them. Organizations like the World Bank, the World Trade Organization, and the United Nations can serve this function. The mobility of capital is a major factor that has constrained the exercise of power by the ruling class since the Industrial Revolution began and explains why rulers prior to the Industrial Revolution had more power and authority over their citizens than those since. Mobility requires that people have some place to go, and international collusion among governments is designed to reduce the attractiveness of migration.

FACTORS OF PRODUCTION AND THE LIMITS OF AUTHORITY

The power of the political elite is constrained to the degree that the masses are able to escape their authority by migrating to another jurisdiction. Economic factors of production have played a large role in determining the limits of authority of the political elite. The increased importance of capital as a factor of production since the beginning of the Industrial Revolution has made it easier for resources to migrate away from jurisdictions in which the ruling class abuses their authority.

Economic history can be divided into three broad periods, each with a different factor of production being the key element in its effect on institutions of governance. In preagricultural societies, labor is the key factor of production, which affords substantial mobility to members of hunter-gatherer societies. The agricultural revolution, which began around 10,000 BC, saw land become the key factor of production, which reduced the mobility of individuals. The emergence of capitalism and the Industrial Revolution undermined the authority of the ruling class as capital displaced land as the key factor of production. The ruling class could continue to defend their geographic borders – their land – but capital can more easily migrate from one location to another. That places constraints on the use of authority by the ruling class beyond those they faced when land was the key factor of production.

The importance of mobility as a constraint on the use of authority has been recognized by the political elite, who in various countries have prevented their citizens from leaving, imposed capital controls to try to prevent capital from leaving, and who have entered into cartel arrangements to prevent countries from enacting policies that make their countries relatively more attractive to capital. The elite few who transact in the political marketplace have substantial power over the masses, who are excluded from the political marketplace. But that power is mitigated to the degree that the mobility of people and resources enables the masses to escape from abuses of power.

CONSTRAINING LEVIATHAN

The first ten chapters describe a society ruled by a small elite, enacting public policies for their own benefit, often at the expense of the masses. One might rightly object that since the Enlightenment, strong governments have laid the foundation for increasing prosperity and increasing freedom, a trend that has lasted hundreds of years. Despite those historical facts, it is also apparent that an elite few do write and enforce the rules, and that the power to do so gives them advantages not available to the masses. The reason the masses have gained more freedom and a higher standard of living is that economic developments have constrained the ability of the elite to abuse their power.

The political elite produce no goods and services for consumption; they rely on the masses to produce goods for themselves and to produce a sufficient surplus to support the ruling class. Among the constraints on elite abuse of power, the most substantial is the increased mobility that capitalism has brought to the masses.

12

Democracy and Authority

Democracy is often viewed as the ultimate check on the abuse of authority. A romantic notion of democracy depicts democratic governments as accountable to their citizens and acting in the best interests of their citizens. The shortcomings of this view of democracy have been discussed at length. All governments are run by an elite few who negotiate in the political marketplace to determine public policy. The masses are excluded from that process because they face high transaction costs, which prevent them from having any influence over the process.

While the votes of all voters determine who exercises the powers of government, any one individual's vote will have no perceptible impact on election outcomes. Thus, voters tend to be rationally ignorant of the alternatives in elections,[1] often vote irrationally,[2] and tend to vote based on factors other than what would be good for them and their fellow citizens.[3] Because they have little incentive to be informed, they tend to adopt their public policy preferences from members of the political elite who tell them what they should think.

Academic analysis of democratic elections generally supports the romantic notion of democracy. In academic models of voting, voters are assumed to have preferences, and parties and candidates adjust their

---

[1] Anthony Downs, *An Economic Theory of Democracy* (New York: Harper & Row, 1957).
[2] Bryan Caplan, *The Myth of the Rational Voter: Why Democracies Choose Bad Policies* (Princeton, NJ: Princeton University Press, 2007).
[3] Geoffrey Brennan and Loren Lomasky, *Democracy and Decision: The Pure Theory of Electoral Preference* (Cambridge: Cambridge University Press, 1993).

platforms to conform with voter preferences.[4] In fact, the direction of causation (mostly) goes in the opposite direction. The political elite tell their supporters what policies they should favor, and citizens follow their leaders, so their public policy preferences conform with the political platforms of the elite rather than the other way around. There are competing elites, as Chapter 13 discusses, so citizens do have a choice about which elites they want to follow, and this may influence the policy platforms candidates and parties try to sell to citizens and voters. This does not alter the fact that citizens and voters adopt the policy preferences offered them by the elite.[5]

In an important way, mobility places greater constraints on the use and abuse of political power than democracy. Citizens and voters have little incentive to be engaged in the political process. It does not matter how they vote, or if they vote, because their one vote will have no effect on an election outcome, or on public policy. However, an individual's decision to move has actual consequences for that individual. People have an incentive to be well-informed about any decision to move because it determines where they will reside. In contrast, when voting, people have no incentive to cast informed votes because the same people will be elected regardless of how they vote. Unlike voting, an individual's decision to move actually affects that individual's life. However, moving is costly – often costly enough to prevent people from migrating to jurisdictions with better political institutions.

E. E. Schattschneider remarks,

> The tendency of the literature of politics is to place a tremendous premium on the role of the interested and to treat indifference as a mortal sin, but the reluctance of the public to press its opinions on the government concerning a great multitude of issues is really not as bad as we may have been led to think; it is a mark of reasonableness and common sense.[6]

Voters must realize that they, as individuals, have no influence over public policy, so it is indeed reasonable to remain disinterested over things that are out of an individual's control.

---

[4] The median voter model, described by Downs, *An Economic Theory of Democracy*, concludes that democratic elections produce the outcome most preferred by the median voter, a conclusion that remains well-accepted in the twenty-first century.

[5] Randall G. Holcombe, *Following Their Leaders: Political Preferences and Public Policy* (Cambridge: Cambridge University Press, 2023) is a book-length explanation of the statements in this paragraph.

[6] E. E. Schattschneider, *The Semisovereign People: A Realist's View of Democracy in America* (New York: Holt, Rinehart, and Winston, 1960), p. 134.

The romantic notion of democracy as a government accountable to its citizens and acting in their interests is, at minimum, an overstatement, but to the extent that it is believed, it legitimizes the actions of the political elite. The idea is not only questionable, it is potentially harmful to the interests of most citizens.

THE IDEOLOGY OF DEMOCRACY

The acceptance of Enlightenment ideas brought with it the demand for democratic government that threatened the status of the ruling class. But while the ideology of democracy threatened to undermine the power of the political class, it was also employed by them to legitimize that power. The adoption of democratic institutions offered a justification for the mandates of the ruling class – the justification that those mandates were chosen by the people. Rather than being run by a king or dictator, democratic institutions are designed to channel the actions of the political elite to further the interests of its citizens. In a powerful defense of that romantic notion of democracy, Jean Jacques Rousseau said, back in 1762,

> The citizen gives his consent to all the laws, including those which are passed in spite of his opposition, and even those which punish him when he dares break any of them.... When in the popular assembly a law is proposed, what the people is asked is not exactly whether it approves or rejects the proposal, but whether it is in conformity with the general will, which is their will. When therefore the opinion that is contrary to my own prevails, this proves neither more nor less than that I was mistaken, and that what I thought was the general will was not so.[7]

Rousseau's idealistic vision of democracy legitimizes the actions of the ruling class by saying that when they negotiate with each other to make policy decisions in the political marketplace, democratic institutions direct their actions to further the general will. Anyone who disagrees is mistaken. While Hobbes argued that the masses should obey the dictates of their rulers to prevent a war of all against all, Rousseau said that the masses should obey the dictates of their rulers because democratic political institutions lead the ruling class to act in the best interest of the masses – to further the general will.

---

[7] Jean Jacques Rousseau, *The Social Contract, Or Principles of Political Right*, Translated by G. D. H. Cole (London: J. M. Dent and Sons, 1923 [orig. 1762]), Book IV, ch. 1, no. 2. While this is a translation from French, note that Rousseau twice refers to people in the singular, reinforcing the view that people have (has?) a common interest.

Is Rousseau's vision of democracy descriptive, or is it propaganda that legitimizes elite rule? The ruling class has an incentive to promote Rousseau's vision of democratic government to the masses, because Rousseau's vision tells citizens that if they disagree that the actions of the ruling class further the general will, they, the citizens, are wrong. To the extent that it is accepted, this ideology of democracy – that democratic governments are accountable to their citizens and act in the interest of their citizens – returns to the ruling class the authority that was threatened by the popularization of Enlightenment ideas. Citizens are obligated to abide by the mandates of their governments not because they have a duty to serve their rulers but because the institutions of democratic governments lead the political elite to act in the public interest.

The ideology of democracy conveys the authority to demand compliance to the ruling class because that ideology declares that democratic institutions give citizens oversight and control of their governments. Democratic governments have the authority to govern because, the ideology of democracy asserts, that government is empowered by the masses and is acting in their interests. Rousseau's statement explains this more clearly than is often the case. Rousseau's reasoning gives the ruling class the legitimate right to mandate the allowable actions of the masses – to require them to do certain things, and prohibit them from doing others. That authority comes because they are the elected representatives of the people.

Robert Michels observes that while voters may choose who holds elective office, after an election, democratically elected leaders gain the same powers as dictators. "In actual fact, directly after the election is finished, the power of the mass of electors over the delegate comes to an end."[8] Michels concludes, "Under representative government the difference between democracy and monarchy, which both are rooted in the representative system, is altogether insignificant – a difference not in substance but in form. The sovereign people elects, in place of a king, a number of kinglets."[9] In democracies, the ruling class derives their authority from what has been referred to as the consent of the governed.

ENLIGHTENMENT AND DEMOCRACY

The Age of Enlightenment, which ran from the mid 1600s up through the early 1800s, brought with it substantial changes in governance,

---

[8] Robert Michels, *Political Parties: A Sociological Study of the Oligarchical Tendencies of Modern Democracy* (Glencoe, IL: Free Press, 1915), p. 45.

[9] Michels, *Political Parties*, p. 43.

along with substantial changes in many other aspects of society. The Industrial Revolution began during that period, perhaps as a result of Enlightenment ideas, or perhaps as one of the causes of Enlightenment ideas. But as Chapter 11 noted, the shift from agricultural economies to industrial economies brought with it a necessary change in the institutions of governance. The ruling class had to deal with a more mobile, and a more productive, citizenry. This, in turn, gave citizens the power to demand more of the ruling class.

The ruling class did not choose to shift the primary form of government from monarchy to democracy. That change was forced upon them. And, it did not occur by somehow requiring that rulers be elected. Rather, the political marketplace was expanded to include representatives of, first, nobility, and later, the general citizenry. Over time, those who were elected gained power relative to those who were not. The process was gradual, as resources became more mobile as the result of industrialization. It was the result of negotiation in a political market. Causation was bidirectional. More democratic political institutions facilitated industrialization, while industrialization forced more democratic political institutions.

Changes were, for the most part, gradual. As some nations industrialized and moved to more democratic political institutions, much of the world remained governed by hierarchical governance structures and rulers who maintained their power through the overt display of force. In places that shifted to more democratic political institutions, change there was also slow. Democracy did not displace monarchy by revolution, but by evolution – the result of bargaining among monarchs and those whose political power came from democratic elections. A more mobile population was able to demand, by degrees, that their representatives have access to the political marketplace.

THE EVOLUTION OF GOVERNANCE AND POWER

While every government is different in its details, Roger Congleton presents a framework that describes the way that all governments tend to be organized.[10] As a general rule, governments are headed by a single chief executive, supported by a council of individuals who also are members of the political elite and share power. Congleton refers to this as a king and council type of political organization. It is descriptive of monarchies,

---

[10] Roger D. Congleton, *Perfecting Parliament: Constitutional Reform, Liberalism, and the Rise of Western Democracy* (Cambridge: Cambridge University Press, 2011).

but also governments that have a president and a legislature, a prime minister and parliament, and dictatorships that have advisors and supporters behind the dictator. Local governments have mayors and city commissions, and state governments have a governor and a state legislature. This general model is descriptive of the organization of most governments. The way that individuals are selected for those positions of political power varies among governments, and the power of the chief executive relative to others in the political elite also varies.

As the world has industrialized over many centuries, the authority of the chief executive has been constrained by an increase in the power of the council, and by an increasing voice given to citizens through democratic institutions. While this has not been universally true – the Kim dynasty in North Korea provides a good counterexample – that trend has been widespread and has accompanied the economic developments that were described in Chapter 11. Just as agricultural societies have the advantage of increased productivity over preagricultural societies, so tend to displace them, so do industrial societies have a productivity advantage over agricultural societies.

Agricultural societies can support larger populations than preagricultural societies, and industrial societies can support larger populations than agricultural societies, so once those transitions are made, going back would require reductions in population and the associated hardships. This does not imply a value judgment that one type of society is better than another, but rather that when a transition is made to a more productive type of economic organization, the population becomes dependent on those economic institutions for their survival.

Societies compete with one another. As democratic institutions emerged, competition often was more than just economic; it was also military. Britain, Spain, France, and other European nations competed to control world markets and to colonize areas outside Europe. And, European nations fought among themselves. The political elite benefit from more productive institutions, which can give themselves more power than their rival elites in other nations. Places that did not see the same economic progress as was occurring in Europe were colonized by the European powers.

PREDEMOCRATIC INSTITUTIONS

While democratic institutions can be traced back at least to ancient Greece, the contemporary concept of representative democracy evolved along with the Enlightenment. Pre-Enlightenment, monarchy was the dominant form of government in the most economically advanced nations. Even as the Enlightenment began, most of the world had preagricultural economies and preagricultural forms of governance. In 1700, with monarchy as the dominant form of government in the most economically productive nations, and with European nations extending their reach, and their rule, throughout the world, it would have been difficult to imagine that a few centuries later, democracy would become the dominant form of world government.

As Roman rule eroded in Europe, governance was run by feudal barons who were supported by knights, for protection and conquest, and by serfs who were attached to the land and obligated to serve their lords. Economic transactions were in-kind, as the serfs produced goods for everyone's consumption in exchange for the protection provided by their rulers. In these agricultural societies in which land was the primary factor of production, the barons had to devote resources to protecting their land and, if they had sufficient strength, to expanding their territory. As a means of protection, barons had an incentive to form alliances with each other, eventually leading to the most powerful barons becoming kings.

Barons paid tribute to the king and provided soldiers in exchange for the king's protection. The arrangement protected them both from foreign invaders and from their neighboring barons. Should disputes arise between barons, the king had the authority to settle them. The barons had obligations to the king, and the king also had obligations to the barons. This arrangement minimized the potential for conflict among the barons by conveying authority to the king. The barons, united under the king, would be in a better position to repel foreign invaders, and to engage in foreign conquests, than they would be if they acted on their own.[11]

The ambitions of the British crown laid the foundation for the more decentralized British government. The king had foreign policy ambitions that required financing and manpower. The king did not have the ability to simply mandate that these obligations be fulfilled. He had to make the case that his operations were in the best interest of the nation, which in practice meant in the best interest of the barons. The king shared more power with the barons in exchange for their providing more resources.

---

[11] Medieval institutions are described by Douglass C. North and Robert P. Thomas, *The Rise of the Western World: A New Economic History* (Cambridge: Cambridge University Press, 1973).

The governments in France and Spain, Britain's primary global rivals, remained more centralized. Throughout Europe, the relationships between king and council – the barons – and the degree to which they shared power were the product of negotiation within a political marketplace, determined by the bargaining power of those involved in the negotiations.

The Roman Catholic Church also provided countervailing power in medieval Europe. The masses recognized religious authority, and the religious elite validated the power of the political elite. Thus, church leaders were able to participate in the political marketplace, and act as a check on the power of the political elite. But, all parties must view political exchanges as beneficial to participate in them. When King Henry VIII of England viewed the Catholic Church as unwilling to meet his terms, he established the Anglican Church as the Church of England in 1534, replacing the Catholic Church's authority with a new church under his supervision.

The king, along with lesser nobility and church leaders, participated in the political marketplace to determine public policy. The masses, who were tied to the land and relied on the ruling class for protection, had little option but to yield to the authority of their rulers. But the balance of power has shifted over time away from the head of state toward the council, to use Congleton's framework.

This is a very Eurocentric description of predemocratic governance. In other parts of the world that had developed past clan-based governance, Congleton's king and council framework was also descriptive, in China, and in central and south America. Taking a Eurocentric view of predemocratic political institutions makes some sense because modern democratic institutions emerged in Europe and were exported around the world. Within Europe, democratic institutions evolved first in Britain.[12]

THE EMERGENCE OF DEMOCRACY IN BRITAIN

Britain provided a template for other emerging democracies, partly because it provided a model of success, and partly because British colonization led to a direct export of British political institutions. Britain had the most democratic political institutions when the Industrial Revolution

---

[12] Congleton, *Perfecting Parliament*, shows the parallels between the development of British democracy and other European democracies.

began, which contributed toward Britain's industrialization. A less authoritarian government offers greater opportunities for entrepreneurship among its citizens. As nations with agricultural economies industrialized, they followed Britain's lead in democratizing their governments, not because the political elite wanted to, but because the increased mobility that came with industrialization forced them to.

The Magna Carta, agreed to in 1215, represents a major development in the political marketplace. People engage in political exchange for their mutual benefit, and the English barons believed that King John was abusing his power, demanding funds for unsuccessful foreign wars and failing to represent the interests of the barons. The king had a bargaining advantage, in that the many barons who pledged allegiance to the king would have to organize to oppose him, presenting a collective action problem for the barons. Even if all barons wanted to confront the king, if only a few were bold enough to actually do so, the king would be able to use his power to put down a few rebels. But the barons presented a united front against the king, giving them a more formal base of power. The Magna Carta created a council of twenty-five barons who advised the king and monitored his activity to assure the nation that he lived up to his part of the agreement.[13] This council of barons evolved into the British Parliament.

One power the council of barons gained was the ability to veto any new taxes. The creation of Parliament produced a formal institution within which transaction costs among members were low. When the king wanted resources, the consent of Parliament was required, which resulted in a gradual shift in power in the political marketplace from the crown to Parliament. As the bargaining power of Parliament increased, the power to veto new taxes enabled them to propose taxes they would not veto. Ultimately, this shifted the power to tax from the crown to Parliament, not as an explicit change in policy, but as the result of a gradual increase in the bargaining power of Parliament. While the old formal political institutions remained, British democracy evolved because of negotiations among the politically powerful in the political marketplace.

Britain had a bicameral parliament going back to the 1300s, with a House of Lords representing nobles and a House of Commons representing local governments.[14] Over time, as kings asked for resources from

---

[13] David Starkey, *Magna Carta: The True Story Behind the Charter* (London: Hodder & Stoughton, 2015).

[14] Details are described in Congleton, *Perfecting Parliament*, ch. 12.

the people, Parliament was able to bargain for more power in exchange for turning over resources to the king, and over time, power shifted from the House of Lords to the House of Commons. This is a good example of institutional evolution as a result of negotiation within the political marketplace. Power shifted away from the crown, toward Parliament, and toward the House of Commons, as the bargaining power of elected bodies increased.

The increasing power of Parliament in the 1600s enabled the body to assemble its own army, and ultimately depose King James II in the Glorious Revolution of 1688–1689, demonstrating the increased power of Parliament relative to the crown. One outcome was the creation of a formal Bill of Rights that established elections and freedom of speech within Parliament.[15] In addition, the approval of Parliament was required for the crown to appoint government ministers.

Much as with the power to tax, this power of approval evolved to the point where the prime minister and other government ministers effectively are appointed by Parliament. The power to veto the appointment of ministers gave Parliament the ability to convey to the crown candidates they would not veto, which then evolved to the point that Parliament was able to tell the crown who should be appointed. The formal arrangement that ministers are appointed by the crown has remained into the twenty-first century, so that nominally ministers are appointed by the crown even though effectively they are chosen by Parliament.

The shift in power has been the result of the increase in bargaining strength of Parliament over time. The bargaining strength of Parliament increased along with the increased productivity of capital, making factors of production more mobile. The emergence of democratic political institutions in Britain was evolutionary rather than revolutionary, operating through negotiations in the political marketplace. The history is well-known. It is more difficult to recognize that the historical evolution that led to more democratic political institutions was the result of a bargaining process in which the bargaining position of elected representatives became increasingly stronger. It was the result of negotiations in the political marketplace.

This pattern repeated itself throughout Europe. Democracy replaced monarchy not by eliminating the monarchs or selecting monarchs by popular vote, but by gradually reducing their power as it was transferred

---

[15] Barry Coward and Peter Gaunt, *The Stuart Age: England, 1603–1714*, 5th ed. (London: Routledge, 2017).

to popularly elected assemblies.[16] Democracy did not become dominant in Europe through revolution, but through evolution.

The broader lesson is that while political institutions are imposed on a society by the political elite, those institutions are the result of negotiations in a political marketplace in which only an elite few are able to transact. The bargaining power of elected representatives grew as the productivity and mobility of those they represented grew.

COMMERCE AND DEMOCRACY

The development of commerce provided an avenue of mobility for the masses. While commerce had been carried on for thousands of years, feudal societies produced most of what they consumed themselves, so advantages of commerce were peripheral to the well-being of the society. But as more goods became available due to the growth of commerce, market exchanges provided a way to gain the money to buy goods. Around 1050–1150, cities began emerging in Europe that undertook manufacturing for the purpose of commerce, allowing individuals to escape the authority of the feudal manor.[17] Thus began the evolution of agricultural societies into industrial ones, laying the foundation for the evolution of autocratic political institutions into democratic institutions.

Participation in the benefits of commercial society requires money. Barons could obtain money by moving some of their land from feudal relationships to sharecropping and tenant farming. This provided income to landholders, but it also provided a way for those who worked the land to earn income. If sharecroppers and tenant farmers were more productive, they could reap much of the benefit, rather than having it go to the ruling class as under feudal institutions. Feudal manors became less economically self-sufficient, but more productive under evolving institutional arrangements, as feudal relationships shifted to market relationships. At the same time, the breakdown in feudal relationships increased the mobility of the masses.

---

[16] As this is being written, monarchies remain in the United Kingdom, Norway, The Netherlands, Denmark, Sweden, Spain, Monaco, Luxembourg, Liechtenstein, Andorra, and Vatican City.
[17] This is discussed by Bernard Bailyn, *The Ideological Origins of the American Revolution* (Cambridge: Cambridge University Press, 1967).

CONSTITUTIONAL CONSTRAINTS

Constitutional rules can complement democratic political institutions to constrain the abuse of power by the elite. The Magna Carta offered an example earlier in this chapter, and the Constitution of the United States provides another example of formal constitutional rules that are designed to constrain the abuse of political power. Constitutional constraints do not have to be formalized as written agreements; they can be established through history and custom – the result of negotiations among the political elite on what powers can be exercised by different individuals. Britain has a constitutionally constrained government without a written constitution, for example.

By themselves, constitutional rules will be ineffective without an enforcement mechanism. One challenge is that the political elite are the ones who have the power of enforcement. One should expect lax enforcement when those who are supposed to be constrained by the rules are also the enforcers. The Constitution of the United States is a prime example. It was designed to limit the powers of government and guarantee the rights of its citizens. While the Constitution of the United States reserves those powers not explicitly given to the U.S. government to the states or to the people, the federal government has clearly gone beyond those bounds. It stretches the imagination to identify anything in the Constitution that gives the federal government the power to run a compulsory retirement program, but the Social Security system was approved by the legislative, executive, and judicial branches of government. Similarly, the commerce clause has been interpreted as classifying just about any economic activity as commerce among the states.

Constitutional rules are not constraints unless they are enforced.

CONSTITUTIONAL POLITICAL ECONOMY

The subfield of constitutional economics, promoted by Nobel laureate James Buchanan and others, is dedicated to identifying constitutional rules that can constrain the powers of government.[18] Work in this area has noted the tendency of government to expand its power and, in so doing, oppress those who are governed.[19] Thus, government must be

---

[18] See James M. Buchanan, "The Domain of Constitutional Economics," *Constitutional Political Economy* 1, no. 1 (December 1990), pp. 1–18.

[19] See James M. Buchanan, *The Limits of Liberty: Between Anarchy and Leviathan* (Chicago, IL: University of Chicago Press, 1975), and Geoffrey Brennan and James

constrained by a set of rules to prevent those in power from abusing it.[20] If those rules are general – they apply to everyone – and if they are durable, so they last beyond the ability of individuals to foresee all their consequences, people will tend to support rules that are beneficial to everyone.[21] Rules are easier to enforce when everyone agrees with them. But when designed as constraints to be placed on those who enforce them, they are likely to be ineffective.

The academic literature on politics as exchange has looked at political exchange at two different levels. One is political agreements that are made within the existing political institutions. The other is agreements that design those political institutions. Those institutions are humanly designed constraints. Buchanan says that economics in general analyzes the choices people make subject to constraints. Constitutional political economy analyzes the choice of constraints. As Buchanan defines it, constitutional decisions are decisions that determine the rules and institutions, and postconstitutional decisions are those made within the rules and institutions.

James Buchanan and Gordon Tullock, in their book *The Calculus of Consent*, offer good examples of politics as exchange at both levels.[22] They discuss the efficiency of logrolling, which is an example of postconstitutional decision-making. Politicians exchange within the existing set of political institutions. In their Chapter 6, they present a generalized theory of constitutions, in which they demonstrate that people might unanimously agree to a political decision rule of less-than-unanimity for postconstitutional decisions. The political decision rules are constitutional decisions. The decisions made within those decision rules are postconstitutional decisions.

Buchanan places heavy emphasis on the desirability of unanimous agreement for constitutional rules. His book, *The Limits of Liberty*,

---

M. Buchanan, *The Power to Tax: Analytical Foundations of a Fiscal Constitution* (Cambridge: Cambridge University Press, 1980).

[20] Geoffrey Brennan and James M. Buchanan, *The Reason of Rules: Constitutional Political Economy* (Cambridge: Cambridge University Press, 1986).

[21] James M. Buchanan and Roger D. Congleton, *Politics by Principle, Not Interest* (Cambridge: Cambridge University Press, 1998). Buchanan's constitutional framework has rested heavily on finding rules to which everyone would agree, under hypothetical circumstances. However, he has recognized that agreement must begin from the status quo, rather than from some idealized starting point. See Michael Munger and Georg Vanberg, "Contractarianism, Constitutionalism, and the Status Quo," *Public Choice* 195, nos. 3/4 (June 2023), pp. 323–339.

[22] James M. Buchanan and Gordon Tullock, *The Calculus of Consent: Logical Foundations of Constitutional Democracy* (Ann Arbor, MI: University of Michigan Press, 1962).

along with John Rawls's *A Theory of Justice*, has laid a foundation for the constitutional political economy research program.[23] Both develop theories about how people might be considered to agree to constitutional rules under hypothetical circumstances. Because of the close connection between Buchanan's use of politics as exchange and the constitutional political economy research program, two points of clarification should be made between Buchanan's normative vision of the desirability of unanimously agreed-upon constitutional rules and the analysis in this volume.

First, the present analysis does not deal with hypothetical political exchanges or agreements. The politics as exchange analyzed in this volume consists of actual political exchanges made among those who face low transaction costs in the political marketplace, and so can actually engage in exchange. It discusses exchanges that actually take place, not exchanges that might take place under hypothetical circumstances.

Second, this analysis suggests that in the actual political marketplace, there is at best a fuzzy distinction between constitutional and postconstitutional decision-making. Much of what occurs in the ordinary everyday political marketplace are negotiations about changing the rules of the game. While there is a clear distinction in theory between decisions about the rules of the game and decisions that are made within those rules, in practice, those decisions are made in the same way, by the same people.

Buchanan developed his device of hypothetical renegotiation of constitutional rules from a position of Hobbesian anarchy, and Rawls developed his device of negotiating rules from behind a veil of ignorance. Those devices are useful for some purposes, but hypothetical devices play no role in the analysis of this volume. In fact, constitutional rules and institutional structures are designed by people who know their interests and negotiate to further them. This idea was controversial when, in 1913, Charles Beard claimed that the authors of the Constitution of the United States designed it to protect their economic interests.[24] More than a century later, the role of individual interests in all political decisions is widely recognized.

---

[23] Buchanan, *The Limits of Liberty*, and John Rawls, *A Theory of Justice* (Cambridge, MA: Belknap Press, 1971).

[24] Charles A. Beard, *An Economic Interpretation of the Constitution of the United States* (New York: Macmillan, 1913).

THE SOCIALLY ASCRIBED CHARACTERISTICS OF AUTHORITY

The shift from monarchy to democracy shifted the basis of political authority from personal characteristics to socially ascribed characteristics. Rather than rulers taking power because they were the descendants of previous monarchs, people assumed power because they were chosen through an institutional process to occupy positions of power. Power came not from who someone was, but what position that person held. This weakened the political elite's hold on power.[25] Ronald Reagan had the powers of the U.S, presidency not because he was Ronald Reagan, but because he had been elected to the office. After his terms, Reagan no longer had the power of the presidency. George H. W. Bush assumed the powers of that position because of the socially ascribed characteristics of the presidency.

Prior to the Enlightenment, people were members of the ruling class because they, personally, were entitled to be rulers. The new ideas and new institutions that came with democracy present a double challenge to the new ruling class. First, they must strive to maintain their positions of power in the face of others who run for office to displace them. Second, rulers must maintain the socially ascribed powers that come with their elected offices. Just as the power monarchs in the 1700s held has dwindled over time to make them into figureheads with no real power, the Enlightenment ideology of democracy threatens to compromise the authority of the ruling class – to make them servants of the public, as they claim to be.

This is the ideal behind competitive elections. Candidates and parties offer policy platforms to voters, and voters select the candidates and parties whose platforms correspond most closely to their preferences.[26] To win elections, candidates and parties must adjust their platforms to conform to what voters want. If this were descriptive, those holding political office would have no power of independent action. Their only option would be to conform to the demands of the voters. If they do not do so, voters will replace them. Their power would be completely constrained by the demands of the voters.

---

[25] This idea is discussed by Douglass C. North, John Joseph Wallis, and Barry R. Weingast, *Violence and Social Orders: A Conceptual Framework for Interpreting Recorded History* (Cambridge: Cambridge University Press, 2009).

[26] This idea is explained by Anthony Downs, *An Economic Theory of Democracy* (New York: Harper & Row, 1957).

The double challenge faced by the political elite can be met by a single strategy. The more secure the political elite can make their hold on their offices, the more power they will have to act independently of the demands of their citizens and voters. This can be done in two ways. One is to design an incumbent advantage into political institutions so that once elected, they are likely to be reelected. The advantages to incumbency, discussed in Chapter 6, are widely recognized. The second way is to try to shift the base of power from the socially ascribed characteristics of the office toward the personal characteristics of the officeholder. To cite an example from the 2020s, Vladimir Putin was elected as Russia's president and assumed the socially ascribed powers that came with the position. Over time, he has been able to shift the basis of his rule to his personal characteristics. If the head of state is a president, another president could be elected, but when the head of state is Putin, there is only one Putin.

INSTITUTIONS DESIGNED TO RETAIN POWER

That romantic notion of democracy suggests that if citizens are dissatisfied with the performance of those they have elected to represent them, at the next election they can replace the incumbents. Periodic elections constrain elected representatives to act in the interests of those they represent. This romantic notion of democracy falls short for several reasons. Chapter 6 discussed some advantages incumbents have designed for themselves to retain power. More fundamentally, incumbency itself offers an advantage. Unless incumbents demonstrate incompetence of obvious abuse of power, they represent the government that citizens are propagandized to support through messages of patriotism. A vote against incumbents is a vote against one's government.

Perhaps the biggest incumbent advantage is a party structure that favors insiders over outsiders. Parties receive campaign contributions (as do individual candidates) and parties generate political support independent of the candidates who are running under the party banner. That support means that party insiders ultimately choose who will run for office and, therefore, who will be elected. The advantage of party politics explains why political parties formed in the United States, despite attempts of the American Founders to inhibit them.

The presidency of Joe Biden provides a clear example of the workings of party politics. In 2020, Donald Trump was the incumbent president, and many Democrats who were competing for their party's nomination were viewed by party insiders as too extreme to beat the incumbent president. Party insiders worked behind the scenes to get others to step aside so Biden, viewed as a more moderate candidate, would be nominated. Behind-the-scenes negotiations are largely invisible to the general public, but the 2024 campaign had a more open curtain.

Biden had won the party's 2024 primaries with little opposition and had more than enough delegates to win the party's nomination, but partly because of Biden's age, party insiders viewed him as too weak a candidate and urged him to step down. In the face of public pressure from his own party members, Biden was adamant that he would run for reelection. He emphasized that he was the choice of the voters in primary elections, and already had the votes locked up to win the nomination at the Party's convention.

Despite visible opposition from members of his own party, Biden made forceful public statements on July 9 and July 11 asserting that he would be the party's candidate in the election. He already had the votes to do so. Then, on July 21, Biden announced that he would drop out of the presidential race, very visibly showing that the party's 2024 presidential candidate – Kamala Harris – was chosen by negotiations among the party's elite – not by the voters. The voters chose Biden; the party's elite chose Harris.

This example reveals the illusion that political leaders in democracies are chosen by the voters. Voters can only vote for candidates who are on the ballot, and the party elite determine who will be their candidates. Competition among elites is discussed further in Chapter 13.

In proportional voting systems that are used in many nations, voters vote for a party rather than an individual candidate, making it even more clear that the party decides who will take office when they win seats. In plurality voting, as used in the United States among other places, individuals can choose to run within a party rather than the party deciding who will run. However, because voters often vote for the party rather than the candidate, and because parties themselves can offer financial and other support, parties largely choose their candidates in plurality systems as well as in proportional systems, as the Biden example illustrates. The electoral process presents the illusion that voters choose who will hold political office, but the political elite decide what choices are offered to voters.

The advantage goes to incumbents, but an appearance of too powerful an incumbent advantage can have negative consequences for incumbents. The appearance that incumbents can be replaced gives the masses the illusion that those who exercise the powers of governance were chosen by the people, and therefore have the legitimate right to exercise that power. Incumbents have institutional advantages in the electoral process, but even if they are replaced, the institutions of governance remain the same. One group of elites replaces another, and the new officeholders gain the same powers as their predecessors.

VOTING: LEGISLATIVE CHOICE VERSUS CITIZEN CHOICE

Democratic political institutions allow citizens to elect their representatives. In that technical sense, those who design public policy are chosen by the masses. The choices they face are limited, however. In elections that use plurality voting, where the candidate who receives the most votes wins, the system naturally evolves into a two-party system.[27] While anyone can choose to run for election in such a system, viable candidates need connections and financing, and the people who supply those things are members of the political elite. So while it is true that anyone can run, only individuals who have the support of the political elite can be viable candidates. It appears that citizen-voters choose their representatives, but they are only able to choose among candidates who have elite support. The elite determine the menu of choices offered to citizen-voters.

In proportional voting systems, people vote for parties rather than individual candidates, and parties are represented in parliament in proportion to the votes they receive. In this system, there is not even the illusion that voters choose their representatives. The parties themselves choose the party members who will serve as elected representatives. Regardless of the electoral system, the political elite determine the choices that are offered to voters. There is no political marketplace in which voters can negotiate to determine candidates or policies. High transaction costs prevent it. Voters may only choose among the alternatives offered them by the political elite.

In contrast to popular voting, the political marketplace allows legislators to negotiate to determine what will be voted on in addition to how individual legislators will vote. In this sense, legislative voting resembles that general equilibrium model of markets discussed earlier in the volume. Participants in the political marketplace decide for themselves what public

---

[27] This idea is referred to as Duverger's law. See Maurice Duverger, *Political Parties: Their Organization and Activity in the Modern State* (London: Methuen, 1964). An explanation is also given by Anthony Downs, *An Economic Theory of Democracy* (New York: Harper & Row, 1957).

policies will be considered, much as firms in markets decide what goods and services to offer. Then, negotiations take place through logrolling and vote trading to produce the public policy outcomes that have the highest value for those who are able to transact in the political marketplace. The yes or no voting at the end of the process looks similar to popular voting. The big difference is that because transaction costs are low, in the political marketplace, the voters themselves decide what will come up for a vote.

Effectively, those in the political marketplace negotiate to arrive at that general equilibrium allocation of resources that maximizes the value to those who participate in political exchanges. At the end of the negotiating process, votes simply reaffirm what had already been decided through political exchange. The result maximizes the welfare of those who are able to negotiate in the political marketplace.

On the surface, it appears that the institutions of voting in legislatures are very similar to the institutions of voting in citizen elections, but a deeper look shows that there is very little similarity. The difference is driven by transaction costs. In legislative voting, where transaction costs are low, a political marketplace allows participants to negotiate the outcome that maximizes their welfare. In citizen voting, high transaction costs prevent negotiation, and citizens can only choose from among alternatives offered them by the elite.

In legislatures, voting serves only to distribute purchasing power among its members. Members then negotiate in the political marketplace to determine what legislation will be voted on, and what they can get given their purchasing power. The choices citizens have when voting are limited. The choices legislators have are unlimited because they can propose anything.

In legislative voting, unlike popular voting, marginal changes are always possible and often occur. "I will vote for your legislation if you include in it $50 million for a facility in my district." If the answer is "I think I can find the votes to pass the legislation at a lower cost," the response can be "How about $30 million for the facility?" In legislative voting, legislators determine what they will vote on in addition to how they will vote. With citizen voting, the political elite determine what choices will be offered to citizens.

MARKETS AND VOTING

Democratic elections offer the appearance that voters choose candidates, parties, and public policies in the same way that, in a market, they choose what goods and services to consume. The concept of politics as exchange, and a political marketplace, furthers this illusion. Academic writing in public choice reinforces this illusion. The parallel between market choice and collective choice through voting is not as great as public choice models make them appear.

The shopping cart analogy has been discussed previously. Choosing between two shopping carts, each filled by someone else, is not the same as choosing for oneself what items go in the cart. It is apparent that the shopper would be better off filling the cart herself rather than having a political candidate make those choices. Even this paints too rosy a picture. Politicians are often vague about what is in their platforms, so extending the shopping analogy, the shopper can see some items at the tops of the carts, but most of what is in the carts is not visible. Even then, while the shopper can vote for her preferred cart, the choice a voter makes is not necessarily what the voter will get. That voter's one vote will not affect the election outcome. Whether she votes for cart A or cart B, the cart she gets will be the same in either case.[28]

Despite the existence of a political marketplace, the parallel between market choice and collective choice through voting breaks down in several ways because of the high transaction costs faced by the masses. First, with voting, the outcome people get is unrelated to the choices they make. This removes the incentive to make informed choices, or even to participate in the choice process. Second, the options among which voters can choose are limited to those offered them by the political elite. The choice set is small and may include only options that are not closely related to what voters would most prefer. Third, the political elite typically offer voters only a vague picture of the public policies they intend to promote if elected.

The political elite want citizens to believe that democratic institutions make the elite accountable to the masses and produce public policies that are in the best interest of the masses. When comparing market institutions with democratic political institutions, it becomes apparent that democratic political institutions fall far short of enabling the masses to choose the public policies they prefer. Their choices are limited to those the elite offer, and candidates and parties rarely lay out specific policies they would attempt to enact. These issues all exist under the assumption that politicians actually intend to do what they promise when they are

---

[28] Some of these ideas are discussed by James M. Buchanan, "Individual Choice in Voting and the Market," *Journal of Political Economy* 62, no. 4 (August 1954), pp. 334–343.

campaigning, an assumption that many would question. There is a political marketplace, but most people are excluded from trading in it.

ASPIRATIONS AND POLICIES

A major factor that stands between the preferences of the masses and the policies enacted by the elite is that the actions of any individual citizen have no effect on public policy outcomes. This means that when voters cast their votes at the ballot box, they know they are not choosing an outcome, but rather expressing a point of view. They may vote for an option at the ballot box that they would not choose if the choice were theirs alone. The utility they get from voting comes solely from expressing an opinion, not choosing an outcome, because their one vote will have no effect on an election outcome.

Gordon Tullock gives a plausible example of an individual who is very uncharitable.[29] The individual may feel he should be charitable, but actually donating to charity is costly. In the voting booth, that individual may choose to vote for a candidate or party that favors redistribution to the less fortunate, getting a good feeling from casting a charitable vote. The individual may feel good by voting for redistribution programs even though, if it was the individual's choice alone, the individual would not choose to fund them. The voter can do so because the act of voting is purely expressive and has no effect on an election outcome.

Geoffrey Brennan and Loren Lomasky extend this idea, offering a hypothetical example to illustrate it.[30] Consider a voter choosing between options A and B. If option B wins, it will cost every voter $500, but expressing support for option B gives every voter a good feeling worth $.05. Because one voter's one vote will not determine which option wins, all voters vote for option B to get the $.05 worth of good feelings. Because all voters are in the same situation, option B wins, and all voters are $499.95 worse off as a result.

Because the connection between what voters choose and what they get is broken in any but the smallest elections, voters tend to vote based on emotion – what makes them feel good – rather than on what option would be best for them and their fellow citizens. One consequence is that

---

[29] Gordon Tullock, "The Charity of the Uncharitable," *Western Economic Journal* 9, no. 4 (December 1971), pp. 379–392.
[30] Geoffrey Brennan and Loren Lomasky, *Democracy and Decision: The Pure Theory of Electoral Preference* (Cambridge: Cambridge University Press, 1993).

candidates and parties design their platforms to have emotional appeal rather than to lay out details of public policies they would favor. Even if voters were trying to choose options that would make them better off, there are many policy issues that often are complex, which stands in the way of their making informed choices. But they know they do not have to make informed choices because one vote will not affect an election outcome. They choose options that make them feel good about expressing support.

This gives an edge to candidates who are charismatic and who seem likeable and knowledgeable. It also guides the way that candidates and parties design their platforms. As a general rule, the message in political platforms is: Things are not as good as they could be, and if you elect me, I will make them better. Campaigns are based on aspirations rather than actual policies. Climate change is a threat, and I will set the goal of limiting greenhouse gas emissions to limit warming. Economic growth is sluggish, and I will enact policies to increase productivity in a sustainable way. Inequality is an issue, and I will help those who are less fortunate. Specific policies to achieve these aspirations tend to be absent from political platforms.[31]

Political campaigns are run on aspirations – goals that have popular support – rather than on actual policies that could be enacted to accomplish those goals. Many people will be in favor of the goals. Who would be against helping the less fortunate, taking action to mitigate climate change, or improving the health care system? Fewer people will be in favor of any specific policies to accomplish those goals, so to maximize support, politicians offer voters aspirations rather than specific policies. Voters feel good about themselves when they support those aspirations, but one result is that this lessens the accountability of the political elite to the masses. Voters choose options that make them feel good, with only a vague idea of what actual public policies candidates will pursue if elected.

CONCLUSION

The political marketplace is more than just an arena in which the political elite bargain among themselves to make public policy. Those political institutions within which those bargains take place have also been the

---

[31] I discuss this in more detail in Randall G. Holcombe, *Following Their Leaders: Political Preferences and Public Policy* (Cambridge: Cambridge University Press, 2023).

product of political negotiation and exchange. The evolution of democratic political institutions since the Enlightenment era has been the result of a shift in bargaining power among those who trade in the political marketplace. Monarchy has been displaced by democracy because of an increase in the bargaining power of democratically elected elites, which in turn has been driven by the increased mobility that capitalism has bought to the masses.

The increased freedom enjoyed by the masses is largely a result of the mobility of capital relative to land as economies have industrialized. Elites are more constrained in their use of power because they want to keep productive assets within their jurisdictions. That has not given individual members of the masses an increased voice in the design of public policy. High transaction costs keep the masses from participating in the political marketplace. Still, there is a widespread perception that democratic institutions empower the masses. The ideology of democracy – the idea that democratic governments are accountable to their citizens and act in the interests of the masses – conveys legitimacy to the political elite. If the masses believe that those who hold political power have gained it legitimately, they are more likely to be compliant citizens who will willingly obey their government's mandates.

There is a danger in overselling the merits of democratic government, but at the same time, one would not want to undersell it. Democracy is a good mechanism for peacefully replacing one group of political elites with another, despite the advantage it gives to those already in positions of power. Those who hold political power in democracies hold it based on the socially ascribed characteristics of their positions rather than based on their personal characteristics. Power goes with the position, not the person who holds the position. Those who hold power can be voted out. But one should not make too much of this. That also means that regardless of who voters select to hold those positions, the power of the political elite will remain essentially unchanged.

13

Constraining Leviathan

Competition among Elites

The institutions of authority and governance necessarily fall under the control of an elite few. The preceding analysis has discussed at length the division between elites and masses, the rulers and the ruled, that necessarily exists because transaction costs stand in the way of most people's ability to participate in the political marketplace. Members of the elite have common interests that often are at odds with the interests of the masses. While members of the elite work together to advance their common interests, they also find themselves competing with each other in different dimensions. Having discussed at length the way the elite work together, this chapter looks at the ways elites compete among themselves for power and influence.

One obvious area in which elites compete with each other is that members of the elite sometimes have different policy goals. To take a clear example from American politics, some want to preserve and expand the right to bear arms, while others want more restrictions on the ownership of firearms. Another example: Some want to expand women's rights to have abortions, while others want more restrictions on it. Coalitions within the elite compete with each other on policy issues – coalitions that often form along established party lines. This aspect of competition, while real, ultimately is not the most significant dimension of competition among members of the elite.

The most significant arena of competition among elites for power, which occurs in two dimensions. First, members of the elite compete among themselves for positions of power. Second, individuals want to expand the scope of power embodied in their current positions, sometimes by encroaching on the scope of power held by others. Elites compete to try to protect and expand their spheres of influence. The more intense, and often vicious, competition among elites occurs as they aspire to move up to more powerful positions by displacing those who currently hold them. Those who are higher up in the hierarchy of power face challengers from within the political elite who want to displace them.

Within legislative bodies, members compete for positions of power – committee assignments and chairmanships. Challengers for political office almost always are themselves members of the political elite who aspire to move up in the hierarchy of power. Even those running for their first office tend to have a background in politics, as legislative aides or party officials. Occasional exceptions are well-known entertainers or sports figures who have acquired name recognition and prominence outside of the political sphere. Their celebrity status gives them access to elites in other areas. It takes connections to get the political support necessary to succeed as a candidate.

Competition among elites, partly over policies but mostly over power, is an essential mechanism that constrains those who hold power from abusing it. Their attempts to preserve and expand their own power lead them to challenge abuses of power by others. Abuse of power by some tends to reduce the power of others. Chapter 11 discussed the importance of mobility within the masses as a constraint on the abuse of power, but mobility is only effective when there is somewhere to go. That means there must be other jurisdictions they could move to that are controlled by different sets of elites.

COMPETITION FOR POLICIES, OR POWER?

Consider some high-profile policy issues debated among political parties in the United States. On the abortion issue, Democrats favor reproductive choice; Republicans oppose abortion. Regarding firearms, Republicans support expanding the right to bear arms; Democrats favor more gun control. On school choice, Republicans are in favor; Democrats are opposed. During the COVID pandemic, Democrats supported vaccine mandates; Republicans opposed them. One curious element in these policy debates is how consistently the views of the political elite fall along party lines.

One of the slogans the proponents of abortion rights have used to support their cause is "My body; my choice." During the COVID pandemic, the opponents of vaccine mandates weaponized the same slogan, asking why those who chant "My body, my choice" when considering abortion issue reject that slogan when considering vaccine mandates. Without wading into a debate on those issues, or whether the slogan applies equally to both issues, the abortion issue seems to have little connection to the vaccine issue beyond the connection just mentioned. Why were the proponents of reproductive choice so consistently opposed to allowing individuals to choose whether to be vaccinated with a vaccine that was rushed into production? With a minimal connection between the issues, wouldn't one anticipate that among those who oppose abortion, their views would be split on mandating the vaccine? Similarly, gun control and abortion rights seem so remotely connected that it would seem reasonable to find that among those who favor reproductive rights, their views would be split on the right to bear arms.

That is not the case. These are partisan issues, and members of the political elite consistently stick with their party's views on them. Members of the political elite are surely more consistently partisan on those issues than the masses. The logic behind that consistency is not due to a set of principles that link them, but rather that party leaders believe that their positions on them are the best way to gain political support. The policy preferences of the political elite do not come from principles, but from the quest for power.

Parties are willing to change their policy positions when they view doing so as advantageous. The Republican party was long considered a supporter of free trade. When Donald Trump campaigned for president in 2016, he ran on a protectionist platform, and the party changed its views. Was President Trump so persuasive that Republicans in lesser positions were convinced by his arguments and adopted his protectionist views? President Trump's persuasion was not based on principle, but on the idea that his protectionist rhetoric could win voter support.[1]

Whether President Trump's protectionist leanings were based on principle is beside the point. The point is that when he became his party's leader, most other members of the party switched their positions on the issue to conform with his. Politicians benefit from the support of their parties, so for the most part they follow the party line on policy issues, lest they lose that support. Republicans brand party members who question the party line RINOs – Republican In Name Only – to try to enforce

---

[1] On the ever-changing policy stances of left and right, see Hyrum Lewis and Verlan Lewis, *The Myth of Left and Right: How the Political Spectrum Misleads and Harms America* (Oxford: Oxford University Press, 2023).

that party discipline. First and foremost, politicians seek power. While differing policy positions among politicians and parties are evident, what they are really competing for is power, not policy outcomes.

If politicians tend to adopt their party's positions on policy issues in the US, that behavior is even more pronounced in countries with proportional representation. Citizens in those countries vote for parties rather than individuals, and the parties choose who will represent their party in parliament. Because parties choose their representatives, those representatives must follow the party line, or be replaced by someone who does. The objective is power, not policy outcomes.

This same partisan consistency tends to exist among citizens and voters, largely because voters adopt policy views offered them by the political elite. Policy issues are numerous and complex, and citizens have other interests – their jobs, their families, and their hobbies – that compete for their attention. Rather than research issues over which they have no influence, they anchor on a candidate, a party, or an ideology and adopt the policy views of their anchors.[2] They rarely recognize that the policy preferences of their anchors are motivated by their anchors' quests for power; the actual policy outcomes are secondary.

This section opened with a discussion of policy positions held by Republicans and Democrats in the early 2020s, when this volume was written. Because those policy positions are designed to gain political support rather than resting on principles, those partisan policy preferences are subject to change if the policy leaders who define them see a political advantage to changing them.

CONSTRAINTS ON THE ELITE

The institutions of authority and governance, to be effective, must have more than just a comparative advantage in the use of force. Those institutions must convey to citizens that they have sufficient power behind them to make resistance appear futile. Effective governance causes citizens to comply with government mandates because of the high cost government would impose on them for noncompliance. Unconstrained, the exercise of that power can be disastrous for the subjects of government. R. J. Rummel estimates that 169 million people were murdered by their own

---

[2] One could write a whole book on this idea, and I have! See Randall G. Holcombe, *Following Their Leaders: Political Preferences and Public Policy* (Cambridge: Cambridge University Press, 2023).

governments in the twentieth century.³ Rummel begins his book by paraphrasing Lord Acton, saying, "Power kills, absolute power kills absolutely." What constrains those in power from abusing it, to the detriment of those subject to that power? In some cases, nothing, as Rummel has documented. Chapters 11 and 12 discussed three factors: mobility, constitutional constraints, and democracy. This chapter considers a fourth: competition among elites.

Democratic institutions and constitutional constraints are desirable, but by themselves, are insufficient, because they need an enforcement mechanism. A problem arises because the enforcers are the political elite, the same people who operate under those institutional constraints. It is very easy for the elite to make the claim that they are following the rules when they are the ones who write and enforce the rules. The American Founders recognized this problem, and their solution was to design a government with a system of checks and balances, so that the power of some elites could stand in the way of any attempted abuse of power by others.

The absolute necessity of a system of checks and balances seems underappreciated by those who see the threat of a Leviathan government. Constitutional rules need an enforcement mechanism to be effective. The idea that democratic oversight will serve the purpose of enforcing constraints on government exercise of power is especially problematic, as Chapter 12 suggested. It legitimizes and enables abuse of power by the ruling class.

POLITICAL PHILOSOPHY AND GOVERNMENT POWER

Political philosophy has largely been written from the vantage point of the citizen. What obligations do citizens have to each other to enable an orderly and productive society? What rules should be in place to constrain the government to act in the interest of its citizens? Social contractarians have made the case that individuals have an obligation to respect the rights of fellow citizens. John Locke made the case that people have natural rights.⁴ Jean Jacques Rousseau made the case that democratic political institutions are designed to advance the general will.⁵

---

[3] R. J. Rummel, *Death by Government* (New Brunswick, NJ: Transaction Publishers, 1994).

[4] John Locke, *Two Treatises of Government* (Cambridge: Cambridge University Press, 1960 [orig. 1690]).

[5] Jean Jacques Rousseau, *The Social Contract, Or Principles of Political Right* (London: J. M. Dent and Sons, 1923 [orig. 1762]).

13 Constraining Leviathan: Competition among Elites

Thomas Hobbes argued that citizens have the obligation to obey the mandates of their rulers to avoid a society that devolves into a war of all against all.[6] More recently, John Rawls offered a theory of justice stating that just rules are those that everyone would agree to if they removed their own personal interests from consideration.[7] A rare exception is Niccolo Machiavelli, who wrote from the standpoint of the rulers rather than the ruled.[8]

Political philosophy, for the most part, considers the way that governments should operate to further the interests of the governed rather than offering a realistic view of how governments actually do operate. One can theorize about a social contract, but there is no social contract, and public policy is designed by an elite few. With regard to the relationship between the elites and the masses, the pre-Enlightenment vision of rulers and ruled, with the ruled obligated to carry out the mandates of the ruling class, is more accurate than a romantic notion of democracy that depicts government as accountable to its citizens. The powerless cannot control the powerful, even if the powerless far outnumber the powerful.

Yet in much of the twenty-first century-world, people enjoy substantial freedom. Their governments protect them from aggression and implement institutions that create a productive and orderly society. Public policies often do promote the public interest. If the masses cannot effectively constrain the elite, how have the interests of the masses been so well preserved? The answer is twofold. First, the interests of the elite and the masses often are the same. Everyone benefits from an orderly and productive society. Second, political institutions create a division of power, so that some elites are able to check and balance the abuse of power by others.

Mobility is an effective constraint only if competing elites offer alternatives to the masses. Constitutional constraints are effective only if those with power are compelled to abide by them. Democracy is effective only if the masses have realistic alternatives. Competition among elites serves those functions.

Members of the elite have many interests in common, and negotiate together in the political marketplace to further those interests. But

---

[6] Thomas Hobbes, *Leviathan* (New York: E. P. Dutton, 1950 [orig. 1651]).
[7] John Rawls, *A Theory of Justice* (Cambridge, MA: Belknap, 1971).
[8] Niccolo Machiavelli, *The Prince* (Chicago, IL: University of Chicago Press, 1985 [orig. 1532]).

members of the political elite, in their quest for power, also compete with each other. The desire to exercise power over others is widespread, and those whose desire for power is most intense self-select into politics because that is where they can gain the most power. Individuals, trying to acquire power for themselves, have an interest in limiting the acquisition of power by others.

PARTIES AND ELECTIONS

Electoral institutions are designed to create competition among elites. In an election, some people win; others lose. To even enter the contest as a serious contender requires the support of elites. At this point in the political process, citizens as a whole have a voice in determining which members of the elite will be awarded the authority that comes with electoral victory. But as Chapter 12 noted, voters tend to be poorly informed and do not have an incentive to vote for options that are in their best interests. Perhaps more significantly, they can only vote for the options offered them by the political elite. The goal of the candidate is to persuade voters, and persuasion is most effective when candidates are personable, appear competent, and offer aspirational platforms, even if those platforms are unrealizable in practice.

A convincing campaign requires the cooperation of others, for financing and for endorsements. The importance of financing requires little defense. Few candidates can afford to finance their own campaigns, so before candidates convince people to vote for them, they must convince people to donate to their campaigns, to get their message out. Endorsements also help by showing that a candidate has support (everyone likes to back a winner) and by refining a candidate's brand. Beyond personal endorsements, interest group endorsements can gain the support of the group's members. Such support is helpful, but in modern politics, party affiliation is a necessary way of gaining the assistance of others.

In parliamentary systems, party affiliation is necessary because parties choose the candidates. In most (but not all) plurality systems, anyone can run, but with rare exceptions, those who win are running as members of major parties. Indeed, while candidates run as individuals with a party affiliation, voters are as likely to vote for the individual's party as they are to vote for the specific individual.

In 2022, John Fetterman was elected to the US Senate by Pennsylvania voters. Fetterman had a history of health problems, including depression during most of his life, and heart issues, and suffered a stroke in May of 2022 prior to the election in November, which made it difficult for him to speak. Opponents hammered on those health issues, but Fetterman was elected anyway, likely because a majority of the voters preferred electing a Democrat to a Republican in what was sure to be a narrow partisan division in the Senate. Surely, many were voting for a Democrat, who happened to be Fetterman, rather than for Fetterman, who happened to be a Democrat.

The American Founders wanted to create a government that was free of parties and factions, but the political system rapidly developed political parties. Parties, as political coalitions, help members of the political elite by enabling them to join forces with allies to combat challengers. Joining a group can work better than battling alone.

THE ELECTORAL COLLEGE

The Electoral College for electing the president was a part of the American Founders' design of a political system that was intended to be free of parties and factions, but within a few decades after the Constitution was written, the modern party system was born as a result of the evolution of the Electoral College. The Constitution specifies that the president is elected by the votes of members of an Electoral College, with those members chosen by the states. The Founders thought that using the Electoral College system rather than selecting the president by popular vote would insulate the selection of the nation's chief executive from popular political pressures. But the Constitution left it up to the states to determine how they selected their electors, and states rapidly moved to popular voting for electors.[9]

The Constitution, as amended, specifies that if a candidate wins a majority of the electoral votes, that candidate becomes the president. If no candidate wins a majority, the names of the three candidates with the highest number of electoral votes are forwarded to the House of Representatives, which selects the president from among those top three electoral vote recipients. The Founders envisioned that because most electors would tend to select "favorite son" candidates from their states, in most cases no candidate would win an electoral majority, and the

---

[9] The Constitution does not now, and never has, given individual citizens the right to vote for president. That right has been conferred by the states. See Randall G. Holcombe, *Liberty in Peril: Democracy and Power in American History* (Oakland, CA: Independent Institute, 2019), Chapter 5 for a more complete history.

House of Representatives would choose the president from among the top electoral vote recipients.

The system never worked as the Founders intended. Up until the election of 1824, presidents won electoral majorities, leaving the House of Representatives out of the process, except in 1800. In that election, John Adams and Thomas Jefferson tied in electoral votes, and the House chose Jefferson. In 1824, Andrew Jackson received the highest number of electoral votes, but fell short of a majority, and the House chose John Quincy Adams, one of their own, as the president.

Jackson's supporters were outraged, arguing that because Jackson had the highest number of electoral votes, the House should have selected him. The House clearly followed the Constitution in its selection, but Jackson's supporters vowed that this would not happen again, and the modern Democratic party was formed specifically to elect Andrew Jackson to the presidency, which they did in 1828.[10] Jackson served two terms and was followed by Martin van Buren, who was instrumental in forming the Democratic party. The Whig party was established to counter the Democrats, and the modern two-party system was borne. When the Republican party rose to prominence in the 1850s, the Whig party disappeared.

Parties have obvious significance in proportional voting systems where they are a part of the formal electoral process. Even when institutions were consciously designed to inhibit the establishment of political parties, they have been established anyway, as a method of forming political coalitions that can help individuals gain power. In the long run, those in power can increase the scope of their power, but in the short run, the pursuit of power is a zero-sum game. In an election, the winner acquires power; the loser does not. An institutional structure that creates winners and losers among the political elite means that elites must compete with each other for political power.

Keeping in mind the multidimensional nature of political competition, elites of all parties have common interests and work together to use their power for their mutual advantage. But the competition for power places a check on its use. In democracies, elites must get elected to assume power, which means appealing to the masses. That check on the abuse of power would work better if the masses had a good idea of what would

---

[10] Jackson's supporters claimed that Adams was selected in a corrupt bargain. The details are explained in Holcombe, *Liberty in Peril*, Chapter 5, which questions the accusation of a corrupt bargain.

be in the public interest and what would be in their own interests, but as Chapter 12 noted, citizens and voters tend to be rationally ignorant and cast their votes based on emotional factors rather than what would be best for them. They vote for the option that makes them feel good about themselves.

COMPETING PARTIES

The formation of the Whig party in the 1830s was a recognition of the importance of party competition in politics. The modern Democratic party, formed to elect Andrew Jackson to the presidency, lowered transaction costs to enable like-minded people – Jackson supporters – to organize and elect, in 1828, the candidate they were unable to elect in 1824. The organized Jackson supporters had an advantage over the less-organized Jackson opponents, just as in general, organized interests have an advantage over unorganized interests. The Whig party was organized for the purpose of opposing the Democratic party – that is, for the purpose of opposing Jackson. Without an organized opposition group, the Democrats would have been much less constrained.

Parties form because they can lower transaction costs among members with common interests. Although the American Founders hoped to discourage the formation of parties and factions, they tend to form anyway, because organized interests have more power than unorganized interests, and the political elite seek power. Without competing parties, a ruling party can abuse that power, prompting the question of how competing parties can be maintained. Germany's Adolf Hitler was democratically elected, as were Venezuela's Hugo Chavez and Russia's Vladimir Putin. Those individuals were able to rise to power based on the socially ascribed characteristics of their offices, and enhance their power once in office, based on their personal characteristics.

Hitler, Chavez, and Putin acquired power because they were elected, but maintained and increased their power because they were Hitler, Chavez, and Putin, not because they were democratically elected. Once in power, they were successful at neutralizing the power of those who opposed them.

One can look at one-party rule in the Soviet Union, in Cuba, in North Korea, and in China to see how it enables political systems without party competition to oppress their citizens. Singapore offers an interesting case because that country's one-party rule has produced a very authoritarian government, but with substantial economic freedom that has produced a prosperous economy.[11] Parties emerge because they facilitate the political elite's pursuit of power. Party competition is an important element in the competition among elites that constrains the abuse of power. The examples in the previous paragraph show that democratic elections do not always produce competition among parties, and that even when party competition exists, it can devolve into single-party rule.

E. E. Schattschneider offers a dissenting viewpoint, suggesting that divided government is ineffective government, and says, "If we believe in majority rule ... party organization and party techniques for getting control of the government are appropriate to democratic government and the measures necessary to the creation of an effective party system are admirable, for we cannot believe that party government is a good thing without also believing in the means appropriate to that end."[12] But, as Chapter 12 argued, we should not believe in majority rule. The interests of the majority can only be protected when those who have access to political power are constrained from abusing it, and the most effective constraint is a division of power among different members of the elite.

POLITICAL COALITIONS

Members of the political elite must cooperate with each other to create and enforce the rules they impose on the masses. This is most obvious in democratic governments, where at many stages, beginning with elections, the elite need majority support. Once elected, the members of legislative bodies negotiate with each other to form majority coalitions to pass legislation. That is how the political marketplace works. Coalitions can be based on parties, but in many cases a subset of individuals with common interests form coalitions to accomplish their ends.

This clearly takes place in proportional voting systems when no single party holds a majority of seats in parliament. Parties, sometimes with clearly different interests, negotiate to form a majority coalition, which allows them to compromise and achieve some of their parties' goals. In

---

[11] Insightful commentary on Singapore is found in Christopher Lingle, *Singapore's Authoritarian Capitalism: Asian Values, Free Market Illusions, and Political Dependency* (Fairfax, VA: Locke Institute, 1996), and by the same author, *The Rise and Decline of the Asian Century: False Starts on the Path to the Global Millennium* (Barcelona: Editions Sirocco, 1997).

[12] E. E. Schattschneider, *The Struggle for Party Government* (College Park: University of Maryland Program in American Civilization, 1948), p. 11.

other cases, interests may cut across party lines. For example, representatives in agricultural districts will have common interests regardless of their party affiliations. In the United States, the Congressional Black Caucus is a coalition of Black legislators who promote issues common to their race.

The formation of coalitions can be an effective method of lowering transaction costs if they are permanent, or at least semipermanent in nature. Much in the same way that economic institutions reduce transaction costs to help connect suppliers with demanders, semipermanent coalitions can lower the transaction costs involved in connecting those with common interests. Because ultimately, majority support is needed to pass legislation, coalitions must form to do so, perhaps temporarily, just to pass one piece of legislation, or perhaps more permanently, to allow that coalition more power in the political process. Except in rare cases in which legislation is unanimously approved, some people are on the winning side while others lose. This competition among elites provides a check on their power.

These concepts apply to dictatorial regimes as well as democracies. While the process is not so transparent in dictatorships, dictators require a coalition of supporters to maintain their power, and if they lose those supporters, they are removed from power. The collapse of many Eastern European dictatorships after the fall of the Berlin Wall in 1989 offers a dramatic example. Muammar Gaddafi, long-time dictator in Libya, similarly lost support, lost power, and was killed in 2011. There is a political marketplace in dictatorships just as in democracies, in which those in the low transaction cost coalition receive government protections and favors in return for their support of the regime.

COMPETITION AND COOPERATION

Because those with political power ultimately rule by force, those with power can use it to their advantage and to the detriment of those without. To sketch out some concepts about the use of power, consider a simple example, extending one presented in Chapter 7, in which three individuals will vote by majority rule to decide how to divide a dollar among them. Individuals can maximize their own take by forming a coalition with another individual to divide the dollar between them. This is represented by the first row in Table 13.1. Two individuals form a coalition by agreeing that each will take half of the dollar, leaving nothing for the third individual.

TABLE 13.1 *The stability of political coalitions*

Voters			
1	2	3	
1/2	½	0	Minimum winning coalition
0	2/3	1/3	
1/3	0	2/3	Cyclical majority
2/3	1/3	0	
1/3	1/3	1/3	Universalism and reciprocity

This outcome is referred to as a minimum winning coalition, which provides the highest payoff to coalition members.[13] The principle holds, and perhaps is more obvious, when there are more voters. Consider an assembly with 100 voters. A minimum winning coalition would consist of 51 voters, splitting the profits among themselves and leaving the other 49 with nothing.

The challenge in forming a minimum winning coalition is that it only takes a few defectors for the coalition to break down. With 51 voters in the minimum winning coalition, if 2 of them left the coalition to join a coalition with the other 49, that new coalition would now be the minimum winning coalition. In the example in Table 13.1, if either one of the coalition members joined with individual 3, the coalition would break down. This is represented in the next row of the table, where individual 3 strikes a deal with individual 2. "If you will join with me, I will increase your share to 2/3, and I will just take 1/3 for myself." Two out of three – a majority – would find themselves better off, so the second row of the table dominates the first by simple majority rule.

Typically, for a minimum winning coalition to endure, members must have something in common besides just wanting the highest payoff possible. If individuals 1 and 2 have ethnic or religious commonalities, for example, they may be able to form a more permanent bond. Otherwise, the minimum winning coalition is likely to break down.

Again looking at the table, if the distribution is like that in the second row, 0, 2/3, 1/3, the first individual could strike a deal with the third, leading to the row below where the first individual gets 1/3 and offers 2/3 to the third individual, leaving the second with nothing. Two out of three

---

[13] This concept is discussed in detail by William H. Riker, *The Theory of Political Coalitions* (New Haven, CT: Yale University Press, 1962).

13 Constraining Leviathan: Competition among Elites 243

would benefit. But then, individual 2 could make a similar offer, producing the outcome of 2/3, 1/3, 0, which would make a majority better off. The third voter could then offer the second row, with the distribution of 0, 2/3, 1/3. The three middle rows of the table form a cyclical majority, a concept discussed in Chapter 7. The third row dominates the second by majority rule, the fourth row dominates the third, and the second row dominates the fourth.[14]

The lesson here is that when democratic governments are deciding among outcomes that are zero-sum games, there is no outcome that dominates all others by simple majority rule. No matter what the status quo, there is always another outcome that would be preferred by a majority, as Chapter 7 noted. This provides some discipline against the abuse of power by the political elite. If outcomes tilt too far toward one subset of the population, political entrepreneurs may be able to mobilize the masses to elect them to replace the current regime.[15]

Look at the second row of the table with the distribution of 0, 2/3, 1/3. It would be easy for the first individual to argue that the second was receiving more than a fair share, prompting a reforming of coalitions leading to the outcome in the third row. Using majority rule, there is always some way to redistribute benefits to produce an outcome a majority would prefer to the status quo. Political competition limits the abuse of power because it provides a check against outcomes that give some obviously more than their fair share.

Faced with the prospect of a cyclical majority, those who trade in the political marketplace might form an agreement to give everyone a relatively equal share of the benefits. This is represented by the bottom row of Table 13.1, in which every individual gets 1/3. This appears more fair. Over the course of a cyclical majority, each individual in the table averages 1/3, sometimes getting 2/3 and sometimes nothing, so a stable outcome with the same average payout may appeal to all.[16] This seems to be descriptive of government spending in many jurisdictions. With

---

[14] Kenneth J. Arrow, *Social Choice and Individual Values* (New York: John Wiley & Sons, 1951) begins his book with an example of a cyclical majority.
[15] James M. Buchanan, "Social Choice, Democracy, and Free Markets," *Journal of Political Economy* 62, no. 2 (April 1954), pp. 114–123, notes that an advantage of a cyclical majority, where it exists, is that it enables a rotation of power so no one coalition is able to dominate the political process and exclude others.
[16] This concept is discussed by Barry R. Weingast, Kenneth A. Shepsle, and Christopher Johnsen, "The Political Economy of Benefits and Costs: A Neoclassical Approach to Distributive Politics," *Journal of Political Economy* 89, no. 4 (August 1981), pp. 642–664.

the exception of some pork-barrel spending – or maybe because of pork-barrel spending – government programs are spread fairly evenly among districts regardless of whether a district is represented by a member of a minority party.

The table illustrates three possible outcomes from democratic decision-making. A minimum winning coalition could form, benefiting those in the coalition but excluding those outside. A cyclical majority could occur in which the status quo is unstable, and the group in power is continually displaced by challengers. Or, participants could all cooperate among themselves for their mutual benefit. Not only are there plausible arguments to support each outcome but also political outcomes that resemble each case can be observed in different times and places.[17]

The first two cases – minimum winning coalitions and cyclical majorities – depict competition among elites. In their quest for power, elites have an incentive to seek others with common interests to negotiate agreements for their mutual benefit while excluding others to maximize their gains. When this happens, there is an opportunity for a political entrepreneur to disrupt the coalition by forming a new coalition that would win the support of a majority. In the examples in the table, all of the winning coalitions are majorities, but in many cases, high transaction costs allow a minority to constitute a winning coalition. When winning coalitions abuse their power, that opens an opportunity for competing elites to take it, which places some constraints on the ruling coalition.

CHECKS AND BALANCES

The institutions of authority and governance are run by a ruling elite who make and enforce the rules that govern the masses. Individual citizens have no power to change those rules. If they are dissatisfied, the best they can do for themselves is move away, and for many people, moving is not a viable option. When unconstrained, the ruling class makes citizens their subjects, and feudal political institutions are the likely outcome. In the twenty-first century, the masses in so many countries fare far better than feudal serfs because the ruling class is constrained in its use of power.

Enlightenment ideas have played a role, but those ideas would have little impact if the ruling class were able to use its power to extract all but a subsistence level of income from the masses, as they have been able to do

---

[17] These ideas are discussed further in Randall G. Holcombe, *Advanced Introduction to Public Choice* (Cheltenham, UK: Edward Elgar, 2016).

13 Constraining Leviathan: Competition among Elites

for most of human history. One thing that has changed since feudal times is the rise in importance, since the beginning of the Industrial Revolution, of capital as a factor of production. The mobility of capital has meant that political elites have had to compete with each other to attract capital, and therefore productivity, to their jurisdictions. Rulers who abuse their power will lose capital, lose wealth and, as a consequence, risk losing their power.

Democratic political institutions provide an excellent mechanism for determining who is able to exercise political power, but those institutions rely on the existence of competing elites. Constitutional rules play an important role in defining the allowable scope of government authority, but they need to be enforced to be effective. Because that power of enforcement is in the hands of the ruling elite, it can only be effective if the power of some elites is able to check and balance the power of others. Democratic political institutions are good for the masses. Constitutional rules that limit the scope of government are good for the masses. But neither can be effective without competing elites who constrain each other from abusing their power.

Because the masses have minimal ability to constrain the ruling elite, a political system in which competing elites check and balance the power of each other is necessary to constrain the abuse of power. Checks and balances require more than just a separation of powers. Mere separation could give some elites absolute control over some powers and other elites absolute control over others.[18] Checks and balances require that the cooperation of competing elites, all of whom are jealously guarding their own power, is necessary for the ruling class to act.[19] Members of the elite have an incentive to protect their own power by preventing other elites from usurping it. This system is evident in the division of governance into legislative, executive, and judicial branches. Public policy measures require that all three branches support those measures. Effective institutional checks create what political scientists call veto players: members of the elite whose actions can block the actions of others, so that their cooperation is necessary for political action to proceed.[20]

---

[18] On this point, see Geoffrey Brennan and Alan Hamlin, "A Revisionist View of the Separation of Powers," *Journal of Theoretical Politics* 6, no. 3 (1994), pp. 345–368.

[19] This idea is developed by Torsten Persson, Gerard Roland, and Guido Tabellini, "Separation of Powers and Political Accountability," *Quarterly Journal of Economics* 112, no. 4 (November 1997), pp. 1163–1202.

[20] See George Tsebelis, *Veto Players: How Political Institutions Work* (Princeton, NJ: Princeton University Press, 2002).

FEDERALISM

This discussion of competition among elites has focused on institutions that place elites within a government to compete with each other. Competing governments also play a role in generating competition among elites. Mobility provides an escape from the abuse of power only if there are alternative locations where they can go. Internationally, one can see the migration of people from nations ruled by oppressive regimes toward those that allow more freedom. Federal systems offer that same type of mobility within their jurisdictions. Within the United States, for example, people are, on net, migrating from New York, Illinois, and California, to Texas and Florida. Within states, people can move from one local jurisdiction to another.

The political elite within states and nations attempt to limit that intergovernmental competition by agreeing to homogenize their policies. Tax treaties among nations are a good example of measures elite among nations can take to prevent other jurisdictions from appearing more desirable than their own. The European Union, while it offers many advantages to its citizens in the form of easy mobility of people and goods, also reduces the advantages of moving by homogenizing policies among the member nations.

Federalism also enables competition among levels of governments. The American Founders viewed that the state governments would be one check against the abuse of power by the federal government. Competing governmental units offer another mechanism that enables competition among elites.

THE CREATIVE DESTRUCTION OF POLITICAL COMPETITION

Chapter 5 noted the desire for stability among the political elite, who want to retain, and if possible, increase, their hold on power. Political competition threatens to destabilize the political power structure. Joseph Schumpeter depicted a capitalist economy as characterized by creative destruction.[21] The same is true of a competitive political environment. Just as incumbent businesses engage in rent-seeking to create barriers to entry into their markets, politicians also conspire with each other to create barriers to entry for those who would challenge their positions of

---

[21] Joseph A. Schumpeter, *Capitalism, Socialism, and Democracy*, 2nd ed. (London: George Allen & Unwin, 1947).

authority.²² Chapter 6 discussed some of the mechanisms the political elite design to preserve their elite positions and prevent their being displaced by challengers – measures that obviously reduce competition for power among elites. The political elite want order and stability, not competition and progress.

Without competition among members of the political elite, those in authority use their power to maintain their positions at the top of the power hierarchy by oppressing those below. Their aim is to prevent potential competitors from gaining sufficient power to challenge them. Venezuela was a relatively prosperous country before Hugo Chavez took over in 1999. His authoritarian rule was continued under Nicolas Maduro, who assumed power in 2013 after the death of Chavez. The country tumbled into economic ruin under their rule. Maduro would have to be delusional to think that his economic policies have furthered the interests of the masses, but his goal is not to benefit the masses. Rather, it is to maintain his own hold on power.

Similarly, Kim Jong-un, Supreme Leader in North Korea since 2011, surely can look across the border to South Korea and see that his authoritarian policies are compromising the well-being of North Koreans, but this is, at best, of secondary importance to Kim. His motivation is to maintain his position as Supreme Leader, and as with Maduro, the lack of political competition has resulted in economic stagnation and decline. Competition among political elites constrains their ability to abuse their power, which fosters economic competition and progress.

The economic and political elites have this in common: they want to preserve the status quo to retain their elite status. They want to prevent the creative destruction that Schumpeter described, and cooperate with an elite few to retain their status.²³ But the economy is always evolving, which necessarily affects the interactions among the economic and political elites.²⁴

---

[22] A more detailed explanation appears in Randall G. Holcombe, "Creative Destruction: Getting Ahead and Staying Ahead in a Capitalist Economy," *Review of Austrian Economics* 35, no. 4 (July 2022), pp. 467–480.

[23] For an experimental analysis, see Konstantin Chatziathanasiou, Svenja Hippel, and Michael Kurschilgen, "Does the Threat of Overthrow Discipline the Elites? Evidence from a Laboratory Experiment," *Journal of Legal Studies* 51, no. 2 (June 2022), pp. 289–320.

[24] A framework for understanding that evolution is presented by Armen A. Alchian, "Uncertainty, Evolution, and Economic Theory," *Journal of Political Economy* 58, no. 3 (June 1950), pp. 211–221. See also Eric D. Beinhocker, *The Origin of Wealth: Evolution, Complexity, and the Radical Remaking of Economics* (Boston: Harvard Business School Press, 2006), for an insightful analysis.

A substantial academic literature explains the interest group politics, rent-seeking, cronyism, and corruption that result from this cooperation between economic and political elites.[25] Over time, rent-seeking members of the economic elite conspire with the political elite to create more regulatory barriers to entry, more targeted subsidies and tax breaks, and more discretion in the enforcement of rules, which increasingly makes profitable business activity the result of political connections rather than satisfying the demands of consumers. The result, Mancur Olson said, is the decline of nations.[26]

The masses are not in a good position to prevent this. Because transaction costs prevent the masses from accessing power, competing elites are necessary to constrain the abuse of power.

CONCLUSION

Public policy is made within a political marketplace to which only an elite few have access. This creates the potential for those elite few who hold political power to abuse it, to the detriment of those who are governed by it. Many mechanisms can constrain the elite from abusing that power, including mobility of factors of production, democratic political institutions, and constitutional rules that limit the scope of government authority. These mechanisms will be insufficient unless they can be enforced. Because the power of enforcement lies with the political elite those mechanisms are designed to constrain, a necessary condition for them to act as constraints is competition among political elites.

Elites compete with each other in many ways. Party competition, competition over public policies, competition for committee memberships and chairmanships, attempts to move up the political chain of command, and attempts to enlarge the scope of power of the positions they currently hold. Competition among elites is also designed into the structure of government through a separation of powers, and through federal systems of government, that enable some members of the elite to check and balance any abuse of power by others.

This volume has noted that members of the elite have more in common with each other than with the masses, or than with challengers

---

[25] The process, along with the academic literature describing it, is discussed in Randall G. Holcombe, *Political Capitalism: How Economic and Political Power Is Made and Maintained* (Cambridge: Cambridge University Press, 2018).

[26] Mancur Olson, Jr., *The Rise and Decline of Nations* (New Haven, CT: Yale University Press, 1982).

who share their political affiliations and views. A Democratic legislator's interests are more aligned with those of Republican legislators than with Democrats who want to challenge Republican legislators in the next election. If this is so, why do members of the elite compete with each other rather than setting aside their differences to cooperate and maintain the status quo? The reason is the quest for power on the part of each individual member of the elite. Bertrand Russell said the quest for power is insatiable, and people who are the most power-hungry self-select into politics, where they can assume positions of authority to exercise power over others. The preservation of freedom for the masses requires a robust system that maintains competition among elites.

14

Politics as Exchange

James Buchanan, who was awarded the Nobel Prize in economics in 1986 for his contributions to the establishment of the public choice research program, cited politics as exchange as a component of the hardcore of public choice. He says, "A research program incorporates acceptance of a hard core of presuppositions that impose limits on the domain of scientific inquiry while, at the same time, insulating such inquiry from essentially irrelevant criticism. The hard core of public choice can be summarized in three presuppositions: (1) methodological individualism, (2) rational choice, and (3) politics-as exchange."[1] As its title suggests, the present volume focuses on that third presupposition.

The statement of those three presuppositions is so brief that each could be interpreted in a variety of ways. Despite Buchanan's depiction of those presuppositions as insulators against criticism, each has been questioned within the public choice research program itself. The questions others have raised about Buchanan's presuppositions are, perhaps, better viewed as elaborations and qualifications of Buchanan's brief statement. Nonetheless, each of those presuppositions warrants elaboration to be fully understood, and without elaboration could be misleading.

PRESUPPOSITIONS

Methodological Individualism

The key idea in this presupposition is that groups do not have preferences, and groups do not make choices. Individuals do. A public choice

---

[1] James M. Buchanan, "Public Choice: The Origins and Development of a Research Program" (Fairfax, VA: Center for Study of Public Choice, 2003). These three presuppositions appear prominently on the website of the Public Choice Society.

14 Politics as Exchange

analysis of government action looks at the individual choices made by individual decision-makers to understand how those actions of individuals shape the activities of government. Saying that government has taken some action, or that voters have chosen one candidate over another, is potentially misleading.[2] Government action must be understood as the result of the actions of individuals within the government.

In politics, however, people sometimes form their political preferences and make choices based on their personal identification as the member of a group.[3] This may be especially true of voters, who may identify themselves along ethnic, racial, gender, or ideological lines and vote based on their group identity. Many voters vote strictly along party lines, revealing that they are acting as members of a group rather than making an individual choice. So, a caveat must be added to this presupposition. Sometimes, people take political actions based on groups they identify with rather than based on their own individual interests.

Rational Choice

This presupposition says that people make choices that they believe are in their best interest. This seems almost self-evidently true. When faced with alternatives, people choose the one they believe will give them the most satisfaction. In politics, however, the most satisfying choice is not always the one someone would prefer to have implemented. The masses must realize that their one vote will not affect an election outcome, and that they, as individuals, have no influence over public policy. Thus, they have little incentive to make informed political choices, and often make political choices that are not in their own interests, or in the public interest.[4]

---

[2] The US presidential elections in 2000 and 2016 provide good examples to illustrate the point. The winner of a presidential election is determined by electoral votes, but in both of those elections, the electoral vote winner was not the popular vote winner. If votes were aggregated by who received the most popular votes, Al Gore would have been elected in 2000 rather than George Bush, and Hillary Clinton would have been elected in 2016 rather than Donald Trump. Voters, as a group, did not prefer one candidate over the other. Some voters preferred one candidate; other voters preferred the other.

[3] See James S. Coleman, *Foundations of Social Theory* (Cambridge, MA: Harvard University Press, 1990) and Randall G. Holcombe, *Following Their Leaders: Political Preferences and Public Policy* (Cambridge: Cambridge University Press, 2023).

[4] This line of reasoning is considered by Geoffrey Bnnan and Loren Lomasky, *Democracy and Decision: The Pure Theory of Electoral Preference* (Cambridge: Cambridge University Press, 1993) and Bryan Caplan, *The Myth of the Rational Voter: Why Democracies Choose Bad Policies* (Princeton, NJ: Princeton University Press, 2007).

Because they realize their political choices have no impact on political outcomes, they may vote for outcomes they would not choose if the choice were theirs alone.

Doing so is rational because of the nature of political choices, but both academics and the general public often take the idea of rational choice to mean that people will choose what is best for them, or is best for society as a whole. This may not be the case with political choices, because what people choose often has no effect on what they get. So here too, a caveat is required. Voters vote for options that make them feel good, which are not necessarily the outcomes they would most like to see prevail. Both academics and the general public often assume that rational choice means choosing the outcome one would most prefer, and if that is what one means by rational choice, political choices often are not rational in that sense.

Politics as Exchange

A primary theme in this volume is that there is a political marketplace in which legislators, lobbyists, interest groups, agency heads, and other well-connected interests engage in politics as exchange. Those well-connected individuals bargain among themselves to create the public policies that govern the interactions among individuals in a society. Within the rules they create, they bargain among themselves for their mutual advantage, just as people do in markets for goods and services. This is politics as exchange. The caveat in this case is that most people are excluded from transacting in the political marketplace, so politics as exchange applies only to an elite subset of the population.

The idea of politics as exchange is often taken to apply not only to those well-connected individuals but also to political activity in general. The thought is that through voting, interest group activity, and citizen participation, the political marketplace allocates resources in a manner similar to the way resources are allocated in markets for goods and services.[5] Buchanan, with coauthor Gordon Tullock, was quoted earlier in this volume in a passage worth repeating because it illustrates an element in the presupposition of politics as exchange that merits further

---

[5] This idea forms the basis of Donald Wittman's critique of the concept of government failure. See Donald A. Wittman, "Why Democracies Produce Efficient Results," *Journal of Political Economy* 97, no. 6 (1989), pp. 395–1424, and *The Myth of Democratic Failure* (Chicago, IL: University of Chicago Press, 1995).

scrutiny. They say, "Collective action is viewed as the action of individuals when they choose to accomplish purposes collectively rather than individually, and the government is seen as nothing more than the set of processes, the machine, which allows collective action to take place."[6] Government is, in fact, much more than this. The analysis in this volume explains why this statement by Buchanan and Tullock presents an overly optimistic view of politics as exchange.

There is a political marketplace in which well-connected individuals – members of the political elite – engage in exchange for their mutual advantage, but transaction costs prevent most people from participating in it. Politics as exchange applies to an elite few. The masses are excluded from the political marketplace in which public policies are designed, but are subject to the public policies that are created there.

A simplistic interpretation of politics as exchange envisions a political marketplace in which citizens collectively exchange to, as Buchanan and Tullock say, accomplish their purposes collectively. It promotes that romantic notion of democracy in which democratic governments are accountable to their citizens and act in their citizens' interests. That is not how the political marketplace operates. Political markets are more like markets for goods that create widespread negative externalities. An auto manufacturer negotiates with a steel mill to buy steel, for example, and air pollution is an external cost imposed on those who live in the vicinity of the mill. As Ronald Coase explains, high transaction costs prevent those who suffer from the pollution from negotiating with the polluter to internalize the externality.[7] Similarly, legislators and lobbyists negotiate with each other in the political marketplace to produce public policies, and third parties who are unable to participate in those negotiations bear the costs.

Participants in the political marketplace do not intend to impose costs on third parties, just as steel manufacturers do not intend to impose the cost of air pollution on third parties. In both cases, those costs are a by-product of their transactions in which those who face low transaction costs negotiate for their mutual benefit.

Buchanan and Tullock were well aware that this depiction of government is an idealization. Well before they wrote the passage just quoted, Buchanan wrote about the inefficiencies of political decision-making and

---

[6] James M. Buchanan and Gordon Tullock, *The Calculus of Consent* (Ann Arbor, MI: University of Michigan Press, 1962), p. 13.
[7] Ronald H. Coase, "The Problem of Social Cost," *Journal of Law & Economics* 3 (1960), pp. 1–44.

Tullock's work has consistently discussed the inefficiencies in political decision-making.[8] But a substantial academic literature depicts democratic government in this way, consistent with that romantic notion of democracy in which government is a mechanism that allows people to cooperate to further their mutual interests.

There is an element of truth in that notion, in that in almost every nation, people are better off living under the protective umbrella provided by their governments than if they had no government at all.[9] In many cases, the ruling class acts in the interests of those they rule because the interests of the rulers and the ruled are the same. Everyone benefits from an orderly and productive society. The danger in these idealistic depictions of government is that they legitimize the use of authority by the political elite and fail to recognize the potential for those who have political power to abuse it.

If unconstrained, those who hold government power can do substantial harm to those they rule and to those outside their borders. Hitler, Stalin, Chavez, and Kim provide examples. So, it is important to understand why government is necessary for an orderly society, why an elite few necessarily make and enforce the rules government imposes on the masses, and why the power of government must be constrained to minimize the abuse of power.

The progress and prosperity that humankind has enjoyed since the beginning of the Industrial Revolution rests on a fragile foundation. It requires institutions of authority and governance to create an orderly and productive society, but absent constraints on the political elite, that power and authority will almost surely be abused. As Lord Acton said,

---

[8] Buchanan compares government unfavorably with markets in James M. Buchanan, "Individual Choice in Voting and the Market," *Journal of Political Economy* 62, no. 4 (August 1954), pp. 334–343 nearly a decade prior to his book with Tullock. Some examples of Tullock's writing on inefficiencies in political decision-making include, "The Welfare Cost of Tariffs, Monopolies, and Theft," *Western Economic Journal* 5, no. 3 (June 1967), pp. 224–232. "The Transitional Gains Trap," *Bell Journal of Economics* 6, no. 2 (Autumn 1975), pp. 671–678, and *The Social Dilemma* (Indianapolis, IN: Liberty Fund, 2005).

[9] Some might disagree with this statement. See, for examples, Murray N. Rothbard, *For a New Liberty: A Libertarian Manifesto* (New York: Macmillan, 1973), David D. Friedman, *The Machinery of Freedom: Guide to Radical Capitalism* (Chicago, IL: Open Court Publishing Company, 1973), and Michael Huemer, *The Problem of Political Authority: An Examination of the Right to Coerce and the Duty to Obey* (New York: Palgrave Macmillan, 2013). But arguments disagreeing with this sentence would further support what is said in the remainder of this paragraph. Steven Pinker, *Enlightenment Now: The Case for Reason, Science, Humanism, and Progress* (New York: Viking, 2018) offers arguments in support of this statement.

power corrupts. Envisioning politics as exchange invites people to view political processes as benign, similar to economic processes in markets for goods and services in which people trade for their own benefit and are led by an invisible hand to further the interests of everyone. Political markets do not have that characteristic.

In markets for goods and services, most of the costs and benefits of exchange are confined to those who voluntarily agree to trade. In political markets, exchanges occur among an elite few, and most of the costs are imposed on the masses who are excluded from the political marketplace. That essential difference makes an uncritical acceptance of the concept of politics as exchange a dangerous proposition.

That dangerous proposition often is uncritically accepted, both by the general public and by academics who study politics. The general public often perceives problems and petitions the government to do something about them, with the thought that the government has both the capability and the incentive to improve things. Meanwhile, academic analyses of democratic decision-making depict the political elite as designing their policies to conform with citizen preferences. Much as with the invisible hand in markets for goods and services, academicians describe the visible hand of government as producing policies that are in the public interest. That view of politics as exchange is too optimistic.

One challenge to the ideas in this volume is that often, it is true that governments further the interests of the masses. When they do so, it is not because those in government are public-spirited civil servants who are looking for ways to improve the lot of the masses, but that they are constrained by various factors to act that way. A public choice approach to politics does not assume that public sector actors are any better or worse than private sector actors. In both cases, people can be opportunistic, which is why societies have police, courts, and prisons to sanction those who violate the rules and harm others.

Even the assumption that those in the public sector have motivations that are no different from those in the private sector may be overly optimistic. People who most desire to exercise power over others will self-select into public sector roles. Those who are most willing to impose costs on some to benefit others have an advantage in an institutional structure that runs based on force, which is why Friedrich Hayek says that the worst get on top.[10] Governments further the public interest when those within government are constrained to do so.

---

[10] Friedrich A. Hayek, *The Road to Serfdom* (London: George Routledge & Sons, 1944), ch. 10.

POLITICAL MARKETS

The existence of a political marketplace is generally recognized, both by academics who study politics and by the general public. People know that legislators make deals among themselves, and that they respond favorably to lobbyists and interest groups that support legislators. The political marketplace is not an analogy, implying that politics is like a marketplace. There is an actual political marketplace and participants do engage in politics as exchange. Recognizing that this is a real market with actual exchanges, an understanding of the way markets for goods and services work can illuminate the way that the political marketplace operates. To facilitate this, Chapter 2 introduced the economic model of competitive general equilibrium to serve as a benchmark. That model describes the theoretically ideal outcome of exchange within competitive markets.

Adam Smith noted the propensity for individuals to truck, barter, and exchange, and the general equilibrium model shows the outcome that would be produced if there were no impediments to exchange, so that every possible mutually beneficial exchange takes place. When that happens, welfare is maximized, in the sense that in competitive general equilibrium, nobody could be made better off without making someone else worse off. This is the outcome that would occur if there were no transaction costs, so there is nothing standing in the way of mutually advantageous exchanges.

Political exchange, like market exchange, requires low transaction costs – low enough that they are not an impediment to mutually advantageous exchanges. Those who transact in the political marketplace face low transaction costs, so are able to negotiate with each other to make mutually advantageous exchanges. Those who are in the low transaction cost group negotiate to allocate resources in a manner that maximizes the value to the members of the group, as the general equilibrium model describes. People who face high transaction costs, which prevent them from trading in the political marketplace, are prone to bear costs imposed on them by the transactions that take place in the political marketplace, as is the case in markets for goods and services that generate externalities.[11]

---

[11] Within that general equilibrium framework, see Francis M. Bator, "The Anatomy of Market Failure," *Quarterly Journal of Economics* 72, no. 3 (August 1958), pp. 351–379 on this point. A comparison of markets for goods and services and political markets is found in Randall G. Holcombe, "The Coase Theorem, Applied to Markets and Government," *The Independent Review* 23, no. 2 (Fall 2018), pp. 249–266.

This point, made by Ronald Coase in his pathbreaking article that emphasized the role of transaction costs in the creation of externalities, applies to political markets just as much as with markets for goods and services.[12] Well-connected individuals who face low transaction costs – legislators, lobbyists, and interest groups – negotiate to maximize the value of their transactions to themselves. Meanwhile, the masses, who face high transaction costs, are excluded from the political marketplace and bear the costs.

While transaction costs can arise from many sources, one factor that results in high transaction costs – the factor emphasized by Coase – occurs when large numbers of people are in the group that would have to transact. Large numbers generate high transaction costs. Because public policies apply to everyone in a jurisdiction, there is no way to get around the problem of large numbers which bring with them high transaction costs.

Markets for goods and services minimize transaction costs by reducing most transactions down to bilateral exchanges in which those who transact bear the costs and benefits of the transactions. People who do not believe that potential exchanges are in their best interest can choose not to participate. The political marketplace produces the institutions of governance and authority that apply to everyone's interactions, and transaction costs prevent everyone from negotiating to determine them. Transaction costs divide citizens into two groups: an elite few who make and enforce the rules, and the masses, who are compelled to follow them.

The size of the elite group who negotiate with each other to design public policy is necessarily small. Transaction costs limit the size of the political elite. The masses are unable to participate in the political marketplace because they face high transaction costs. Most people are aware of this division between the rulers and the ruled. By analyzing it within an economic framework, it becomes apparent not only that the division exists but also that because of transaction costs, it must exist.

CAN GOVERNANCE BECOME MORE INCLUSIVE?

Political systems have evolved substantially since the 1700s, when monarchies were the dominant form of government in the most developed nations. In an age of monarchy, it would have been difficult to foresee the widespread adoption of democratic political institutions. Looking

---

[12] Ronald H. Coase, "The Problem of Social Cost," *Journal of Law & Economics* 3 (1960), pp. 1–44.

ahead, perhaps there are ways to overcome the transaction costs created by large numbers so that governments can move away from being controlled by an elite few toward more egalitarian institutions. There are (at least) three problems that must be overcome for that to happen.

Information

Taking a brief detour into science fiction, one can imagine that artificial intelligence (AI) develops to the point where everyone could type their views, or even speak their views, into a computer network, and that AI would aggregate those views and compute the collective outcome that would result from everyone being able to negotiate in a no-transaction cost setting. One problem is that the information that would need to be utilized to undertake such a computation would not be available to anyone.

Referring back to the general equilibrium framework that was used as a benchmark, markets generate the information that leads to a welfare-maximizing outcome because people actually give up something of value to get something in return, which provides information on intensity of preference – information would not be available in the absence of a market. The value of goods and services is not some magnitude that is "out there" waiting to be discovered. Rather, that value is determined through the process of market exchange. Information produced through the process of exchange cannot be known prior to the process that produces it.

The same is true of political exchange. In determining a set of rules and institutions that apply to everybody, nobody will get exactly the outcome he or she wants. People will have to compromise, giving up a little on some issues to gain something on others, and the outcome of that negotiation to produce a "social contract" cannot be known without the negotiation taking place.[13] Some mechanism must be devised to reveal the intensity of people's political preferences.[14] In the absence of an actual negotiation, it is difficult to imagine such a mechanism – a mechanism that would reveal how much an individual would be willing to compromise on one issue to get more of what the individual wants on another. Meanwhile, high transaction costs prevent an actual negotiation from taking place.

---

[13] This issue is discussed by Friedrich A. Hayek, "The Use of Knowledge in Society," *American Economic Review* 35 (1945), pp. 519–530.
[14] For a possible mechanism that could reveal preference intensity, see T. Nicolaus Tideman and Gordon Tullock, "A New and Superior Process for Making Social Choices," *Journal of Political Economy* 84, no. 6 (December 1976), pp. 1145–1159.

This negotiation actually does take place in the political marketplace, where participants give up something to gain something of greater value to them. The problem, from the standpoint of society at large, is that most people are excluded from participating in the political marketplace, making it impossible to discover the actual value of public policies.

Implementation

If a mechanism were designed that would make the system of governance more inclusive, another problem is that someone would have to implement the system. This is problematic because the people who have the power to do so would not choose to give up their own power to see it through. It is easy to think of ways that, in the abstract, the political decision-making process can be improved. It is more difficult, in the real world, to enable changes that would empower the masses when those changes would reduce the power of the powerful. Even if changes could be conceived, implementing them would be a challenge if those who had the power to do so would lose power in the process. The powerful do not want to give up their power to make the political process more inclusive.

One response to this problem is that such changes have taken place over past centuries. These changes have occurred because the masses have become more mobile and because the masses have gained control over more resources. The political elite did not choose to give up some of their power; they were forced to.

Changes in economic conditions can lead to changes in political systems. Even as political systems have become more democratic, and citizens in democracies have become more free, this has had little effect on the size of the political elite or the division between elites and masses. The main consequence has been an increase in competition for entry into elite status, not an increase in the size of the elite. One does not have to imagine the power of the elite being diluted over time, because that has actually happened as a result of changes in economic conditions. That may continue to happen, but it will not create an open door to expand the size of the elite.

Incentives to Participate

A third problem is that if transaction costs were somehow lowered to allow more people to participate in the political marketplace, the impact of each individual's participation would be proportionately lower, reducing the incentive to participate. With the current political institutions, each member of the political elite can have a visible impact on public policy. If millions of people had equal opportunities to participate, each individual's impact would be too small to notice.

This gives rise to the rational ignorance that characterizes democratic participation in contemporary politics. If each individual's preferences have an imperceptible impact, nobody has an incentive to meaningfully participate. This goes beyond the issue of transaction costs. Even if there were no transaction costs, individuals would have little voice if they were one of a thousand, or a million, of those who participated equally.

The problem stems from the fact that one set of public policies applies to everyone. People cannot opt out from the authority of government. They can choose not to transact in markets for goods and services if the terms of a potential exchange do not look favorable, but the same is not true for institutions of governance.

The problems of information, implementation, and incentives reinforce the conclusion that the institutions of governance necessarily are controlled by an elite few. The idea that government can somehow be controlled by the masses is wishful thinking. The abuse of political power cannot be controlled by making political institutions more democratic, or by somehow increasing citizen participation. Transaction costs prevent it. Competition among elites is essential because those are the people who have power. They have the incentive to use their power to control the power of others in order to maintain and possibly increase their own power.

INSTITUTIONS OF AUTHORITY

Although institutions of authority provide advantages to the elite relative to the masses, the masses tolerate those institutions for several reasons. One reason is that they have little choice. Those in authority have the capacity to credibly threaten to impose high costs on those who do not comply with their rules, making resistance futile. Another reason is that the masses are better off living within an orderly and productive society that relies on government authority. The institutions of organization that produce an orderly and productive society require institutions of authority and governance to define and enforce people's rights. The necessity of these institutions of authority can be seen within the general equilibrium framework that provided a benchmark for welfare-enhancing social interaction.

The benefits of institutions of authority are recognized by the general public, who willingly defer to the authority of government. The elite promote those benefits through messages of patriotism and propaganda. Sporting events often begin with a rendition of the national anthem and, in larger events, flybys of military aircraft, which are cheered by those in attendance.[15] Voluntary displays of patriotism in nations around the world indicate that even while citizens are forced to comply with institutions of authority, they actively support those institutions.

That citizen support is reinforced by academic support. The basic framework for academic support is the prisoners' dilemma model in game theory, which demonstrates the possibility that individuals who act in their own narrow interests can produce a suboptimal social outcome. Everyone could be better off if they were forcibly prevented from undertaking actions that would be best for themselves and acting in the public interest. These game-theoretic models are further supported by models of voting and collective decision-making that depict democratic processes as leading to outcomes that increase the general welfare.

Those models of governance are descriptive, and the general public's perception of governmental authority is accurate, to the extent that those with political power face constraints that prevent them from abusing it. Citizens and academics in Western democracies tend to underestimate the value of constraints on the political elite, not perceiving how fragile those political institutions are. Those institutions rely on a balance of power that can easily be tipped, as Putin's Russia, Maduro's Venezuela, and Xi's China show.

To the question of why the masses appear to willingly accept the authority of the political elite, it does not matter whether institutions of authority are actually necessary for an orderly and productive society, but rather whether the masses think they are. If the masses believe that government authority is necessary for an orderly and productive society, they will accept that authority regardless of whether they are correct in their belief. Even if they do not believe that authority is necessary, they may still yield to it if they believe resistance would be futile. The danger in the arguments that the masses must yield to the authority of the elite is that they apply to the governments of Russia, Venezuela, China, and North Korea just as much as they apply to those in Western Europe.

---

[15] This is discussed at length by Christopher J. Coyne and Abigail R. Hall, *Manufacturing Militarism: U.S. Government Propaganda in the War on Terror* (Stanford, CA: Stanford University Press, 2021).

THE PURSUIT OF POWER

The necessary division between the rulers and the ruled conveys authority and power to those in the ruling class. People in general seek power, and the people who most desire to acquire power will self-select into the political marketplace. Much of this volume has discussed how the political elite cooperate with each other, and cooperate with the economic elite, for their mutual benefit. The political and economic elite are able to negotiate within the political marketplace because they face low transaction costs. What the elite trade in the political marketplace is access to power. They are negotiating for the right to mandate that people comply with their orders.

Members of the political elite do not just have power. It is not given to them. They must compete to get it. The competition for political power is, in the short run, a zero-sum game. One person's gain in power is another's loss. In the long run, those with power can increase their scope of power, adding to the power of the elite and reducing the freedom of the masses. The political elite seek power both by trying to increase the scope of power in their current positions and by moving up the power hierarchy by displacing those above them.

Note the difference between economic power and political power in this regard. People compete to gain political power by depriving others of it. Some people gain; others lose. Economic power is exercised by finding people who agree to cooperate with each other for their mutual benefit. While one might assume that people in politics are, as individuals, much like those who trade in goods and services, consider the differences in personalities between people who aspire to gain power by taking it from others compared with those who aspire to gain economic power through mutually advantageous and voluntary exchange.

The interests of the elite are, for the most part, held in common, and they cooperate with each other in the political marketplace to further those interests. But in one area, the pursuit of power, their interests conflict. The possibility of competing elites is the best opportunity for political institutions to prevent the abuse of power by those who hold it.

ECONOMIC AND POLITICAL INSTITUTIONS

Living conditions have become much better for the masses since the Enlightenment. The Enlightenment concept that government should serve its citizens, rather than citizens serving their governments, is a powerful one, and ideas do matter. But this idea is an aspiration, and it requires some institutional mechanisms behind it to make it operational. The ruling class will not give up its power for a slogan.

To maintain and enhance the institutional environment for the masses, it is necessary to understand why the well-being of the masses has increased so substantially since the Enlightenment. Setting aside slogans, economic institutions and political institutions have evolved to benefit the masses. Feudal economies have been displaced by market institutions, and monarchies have given way to democratic political institutions. These developments did not occur because people wished they would. They occurred because of a shift in the balance of power that constrained the political elite.

The institutional developments that have constrained the exercise of power by the elite have largely been economic ones. In agricultural societies that led the development of civilization for thousands of years, power came from control of land, and the elite gained control of land through conquering it by force. People were tied to the land, and land was the primary factor of production. Control over land gave the elite control over the people who worked the land. As the Industrial Revolution progressed, capital displaced land as the primary factor of production, and capital, unlike land, is mobile. To maintain power, the ruling class had to recognize the interests of capitalists and entrepreneurs, or lose those individuals and their capital, because they could move to more favorable jurisdictions. Economic changes eroded the power of the political elite.

Unlike land, which is fixed in quantity, capital can grow through investment. The most effective way for the political elite to increase the amount of capital under their control is not to take it from someone else, as is the case with land, but to create conditions favorable for innovation and investment. Mobility for the masses imposes constraints on the abuse of power by the elite.

Governments exercise their powers within given geographic boundaries. In agricultural societies, those geographic boundaries kept the key factor of production – land – under the control of the ruling class. In industrial societies, government authority remains restricted to geographic boundaries, but the key factor of production – capital – is mobile, lessening the ability of those with power to abuse it. The fact that land cannot move to another jurisdiction but capital can has been a major factor that has increased constraints on the political elite since the beginning of the Industrial Revolution.

As with economic institutions, the development of democratic political institutions came through a shifting in the balance of power. This is most evident in Britain, which retains its monarchy into the twenty-first century, but which has greatly diminished the power of the monarch. The power of the crown was negotiated away over a period of centuries, as the crown was forced to compromise with other holders of power. Democratic political institutions arose as a result of a competition among ambitious individuals to ascend into the ranks of the political elite. Democratic political institutions have been the result of evolution, not revolution.

Chapters 11–13 have discussed institutional features that can constrain the abuse of political power. The most important is competition among elites to enable the power of some to check and balance the power of others. This is essential because in the absence of competing elites, all other institutional features will be ineffective. Institutional constraints need an enforcement mechanism, and that authority rests with the elite. The mobility of the masses is important, but this mobility constrains the elite only because the masses can move from the jurisdiction of one set of elites to a jurisdiction controlled by another. Without competing elites, mobility would offer the masses no escape.

Separation of powers within government and a federal system of government have many benefits. The primary benefit is that it generates competition among elites. Representatives aspire to become Senators. Senators and governors aspire to become presidents. This competition among elites pushes those who want votes to appeal to the voters. The importance of constitutional constraints on the use of power, and of democratic political institutions, has been widely recognized. Less recognized, but no less important, is the mobility of people, goods, and capital. A protectionist agenda often has political appeal, but protectionism reduces mobility and lessens constraints on the political elite.

POPULISM

Populism is based on the claim that government is run by an elite few for their benefit. Populist politicians pledge that if they are put in control, they will return control of government to the citizens who are being governed. This is a powerful message because its main premise is true: government is run by an elite few. Populism as a political movement has no policy content. Political leaders from left to right have been identified as populists, ranging from Donald Trump in the United States, Boris

Johnson in the United Kingdom, Daniel Ortega in Nicaragua, Hugo Chavez in Venezuela, and Benjamin Netanyahu in Israel.[16] Hannah Arendt lists both Adolf Hitler and Joseph Stalin as populist leaders.[17] There is no populist ideology; just the claim that government is being run by an elite few, and that if put into power, populist leaders will make government accountable to the masses.

The term populism was first used in the late 1800s to describe a political movement in the United States, but the idea predates the term's first use. Karl Marx and Friedrich Engels, in *The Communist Manifesto*, made the claim that government works for the benefit of the elite, saying, "The executive of the modern state is but a committee for managing the common affairs of the whole bourgeoisie."[18]

The element of truth in the populist claim is that government is run by an elite few, a claim obvious enough that ordinary citizens can see it is true. One can see the appeal of populist rhetoric. While populists claim that this will change if they rise to power, it cannot. Transaction costs prevent it. When populist rulers take over, one set of elites just replaces another. The ultimate goal of populist politicians, and politicians more generally, is to increase their power, so populist politicians' goals can be achieved even if their promises cannot.

THE MARKETPLACE FOR IDEAS

At the conclusion of his *General Theory of Employment, Interest, and Money*, John Maynard Keynes wrote, "the ideas of economists and political philosophers, both when they are right and when they are wrong, are more powerful than is commonly understood. Indeed, the world is ruled by little else. ... soon or late, it is ideas, not vested interests, which are dangerous for good or evil."[19] The preceding analysis has placed heavy emphasis on the influence of interests and, in particular, the ability of the elite to act on and further their interests via the political marketplace, while the interests of the masses, unorganized because

---

[16] See Randall G. Holcombe, "Populism: Promises and Problems," *The Independent Review* 26, no. 1 (Summer 2021), pp. 27–37, for a discussion and list of populist leaders.
[17] Hannah Arendt, *The Origins of Totalitarianism* (Cleveland, OH: World Publishing Company, 1958).
[18] Karl Marx and Friedrich Engels, *The Communist Manifesto*, Authorized translation (New York: International Publishers [German original, 1848]), pp. 10–11.
[19] John Maynard Keynes, *The General Theory of Employment, Interest, and Money* (New York: Harcourt, Brace, and Company, 1936), pp. 383–384.

they face transaction costs too high to organize, are underrepresented. As Enlightenment ideas along with the Industrial Revolution brought increased freedom and prosperity to the masses, Chapter 11 emphasized the importance of increased mobility that gave the masses more freedom while constraining the abuse of power by the elite. One could conjecture that Enlightenment ideas would not have had a chance were it not for industrialization and increased mobility allowing them to be heard.

But Enlightenment ideas did have a substantial influence, because they provided a framework for institutionalizing the expanding opportunities that industrialization and increased mobility brought to the masses. As economic advances enabled the masses more freedom from the mandates of their rulers, Enlightenment ideas explained both why the masses were entitled to this freedom, and provided a framework for designing institutions that preserved their freedom.

The task of securing the freedom of the masses can never be completed, because there will always necessarily be a ruling elite, and members of the ruling class will always seek ways of expanding their power and using it to their advantage. Before this threat to the freedom of the masses can be countered, it must be recognized.

Institutionally, this means recognizing the inevitability of a ruling elite, along with the recognition that their interests often are at odds with the interests of the masses. This volume has discussed institutional constraints that can counter these institutional factors, emphasizing the importance of competition among elites, and discussing mobility, constitutional rules, and democratic decision-making. Absent these constraints, the ruling elite will abuse their power to the detriment of the masses. History, right up into the twenty-first century, shows that to be true.

Institutions to protect the masses require ideas to support them, and too often, popular ideas undermine the interests of the masses. The romantic vision of democracy as a system that is accountable to its citizens and that acts in their interests has been mentioned repeatedly. This romantic notion is supported by public choice models of voting, which depict a democratic process that produces results corresponding to the preferences of voters. The romantic notion of democracy is supported by academics just as much as by the general public. Democracies can be just as oppressive as autocracies if the ruling class is not constrained in other ways. This volume has focused on another idea, politics as exchange, which has the potential to undermine the interests of the masses if interpreted too broadly.

The danger in this concept is that it is not entirely incorrect. There is a political marketplace in which exchange takes place to determine public policy. Unlike the market for goods and services, which is open to everyone and in which everyone benefits, the political marketplace is limited to an elite few who benefit in much the same way as those who transact in the market for goods and services. Those benefits are often paid for by costs imposed on the masses, who are excluded from the political marketplace. Understanding how the political marketplace actually works, rather than how we wish it would work, can go some distance toward preventing it from being abused.

The marketplace for ideas is primarily an academic marketplace, at least initially. But ultimately, ideas dominate interests. Since the Enlightenment, governments have done many good things for people, but also many bad things. The authority of government is necessary for an orderly and prosperous society, but recognizing the inevitability that it is controlled by a small ruling elite, there are good reasons to be apprehensive when that ruling elite seeks to extend the scope of its powers.

References

Acemoglu, Daron, and James Robinson. *The Narrow Corridor: States, Societies, and the Fate of Liberty.* New York: Penguin, 2019.

Achen, Christopher H., and Larry M. Bartels. *Democracy for Realists: Why Elections Do Not Produce Responsive Government.* Princeton, NJ: Princeton University Press, 2016.

Alchian, Armen A. "Uncertainty, Evolution, and Economic Theory." *Journal of Political Economy* 58, no. 3 (June 1950): 211–221.

Aligica, Paul Dragos, Peter J. Boettke, and Vlad Tarko. *Public Governance and the Classical-Liberal Perspective: Political Economy Foundations.* Oxford: Oxford University Press, 2019.

Antunes, Catia, and Jos Gommans. *Exploring the Dutch Empire: Agents, Networks, and Institutions, 1600–2000.* London: Bloomsbury, 2015.

Arendt, Hannah. *The Origins of Totalitarianism.* Cleveland, OH: World Publishing Company, 1958.

Arrow, Kenneth J. "General Economic Equilibrium: Purpose, Analytic Techniques, Collective Choice." *American Economic Review* 64, no. 3 (June 1974): 253–272.

Arrow, Kenneth J. *Social Choice and Individual Values.* New York: John Wiley & Sons, 1951.

Arrow, Kenneth J., and Gerard Debreu. "Existence of an Equilibrium for a Competitive Economy." *Econometrica* 27, no. 3 (1954): 265–290.

Axelrod, Robert. *The Evolution of Cooperation.* New York: Basic Books, 1984.

Babcock, Richard F. *The Zoning Game: Municipal Practices and Policies.* Madison, WI: University of Wisconsin Press, 1966.

Bailyn, Bernard. *The Ideological Origins of the American Revolution.* Cambridge: Cambridge University Press, 1967.

Bator, Francis M. "The Anatomy of Market Failure." *Quarterly Journal of Economics* 72, no. 3 (August 1958): 351–379.

Bator, Francis M. "The Simple Analytics of Welfare Maximization." *American Economic Review* 47, no. 1 (March 1957): 22–59.

Beard, Charles A. *An Economic Interpretation of the Constitution of the United States.* New York: Macmillan, 1913.

Bearle, Adolf A., and Gardner C. Means. *The Modern Corporation and Private Property.* New York: Harcourt, Brace, and World, 1934.

Becker, Gary S. "A Theory of Competition among Pressure Groups for Political Influence." *Quarterly Journal of Economics* 98, no. 3 (August 1983): 371–400.

Beinhocker, Eric D. *The Origin of Wealth: Evolution, Complexity, and the Radical Remaking of Economics.* Boston: Harvard Business School Press, 2006.

Benson, Bruce L. *The Enterprise of Law: Justice without the State.* Oakland, CA: Pacific Research Institute for Public Policy, 1990.

Bergson, Abram. "A Reformulation of Certain Aspects of Welfare Economics." *Quarterly Journal of Economics* 52, no. 2 (February 1938): 310–334.

Bergson, Abram. "On the Concept of Social Welfare." *Quarterly Journal of Economics* 68, no. 2 (May 1954): 233–252.

Brennan, Geoffrey, and Alan Hamlin. "A Revisionist View of the Separation of Powers." *Journal of Theoretical Politics* 6, no. 3 (1994): 345–368.

Brennan, Geoffrey, and James M. Buchanan. *The Power to Tax: Analytical Foundations of a Fiscal Constitution.* Cambridge: Cambridge University Press, 1980.

Brennan, Geoffrey, and James M. Buchanan. *The Reason of Rules: Constitutional Political Economy.* Cambridge: Cambridge University Press, 1986.

Brennan, Geoffrey, and Loren Lomasky. *Democracy and Decision: The Pure Theory of Electoral Preference.* Cambridge: Cambridge University Press, 1993.

Browning, Edgar K. "Inequality and Poverty." *Southern Economic Journal* 55, no. 4 (April 1989): 819–830.

Buchanan, James M. "Afraid to be Free: Dependency as Desideratum." *Public Choice* 124, nos. 1/2 (July 2005): 19–31.

Buchanan, James M. "An Economic Theory of Clubs." *Economica n.s.* 32, no. 126 (February 1965): 1–14.

Buchanan, James M. "Individual Choice in Voting and the Market." *Journal of Political Economy* 62, no. 4 (August 1954): 334–343.

Buchanan, James M. "Politics, Policy, and the Pigouvian Margins." *Economica n.s.* 29, no. 113 (February 1962): 17–28.

Buchanan, James M. "Public Choice: The Origins and Development of a Research Program." Fairfax, VA: Center for Study of Public Choice, 2003.

Buchanan, James M. "Public Choice: Politics without Romance: A Sketch of Positive Public Choice Theory and Its Normative Implications." In *The Collected Works of* James M. Buchanan, vol. 1 (1999): 45–59.

Buchanan, James M. "Public Finance and Public Choice." *National Tax Journal* 28, no. 4 (December 1975): 383–394.

Buchanan, James M. "Social Choice, Democracy, and Free Markets." *Journal of Political Economy* 62, no. 2 (April 1954): 114–123.

Buchanan, James M. "The Domain of Constitutional Economics." *Constitutional Political Economy* 1, no. 1 (December 1990): 1–18.

Buchanan, James M. *The Limits of Liberty: Between Anarchy and Leviathan.* Chicago, IL: University of Chicago Press, 1975.

Buchanan, James M., and Roger D. Congleton. *Politics by Principle, Not Interest.* Cambridge: Cambridge University Press, 1998.

Buchanan, James M., and Gordon Tullock. *The Calculus of Consent.* Ann Arbor: University of Michigan Press, 1962.

Caplan, Bryan. *The Myth of the Rational Voter: Why Democracies Choose Bad Policies.* Princeton, NJ: Princeton University Press, 2007.

Case, Anne, and Angus Deaton. *Deaths of Despair and the Future of Capitalism.* Princeton, NJ: Princeton University Press, 2020.

Chakraborty, Rabindra Nath. "Sharing Culture and Resource Conservation in Hunter-Gatherer Societies." *Oxford Economic Papers* 59, no. 1 (January 2007): 63–88.

Chatziathanasiou, Konstantin, Svenja Hippel, and Michael Kurschilgen. "Does the Threat of Overthrow Discipline the Elites? Evidence from a Laboratory Experiment." *Journal of Legal Studies* 51, no. 2 (June 2022): 289–320.

Christensen, Clayton. *The Innovator's Dilemma: When New Technologies Cause Great Firms to Fail.* Cambridge, MA: Harvard Business Review Press, 1997.

Coase, Ronald H. "The Nature of the Firm." *Economica n.s.* 4, no. 16 (November 1937): 386–405.

Coase, Ronald H. "The Problem of Social Cost." *Journal of Law & Economics* 3 (1960): 1–44.

Coleman, James S. *Foundations of Social Theory.* Cambridge, MA: Harvard University Press, 1990.

Commons, John R. *Institutional Economics: Its Place in Political Economy.* New York: Macmillan, 1934.

Commons, John R. *The Legal Foundations of Capitalism.* Madison, WI: University of Wisconsin Press, 1924.

Congleton, Roger D. *Perfecting Parliament: Constitutional Reform, Liberalism, and the Rise of Western Democracy.* Cambridge: Cambridge University Press, 2011.

Congleton, Roger D., and Arye L. Hillman, eds. *Companion to the Political Economy of Rent-Seeking.* Cheltenham, UK: Edward Elgar, 2015.

Coward, Barry, and Peter Gaunt. *The Stuart Age: England, 1603–1714*, 5th ed. London: Routledge, 2017.

Coyne, Christopher J. and Abigail R. Hall. *How to Run Wars: An Confidential Playbook for the National Security Elite.* Oakland, CA: Independent Institute, 2024.

Coyne, Christopher J., and Abigail R. Hall. *Manufacturing Militarism: U.S. Government Propaganda in the War on Terror.* Stanford, CA: Stanford University Press, 2021.

Crain, W. Mark. "On the Structure and Stability of Political Markets." *Journal of Political Economy* 85, no. 4 (August 1977): 829–842.

de Jouvenel, Bertrand. *On Power: Its Nature, and the History of Its Growth.* New York: The Viking Press, 1949.

Delsol, Jean-Philippe, Nicolas Lecaussin, and Emmanual Martin, eds. *Anti-Piketty: Capital for the 21st Century.* Washington, DC: Cato Institute, 2017.

de Soto, Hernando. *The Other Path: The Invisible Revolution in the Third World.* New York: Harper & Row, 1989.

Diamond, Jared. *The World Until Yesterday: What Can We Learn from Traditional Societies?* New York: Viking, 2012.

Diamond, Peter A., and James A. Mirrlees. "Optimal Taxation and Public Production: I and II." *American Economic Review* 81 (March): 8–27 (June 1971): 261–278.

Dixit, Avinash. "Governance Institutions and Economic Activity." *American Economic Review* 99, no. 1 (March 2009): 5–24.

Downs, Anthony. *An Economic Theory of Democracy.* New York: Harper & Row, 1957.

Dunbar, Robin L. M. "Neocortex Size as a Constraint on Group Size in Primates." *Journal of Human Evolution* 22, no. 6 (1992): 469–493.

Duverger, Maurice. *Political Parties: Their Organization and Activity in the Modern State.* London: Methuen, 1964.

Edelman, Murray. *The Symbolic Uses of Politics.* Urbana, IL: University of Illinois Press, 1964.

Epstein, Richard A. *Takings: Private Property and the Power of Eminent Domain.* Cambridge, MA: Harvard University Press, 1985.

Foldvary, Fred. *Public Goods and Private Communities: The Market Provision of Social Services.* Aldershot, UK: Edward Elgar, 1994.

Forde, Daryll, and Mary Douglas. "Primitive Economies," ch. 2 in George Dalton, ed., *Tribal and Peasant Economies: Readings in Economic Anthropology.* Garden City, NY: Natural History Press (1967): 13–28.

Frank, Robert H. *Luxury Fever: Weighing the Cost of Excess.* Princeton, NJ: Princeton University Press, 2000.

Friedman, David D. *The Machinery of Freedom: Guide to Radical Capitalism.* Chicago, IL: Open Court Publishing Company, 1973.

Friedman, Walter A. *American Business History: A Very Short Introduction.* Oxford: Oxford University Press, 2020.

Furbotn, Erik G, and Rudolph Richter. *Institutions and Economic Theory: The Contributions of the New Institutional Economics.* Ann Arbor, MI: University of Michigan Press, 2000.

Galbraith, John Kenneth. *The Anatomy of Power.* Boston: Houghton Mifflin Company, 1983.

Graaf, J. de V. *Theoretical Welfare Economics.* Cambridge: Cambridge University Press, 1957.

Graeber, David, and David Wengrow. *The Down of Everything: A New History of Humanity.* New York: Aarrar, Straus and Giroux, 2021.

Grofman, Bernard, ed. *Political Gerrymandering and the Courts.* New York: Agathon Press, 1990.

Hardin, Garrett. "The Tragedy of the Commons." *Science* 162, no. 3859 (December 13, 1968): 1243–1248.

Hayek, Friedrich A. *Individualism and Economic Order.* London: Routledge and Kegan Paul, 1944.

Hayek, Friedrich A. *The Fatal Conceit: The Errors of Socialism.* Chicago, IL: University of Chicago Press, 1988.

Hayek, Friedrich A. *The Road to Serfdom.* London: George Routledge & Sons, 1944.

Hayek, Friedrich A. "The Use of Knowledge in Society." *American Economic Review* 35 (1945): 519–530.

Heilbroner, Robert L. *The Making of Economic Society*. Englewood Cliffs, NJ: Prentice-Hall, 1962.
Hicks, John R. *Value and Capital*. Oxford, UK: Clarendon Press, 1939.
Hobbes, Thomas. *Leviathan*. New York: E. P. Dutton, 1950 [orig. 1651].
Hochman, Harold M., and James D. Rodgers. "Pareto Optimal Redistribution." *American Economic Review* 59, no. 4, Part 1 (1969): 542–557.
Holcombe, Randall G. *Advanced Introduction to Public Choice*. Cheltenham, UK: Edward Elgar, 2016.
Holcombe, Randall G. "A Note on Seniority and Political Competition." *Public Choice* 61, no, 3 (June 1989): 285–288.
Holcombe, Randall G. *Coordination, Cooperation, and Control: The Evolution of Economic and Political Power*. Cham, Switzerland: Palgrave Macmillan, 2020.
Holcombe, Randall G. "Contractarian Ideology and the Legitimacy of Government." *Journal of Institutional Economics* 17, no. 3 (June 2021): 379–391.
Holcombe, Randall G. "Creative Destruction: Getting Ahead and Staying Ahead in a Capitalist Economy." *Review of Austrian Economics* 35, no. 4 (July 2022): 467–480.
Holcombe, Randall G. *Entrepreneurship and Economic Progress*. London: Routledge, 2007.
Holcombe, Randall G. *Following Their Leaders: Political Preferences and Public Policy*. Cambridge: Cambridge University Press, 2023.
Holcombe, Randall G. *From Liberty to Democracy: The Transformation of American Government*. Ann Arbor, MI: University of Michigan Press, 2002.
Holcombe, Randall G. "Government: Unnecessary but Inevitable." *The Independent Review* 8, no. 3 (Winter 2004): 325–342.
Holcombe, Randall G. *Liberty in Peril: Democracy and Power in American History*. Oakland, CA: Independent Institute, 2019.
Holcombe, Randall G. *Political Capitalism: How Economic and Political Power Is Made and Maintained*. Cambridge: Cambridge University Press, 2018.
Holcombe, Randall G. "Political Entrepreneurship and the Democratic Allocation of Resources." *Review of Austrian Economics* 15, nos. 2/3 (June 2002): 143–159.
Holcombe, Randall G. "Populism: Promises and Problems." *The Independent Review* 26, no. 1 (Summer 2021): 27–37.
Holcombe, Randall G. "Political Incentives for Rent Creation." *Constitutional Political Economy* 28, no. 1 (March 2017): 62–78.
Holcombe, Randall G. "Principles and Politics: Like Oil and Water." *Review of Austrian Economics* 22, no. 2 (June 2008): 151–157.
Holcombe, Randall G. "The Coase Theorem, Applied to Markets and Government." *The Independent Review* 23, no. 2 (Fall 2018): 249–266.
Holcombe, Randall G. *The Economic Foundations of Government*. New York: New York University Press, 1994.
Holcombe, Randall G. "The Economic Theory of Rights." *Journal of Institutional Economics* 10, no. 3 (September 2014): 471–491.
Holcombe, Randall G. "The Transformative Impact of Rent-Seeking on the Study of Public Choice." *Public Choice* 196, nos. 1/2 (July 2023): 157–167.

Holcombe, Randall G. "Why Does Government Produce National Defense?" *Public Choice* 137, nos. 1/2 (October 2008): 11–19.

Holcombe, Randall G., and Christopher J. Boudreaux. "Regulation and Corruption." *Public Choice* 164, no. 1 (July 2015): 75–85.

Holcombe, Randall G., and DeEdgra W. Williams. "The Cartelization of Local Governments." *Public Choice* 149, nos. 1/2 (October 2011): 65–74.

Holcombe, Randall G., and Glenn R. Parker. "Committees in Legislatures: A Property Rights Perspective." *Public Choice* 70, no. 1 (April 1991): 11–20.

Huemer, Michael. *The Problem of Political Authority: An Examination of the Right to Coerce and the Duty to Obey*. New York: Palgrave Macmillan, 2013.

Hughes, Jonathan R. T. *The Governmental Habit: Economic Controls from Colonial Times to the Present*. New York: Basic Books, 1977.

Hume, David. *A Treatise on Human Nature*, 2nd ed., Sir Lewis Amherst Selby-Bigge, and P. H. Nidditch (eds.). Oxford: Oxford University Press, 1978 [orig. 1739–40].

Ikeda, Sanford. *Dynamics of the Mixed Economy: Toward a Theory of Interventionism*. London: Routledge, 1997.

Jensen, Michael C., and William H. Meckling. "Theory of the Firm: Managerial Behavior, Agency Costs, and Ownership Structure." *Journal of Financial Economics* 3, no. 4 (October 1976): 305–360.

Kelman, Steven. "'Public Choice' and Public Spirit." *The Public Interest* 87 (Spring 1987): 80–94.

Keynes, John Maynard. *The General Theory of Employment, Interest, and Money*. New York: Harcourt, Brace, and Company, 1936.

Kinsella, N. Stephan. *Against Intellectual Property*. Auburn, AL: Ludwig von Mises Institute, 2008.

Kirzner, Israel. *Competition and Entrepreneurship*. Chicago, IL: University of Chicago Press, 1973.

Koford, Kenneth J. "Centralized Vote Trading." *Public Choice* 39, no. 2 (1982): 245–268.

Koppl, Roger. *Big Players and the Economic Theory of Expectations*. Houndmills, Basingstoke, Hampshire, UK: Palgrave Macmillan, 2002.

Krueger, Anne O. "The Political Economy of the Rent-Seeking Society." *American Economic Review* 64 (1974): 291–303.

Kukathas, Chandran. *The Liberal Archipelago: A Theory of Diversity and Freedom*. Oxford: Oxford University Press, 2007.

Kurrild-Klitgaard, Peter. *Rational Choice, Collective Action, and the Paradox of Rebellion*. Copenhagen: University of Copenhagen Institute of Political Science, 1997.

Lange, Oskar, and Fred M. Taylor. *On the Economic Theory of Socialism*. Minneapolis, MN: University of Minnesota Press, 1938.

Lerner, Abba P. *The Economics of Control: Principles of Welfare Economics*. New York: Macmillan, 1944.

Levi, Margaret. *Of Rule and Revenue*. Berkeley, CA: University of California Press, 1988.

Lewis, Hyrum, and Verlan Lewis. *The Myth of Left and Right: How the Political Spectrum Misleads and Harms America*. Oxford: Oxford University Press, 2023.

Lichbach, Mark Irving. *The Rebel's Dilemma*. Ann Arbor, MI: University of Michigan Press, 1995.

Lingle, Christopher. *The Rise and Decline of the Asian Century: False Starts on the Path to the Global Millennium*. Barcelona: Editions Sirocco, 1997.

Lingle, Christopher. *Singapore's Authoritarian Capitalism: Asian Values, Free Market Illusions, and Political Dependency*. Fairfax, VA: Locke Institute, 1996.

Locke, John. *Two Treatises of Government*. Cambridge: Cambridge University Press, 1960 [orig. 1690].

Lofgren, Mike. *The Deep State: The Fall of the Constitution and the Rise of a Shadow Government*. New York: Penguin Random House, 2016.

Machiavelli, Niccolo. *The Prince*. Chicago, IL: University of Chicago Press, 1985 [orig. 1532].

Malthus, Thomas Robert. *An Essay on the Principle of Population*. London: J. Johnson, 1798.

Malthus, Thomas Robert. *Principles of Political Economy*. London: William Pickering, 1836.

Martis, Kenneth C. *The Historical Atlas of United States Congressional Districts: 1789–1983*. New York: Free Press, 1982.

Marx, Karl. *Capital: A Critique of Political Economy*. Chicago, IL: Charles H. Kerr & Company, 1906.

Marx, Karl, and Friedrich Engels. *The Communist Manifesto*. New York: International Publishers, 1948 [orig. 1848].

McChesney, Fred S. *Money for Nothing: Politicians, Rent Extraction, and Political Extortion*. Cambridge, MA: Harvard University Press, 1997.

McChesney, Fred S. "Rent Extraction and Rent Creation in the Economic Theory of Regulation." *Journal of Legal Studies* 16, no. 1 (January 1987): 101–118.

McConnell, Grant. *Private Power and American Democracy*. New York: Alfred A. Knopf, 1966.

McKenzie, Richard B., and Dwight R. Lee. *Quicksilver Capital: How the Rapid Movement of Wealth Has Changed the World*. New York: Free Press, 1991.

Medima, Steven G. "The Coase Theorem at Sixty." *Journal of Economic Literature* 53, no. 4 (December 2020): 1045–1128.

Michels, Robert. *Political Parties: A Sociological Study of the Oligarchical Tendencies of Modern Democracy*. Glencoe, IL: Free Press, 1915.

Mills, C. Wright. *The Power Elite*. New York: Oxford University Press, 1956.

Minasian, Jora R. "Television Pricing and the Theory of Public Goods." *Journal of Law & Economics* 7 (October 1964): 71–80.

Mirrlees, James A. "An Exploration in the Theory of Optimum Income Taxation." *Review of Economic Studies* 38 (1971): 175–208.

Mirrlees, James A. "Optimal Tax Theory – A Synthesis." *Journal of Public Economics* 6, no. 4 (1976): 327–358.

Mises, Ludwig von. *Human Action: A Treatise on Economics, Scholar's Edition*. Auburn, AL: Ludwig von Mises Institute, 1998.

Mises, Ludwig von. *Socialism: An Economic and Sociological Analysis*. New Haven, CT: Yale University Press, 1951.

Mosca, Gaetano. *The Ruling Class*. New York: McGraw Hill, 1939.

Munger, Michael, and Georg Vanberg. "Contractarianism, Constitutionalism, and the Status Quo." *Public Choice* 195, nos. 3/4 (June 2023): 323–339.

Neal, Larry, and Rondo Cameron. *A Concise Economic History of the World: From Paleolithic Times to the Present*, 5th ed. New York: Oxford University Press, 2016.

Niskanen, William A. *Bureaucracy and Representative Government*. Chicago, IL: Aldine-Atherton, 1971.

North, Douglass C. "A Transaction Cost Theory of Politics." *Journal of Theoretical Politics* 2, no. 4 (1990): 355–367.

North, Douglass C. "Institutions." *Journal of Economic Perspectives* 5, no. 1 (Winter 1991): 97–112.

North, Douglass C. *Structure and Change in Economic History*. New York: Norton, 1981.

North, Douglass C., and Robert P. Thomas. *The Rise of the Western World: A New Economic History*. Cambridge: Cambridge University Press, 1973.

North, Douglass C., John Joseph Wallis, and Barry R. Weingast. *Violence and Social Orders: A Conceptual Framework for Interpreting Recorded History*. Cambridge: Cambridge University Press, 2009.

Olson, Mancur, Jr. *The Logic of Collective Action*. Cambridge, MA: Harvard University Press, 1965.

Olson, Mancur, Jr. *The Rise and Decline of Nations*. New Haven, CT: Yale University Press, 1982.

Osborne, David, and Ted Gaebler. *Reinventing Government: How the Entrepreneurial Spirit Is Transforming the Public Sector*. Reading, MA: Addison-Wesley, 1992.

Ostrom, Elinor. *Governing the Commons: The Evolution of Institutions for Collective Action*. Cambridge: Cambridge University Press, 1990.

Paine, Thomas. "Common Sense." [1776]. Ch. 15 in Moncure Daniel Conway, *The Writings of Thomas Paine*, vol. 1. New York: G. P. Putnam's Sone, 1894: 67–120.

Persson, Torsten, Gerard Roland, and Guido Tabellini. "Separation of Powers and Political Accountability." *Quarterly Journal of Economics* 112, no. 4 (November 1997): 1163–1202.

Pierre, Jon, and B. Guy Peters. *Advanced Introduction to Governance*. Cheltenham, UK: Edward Elgar, 2021.

Piketty, Thomas. *Capital in the Twenty-First Century*. Cambridge, MA: Harvard University Press, 2014.

Pinker, Steven. *Enlightenment Now: The Case for Reason, Science, Humanism, and Progress*. New York: Viking, 2018.

Pinker, Steven. *The Better Angels of Our Nature: Why Violence Has Declined*. New York: Viking, 2011.

Rawls, John. *A Theory of Justice*. Cambridge, MA: Belknap, 1971.

Ricardo, David. *Principles of Political Economy and Taxation*, 3rd ed. London: John Murray, 1821 [1st ed. 1817].

Richman, Barak D. *Stateless Commerce: The Diamond Network and the Persistence of Relational Exchange*. Cambridge, MA: Harvard University Press, 2017.

Riker, William H. *The Theory of Political Coalitions.* New Haven, CT: Yale University Press, 1962.

Rohde, David. *In Deep: The FBI, CIA, and the Truth about America's "Deep State."* New York: W. W. Norton, 2020.

Rothbard, Murray N. *For a New Liberty: A Libertarian Manifesto.* New York: Macmillan, 1973.

Rothbard, Murray N. *The Ethics of Liberty.* Atlantic Highlands, NJ: Humanities Press, 1982.

Rousseau, Jean-Jacques. *Discourse on the Origin of Inequality.* Indianapolis, IN: Hackett Publishing Company, 1992 [orig. 1755].

Rousseau, Jean Jacques. *The Social Contract, Or Principles of Political Right.* Translated by G. D. H. Cole. London: J. M. Dent and Sons, 1923 [orig. 1762].

Rummel, R. J. *Death by Government.* New Brunswick, NJ: Transaction Publishers, 1994.

Russell, Bertrand. "What Desires Are Politically Important?" Nobel Lecture, December 11, 1950, found at www.nobelprize.org/prizes/literature/1950/russell/lecture.

Sachs, Jeffrey D. and Andrew M. Warner. "Natural Resources and Economic Development: The Curse of Natural Resources." *European Economic Review* 45 (2001): 827–838.

Saez, Emmanuel, and Gabriel Zucman. *Triumph of Injustice: How the Rich Dodge Taxes and How to Make Them Pay.* New York: W. W. Norton, 2019.

Sahlins, Marshall. "Notes on the Original Affluent Society." In Richard B. Lee and Irven DeVore, eds., *Man the Hunter: The First Intensive Survey of a Single, Crucial Stage of Human Development—Man's Once Universal Hunting Way of Life.* Chicago, IL: Aldine Publishing Company (1968): 85–99.

Samuelson, Paul A. "A Diagrammatic Exposition of a Theory of Public Expenditure." *Review of Economics and Statistics* 37 (November 1955): 350–356.

Samuelson, Paul A. *Economics,* 9th ed. New York: McGraw Hill, 1973.

Samuelson, Paul A. *Foundations of Economic Analysis.* Cambridge, MA: Harvard University Press, 1947.

Samuelson, Paul A. "The Pure Theory of Public Expenditure." *Review of Economics and Statistics* 36 (November 1954): 387–389.

Schattschneider, E. E. *Party Government.* New York: Reinhart & Company, 1959.

Schattschneider, E. E. *The Semisovereign People: A Realist's View of Democracy in America.* New York: Holt, Rinehart, and Winston, 1960.

Schattschneider, E. E. *The Struggle for Party Government.* College Park: University of Maryland Program in American Civilization, 1948.

Schumpeter, Joseph A. *Capitalism, Socialism, and Democracy,* 2nd ed. London: George Allen & Unwin, 1947.

Schweizer, Peter. *Extortion: How Politicians Extract Your Money, Buy Votes, and Line Their Own Pockets.* Boston: Houghton Mifflin, 2013.

Schweizer, Peter. *Secret Empires: How the American Political Class Hides Corruption and Enriches Family and Friends.* New York: Harper, 2018.

Sinclair, Upton. *The Jungle.* New York: Doubleday, Page & Co., 1906.

Skarbek, David. *The Social Order of the Underworld: How Prison Gangs Govern the American Penal System.* Oxford, UK: Oxford University Press, 2014.

Smith, Adam. *The Wealth of Nations.* New York: Modern Library, 1937 [orig. 1776].

Smith, Eric Alden, and Brian F. Codding. "Ecological Variation and Institutionalized Inequality in Hunter-Gatherer Societies." *PNAS* 118, no. 13 (2021) e2016134118.

Solow, Robert M. "A Contribution to the Theory of Economic Growth." *Quarterly Journal of Economics* 70 (1956): 65–94.

Starkey, David. *Magna Carta: The True Story behind the Charter.* London: Hodder & Stoughton, 2015.

Stigler, George J. "Director's Law of Public Income Redistribution." *Journal of Law & Economics* 13, no. 1 (April 1970): 1–10.

Stigler, George J. "The Theory of Economic Regulation." *Bell Journal of Economics and Management Science* 2, no. 1 (1971): 3–21.

Stigler, George J. *The Theory of Price*, 3rd ed. New York: Macmillan, 1966.

Stiglitz, Joseph E. *The Price of Inequality: How Today's Divided Society Endangers the Future.* New York: W. W. Norton, 2012.

Stockman, David A. *The Great Deformation: The Corruption of Capitalism in America.* New York: Public Affairs Press, 2013.

Suzman, James. *Affluence without Abundance: The Disappearing World of the Bushmen.* New York: Bloomsbury, 2017.

Tideman, T. Nicolaus, and Gordon Tullock. "A New and Superior Process for Making Social Choices." *Journal of Political Economy* 84, no. 6 (December 1976): 1145–1159.

Tiebout, Charles M. "A Pure Theory of Local Expenditures." *Journal of Political Economy* 64, no. 5 (October 1956): 416–424.

Tsebelis, George. *Veto Players: How Political Institutions Work.* Princeton, NJ: Princeton University Press, 2002.

Tullock, Gordon. "The Charity of the Uncharitable." *Western Economic Journal* 9, no. 4 (December 1971): 379–392.

Tullock, Gordon. *The Economics of Income Redistribution*, 2nd ed. New York: Springer, 1997.

Tullock, Gordon. *The Politics of Bureaucracy.* Washington, DC: Public Affairs Press, 1965.

Tullock, Gordon. *The Social Dilemma.* Indianapolis, IN: Liberty Fund, 2005.

Tullock, Gordon. "The Transitional Gains Trap." *Bell Journal of Economics* 6, no. 2 (Autumn 1975): 671–678.

Tullock, Gordon. "The Welfare Cost of Tariffs, Monopolies, and Theft." *Western Economic Journal* 5, no. 3 (June 1967): 224–232.

Wagner, Richard E. *Fiscal Sociology and the Theory of Public Finance.* Cheltenham, UK: Edward Elgar, 2007.

Wagner, Richard E. *Politics as Peculiar Business: Insights from a Theory of Entangled Political Economy.* Cheltenham, UK: Edward Elgar, 2016.

Waldo, Dwight. *The Administrative State: A Study of the Political Theory of American Public Administration.* New York: Ronald Press Co., 1948.

Walras, Leon. *Elements of Pure Economics.* London: Routledge, 2003 [orig. 1874].

Weber, Max. "Politics as a Vocation." In H. H. Gerth and C. Wright Mills, eds., *From Max Weber: Essays in Sociology*. New York: Oxford University Press, 77–128.

Weingast, Barry R., Kenneth A. Shepsle, and Christopher Johnsen. "The Political Economy of Benefits and Costs: A Neoclassical Approach to Distributive Politics." *Journal of Political Economy* 89, no. 4 (August 1981): 642–664.

Williamson, Oliver E. "A Comparison of Alternative Approaches to Economic Methodology." *Journal of Institutional and Theoretical Economics* 146, no. 1 (1990): 595–613.

Williamson, Oliver E. *The Mechanisms of Governance*. New York: Oxford University Press, 1996.

Wilson, Woodrow. "The Study of Administration." *Political Science Quarterly* 2, no. 2 (June 1887): 197–222.

Wittman, Donald A. *The Myth of Democratic Failure*. Chicago, IL: University of Chicago Press, 1995.

Wittman, Donald A. "Why Democracies Produce Efficient Results." *Journal of Political Economy* 97, no. 6 (1989): 1395–1424.

Yeager, Leland B. *Ethics as a Social Science: The Moral Philosophy of Social Cooperation*. Cheltenham, UK: Edward Elgar, 2001.

Yeager, Leland B. "Rights, Contract, and Utility in Policy Espousal." *Cato Journal* 5, no. 1 (1985): 259–294.

Index

Acemoglu, Daron, 68
Acton, Lord, 234
Adams, John, 238
Adams, John Quincy, 238
administrative state, 121
affirmative action, 159
agricultural revolution, 184–185
American Association of Retired Persons, 133
anarchy, libertarian, 16
Anglican Church, 214
Archer Daniels Midland, 128
Arendt, Hannah, 265
Arrow, Kenneth J., 146
artificial intelligence, 258
autocracy, 71
Axelrod, Robert, 43

Bailyn, Bernard, 167
basketball, rules of, 92
Beard, Charles A., 220
Berlin Wall, 28, 92, 180, 204, 241
  and yardstick competition, 177
Bezos, Jeff, 155
Biden, Joe, 90, 222
Black Caucus, 241
Bloomberg, Michael, 132
Brennan, Geoffrey, 227
bridge to nowhere, 1
Britain, democracy in, 214
Buchanan, James M., 14, 59, 61, 68, 92, 131, 149, 219, 250, 252–253
  and constitutional political economy, 218

Bush, George H. W., 101, 221
Bush, George W., 109

California rule, 134
Cameron, Rondo, 190
Carter, Jimmy, 101
Case, Anne, 161
Castro, Fidel, 73, 93, 100, 180
central economic planning, 25
Chakraborty, Rabindra, 187
Chavez, Hugo, 103, 204, 239, 247, 265
church as a check on power, 90
Church Committee, 122
circular reference. *See* reference, circular
Civil Aeronautics Board, 142
Coase, Ronald H., 37, 134, 253, 257
Coase theorem, 7, 57
  and general equilibrium, 26
Codding, Brian F., 190
cognitive dissonance, 136
Cold War, 71
collective bargaining, 23
comfort women, 54
common pool problem, 96
Commons, John R., 63, 150, 160
competition, political vs. economic, 53
Congleton, Roger D., 211
congressional committees, 97
Constitution of the United States
  Article I, Section 8, 165
  commerce clause, 166
  Sixteenth Amendment to, 89
  Tenth Amendment, 165
constitutional rules, effectiveness of, 218

contracts, 35, 39
  enforcement of, 40
copyright law, 56, 66, 151, 153
creative destruction, 84, 246
cyclical majority, 108, 243

de Jouvenel, Bertrand, 76
Deaton, Angus, 161
Debreu, Gerard, 146
deep state, 124
democracy
  as a constraint on power, 90
  romantic notion of, 4, 207, 209, 222, 266
DeSantis, Ron, 166
Diamond, Jared, 189
diamond traders, and informal institutions, 44
Disney company, 60, 166
division of power, 104
Dodd-Frank, 172
Douglas, Mary, 187
Dunbar's number, 88, 113, 187, 190, 193–194
Dutch East India Company, 199

Electoral College, 237
elite rule, popular support for, 16
Engels, Friedrich, 265
Enlightenment, 16, 167, 210, 244, 262, 266
  and democracy, 211
  philosophy of, 168
Environmental Protection Agency, 119, 121
environmental regulations, 11
ethanol mandate, 8, 109, 128, 140
European Union, 246
Everytown for Gun Safety, 132

Federal Aviation Administration, 120
Federal Reserve System, 172
federalism, 177, 246
Fetterman, John, 236
Ford, Henry, 155, 159
Forde, Daryll, 187
free trade, 232
French Revolution, 167
Friedman, David, 174
Friedman, Milton, 162
Furubotn, Erik G., 53

Gaddafi, Muammar, 73, 241
Galbraith, John Kenneth, 75
Gates, Bill, 66, 155
general equilibrium, 19, 67
  and economic progress, 27
  in real-world economies, 25
  value of, 26
gerrymandering, 99
gluts, 19
governance
  definition of, 53
  distinguished from government, 59, 62–63
governance, corporate, 69
Graeber, David, 186, 193
Gravina Island, 1
Great Depression, 170

Harley-Davidson, 109, 139
Harris, Kamala, 223
Hayek, Friedrich A., 255
Henry VIII, 214
Hitler, Adolf, 103, 239, 265
Hobbes, Thomas, 51, 67, 73, 78, 145, 235
  compared to Rousseau, 209
Hoover, J. Edgar, 122
Hume, David, 8

incumbency, advantages of, 100
Industrial Revolution, and mobility, 184
institutional economics, 63
institutions
  of authority, 21
  as constraints, 17
  formal and informal, 87
  functions of, 22, 33
  informal, 43, 45
  to match suppliers with demanders, 34
  of organization, 21, 34
  and transaction costs, 50
intangible property, 56
intellectual property, 56, 65, 151, 153
interest groups, 6
  and cognitive dissonance, 138
  organized and unorganized, 127
  and political extortion, 141
interest groups, and expressive preferences, 135
intergovernmental grants, 178

Jackson, Andrew, 238
Jefferson, Thomas, 238

Index

Jensen, Michael C., 38
Johnson, Boris, 102, 265

Keynes, John Maynard, 265
Kim Jong-un, 73, 93, 102, 247
Kirzner, Israel, 28
Koppl, Roger, 139
Korea, 204, 247
Krueger, Anne O., 110

land reform, 56
legislation
  as an "all-or-nothing" sale, 117
  bundled, 116
  creation of, 4
legislatures, voting in, 4
legitimacy, perception of, 72
Lenin, Vladimir, 73, 100, 180
limited liability corporation, 64–65
Locke, John, 167, 234
Lofgren, Mike, 122
logrolling, 1, 18, 113
Lomasky, Loren, 227

Machiavelli, Niccolo, 235
Maduro, Nicolas, 90, 247
Magna Carta, 215
Malthus, Thomas Robert, 155, 195, 201
market exchange, compared with political exchange, 9
market failure, 46, 169
  as profit opportunity, 170
Marx, Karl, 151, 161, 198, 201, 265
Meckling, William H., 38
methodological individualism, 250
Michels, Robert, 76, 210
Microsoft, 66
milker bills, 2
Mills, C. Wright, 75
minimum winning coalition, 242
Mosca, Gaetano, 168, 179
Musk, Elon, 77

National Rifle Association, 131
Nature Conservancy, 137
Neal, Larry, 190
Netanyahu, Benjamin, 265
New Deal, 170
North, Douglass C., 12, 22, 35, 52, 68, 100

Occupational Safety and Health Administration, 64
Olson, Mancur, 128
Ortega, Daniel, 265

Paine, Thomas, 182
patents, 56, 66, 151
Piketty, Thomas, 151, 155, 161, 202
Pinker, Steven, 16, 67, 78
policy advisors, 47
  choice of, 172
political capital, 116
political elites, 6
  definition of, 6
political entrepreneurs, 106, 131, 133, 244
political marketplace, access to, 5
polycentricity, 203
populism, 264
pork-barrel projects, 1
power
  political, 72
  quest for, 77
prisoners' dilemma, 72, 261
progress, rate of, 196
propaganda, and education, 175
property rights, 56
public choice research program, 250
public goods, 62, 172
Pure Food and Drug Act, 170
Putin, Vladimir, 90, 102, 157, 222, 239

rational choice, 251
rational ignorance, 6, 58, 260
  and interest groups, 135–136
Rawls, John, 146, 220, 235
Reagan, Ronald, 109, 221
redistribution
  and institutions, 151
  legitimacy of, 145
  as a part of a social contract, 146, 149
  as a social responsibility, 149
  and social welfare, 146
  through regulation, 154
reference, circular. See circular reference
regulation, 176
  purpose of, 15
regulatory capture, 120
regulatory takings, 11
rent creation, 108, 111
  and political extortion, 141

rent-seeking, 36, 105
resource curse, 202
revenue sharing, 178
revolution, 92, 180
　as a constraint, 91
Ricardo, David, 201
Richter, Rudolph, 53
rights
　enforcement of, 53–54
　positive theory of, 55
Robinson, James, 68
Rockefeller, John D., 155
Rohde, David, 122
Roman Catholic Church, 214
Roosevelt, Franklin D., 101, 103
Rothbard, Murray, 174
Rousseau, Jean Jacques, 169, 209, 234
Rule of law, 82
Rummel, R. J., 233
Russell, Bertrand, 75

Saez, Emmanuel, 161
Sahlins, Marshall, 186, 189
Samuelson, Paul A., 24, 172
Schattschneider, E. E., 130, 208, 240
Schumpeter, Joseph A., 27–28, 83, 197, 246
seniority in politics, 98
separation of powers, 90, 245
Sierra Club, 137
Sinclair, Upton, 170
Singapore, 239
single-member districts, 95
slavery, 54
Smith, Eric Alden, 190
Smith, Adam, 17, 19, 31, 75, 194, 256
social contract, 73, 192, 235, 258
Social Security, 89, 160, 165–166
socialist calculation debate, 25
Stalin, Joseph, 73, 265
Stigler, George J., 120, 154, 179
Stiglitz, Joseph E., 81, 161
Suzman, James, 187

Tiebout, Charles M., 184
transaction costs, 7, 13, 57
　and bilateral exchange, 37
　and firms, 37
　and general equilibrium, 20
　and interest groups, 129
　and large numbers, 10
　and logrolling, 113
　and the political elite, 43
Transportation Security Administration, 171
Trump, Donald, 90, 101, 122, 222, 232, 264
Tullock, Gordon, 59, 61, 91, 141, 219, 227, 252, 254

United Auto Workers, 64

van Buren, Martin, 238
veil of ignorance, 93
Venezuela, 204
voting
　legislative vs. popular, 224
　proportional vs. plurality, 223

Wagner, Richard E., 9, 123
Wallis, John Joseph, 100
Walras, Leon, 19, 24
Walton, Sam, 159
Weber, Max, 75
Weingast, Barry R., 100
Wengrow, David, 186, 193
Wetherell, T. K., 116
Whig party, 238–239
Wickard v. Filburn, 165
Williamson, Oliver E., 36, 44, 63, 154
Wilson, Woodrow, 119
Winfrey, Oprah, 158
Wittman, Donald, 136
World Trade Organization, 205

Xi Jinping, 102

zoning regulations, 11
Zucman, Gabriel, 161

For EU product safety concerns, contact us at Calle de José Abascal, 56–1°, 28003 Madrid, Spain or eugpsr@cambridge.org.